The colour dictionary of CAMELLIAS

The colour dictionary of CAMELLIAS

Stirling Macoboy

LANSDOWNE PRESS
Sydney · Auckland · London · New York

*Dedicated to the memory
of Eben Gowrie Waterhouse,
a gentleman, a camellian and a scholar.
This book was first published in 1981,
the centenary year of his birth.*

Published by Lansdowne Press
a division of RPLA Pty Limited
176 South Creek Road, Dee Why West, NSW, Australia 2099
First published 1981
© Copyright Stirling Macoboy 1981
Photographs of *Camellia reticulata* in New Zealand © T. L. Durrant
Painting of *Camellia chrysantha* © Paul Jones 1981
Unless specifically credited, all camellia
   photographs are by the author.
Produced in Australia by the Publisher
Typeset in Australia by Savage & Co. Pty Ltd, Brisbane
Printed in Hong Kong

National Library of Australia Cataloguing-in-Publication Data

Macoboy, Stirling
   The colour dictionary of camellias.

   Bibliography.
   Includes indexes.
   ISBN 0 7018 1499 3.

   1. Camellia. I. Title.

635.9'33166

Half title page: Camellia japonica Gigantea
Facing title page: Mixed modern Japanese camellias
Title page: Camellia reticulata Buddha
Above: Camellia japonica Guilio Nuccio Variegated

PREFACE

For over 45 years I have had the good fortune to be associated with camellias — not only as a nurseryman and grower, but also as an interested collector and hybridiser. I can remember the excitement (in the 1930s and 1940s) of discovering long-lost varieties from the 1800s. These were in great demand, because until that time we had but few varieties of *C. japonica*, a mere scattering of *C. sasanqua* and one only *C. reticulata*, the tried and true *Captain Rawes*. Three only known species! But the interest of the hobbyist demanded so much more that many growers were stimulated into hybridising, and the development of their own new varieties. Even today, when the trickle of new cultivars has become a flood, the interested gardener still thrills at the sight of a new and different camellia.

I can also remember how difficult it was to find any written material about the camellia and its culture. However, because of the intense interest from both hobbyist and grower, and because of the willingness of camellia lovers to share their experiences and knowledge with others, articles and pamphlets began to be published.

In all these years, progress has been constant and steady. A number of camellia society journals have appeared, new books have been written — each contributing in its own way to the advancement of the camellia.

Now, here is another great step forward. The book in which this preface appears deals with almost 2,000 camellia cultivars from many times and many places. Over 1,000 of them are described in detail. Around 500 are illustrated in colour. Also described and illustrated are 45 camellia species and the various camellia relatives, which should be of great value in the future to camellia hybridisers.

I can remember when we first had *C. lutchuensis*, a camellia species that was very fragrant. This suggested we could have new scented camellia cultivars. Now, this is happening! And not only is there fragrance, but recently discovered, and beautifully illustrated in this book is the new golden species, *C. chrysantha*, a long-awaited dream come true!

This new discovery will be of utmost value, both to hybridists and home gardeners, because it is the breakthrough to a whole spectrum of new colours; not only yellows, but salmons, corals and quite possibly orange and tawny shades.

The camaraderie of camellia lovers is unequalled. It spans oceans and transcends both national and linguistic boundaries. Never in the world has a single flower brought together more people from different walks of life than has the camellia.

The preparation of this book has required the knowledge, the artistic talents of many of them.

I am honoured and proud to have had them as my friends for a many years.

Julius Nuccio

Chaney Trail,
Altadena, California.

Over the last quarter of a century, the Nuccio family's camellia nursery in the hills behind Pasadena, California, has become Mecca for camellia lovers all over the world. From the gentle green fingers of this remarkable Italo-American family has flowed an almost unbroken stream of prize-winning camellia varieties, many of them (Guilio Nuccio; Katharine Nuccio; Nuccio's Gem, Jewel, Pearl and Ruby) endorsed with the family name. Others of their 30 or so cultivars illustrated in this book are Bob Hope, Debut, Elegans Champagne, Francie L., Grand Slam, Midnight, Silver Waves and Wildfire. Julius Nuccio is the present patriarch of the clan.

CONTENTS

AN INTRODUCTION

Even today, in some quiet out of the way setting in Japan, a Western visitor may run across the same curious little ceremony that I witnessed in March 1980 in a large park near the heart of bustling Tokyo.

A young Japanese couple, quite oblivious to the presence of a stranger, knelt at the foot of a gnarled old tree with greyish bark and shining leaves. The boy clapped his hands sharply, once, twice, as if for attention. They then bowed deeply, touching an old root with their foreheads and tensed, as if drawing strength from the tree itself.

The tree was a camellia or *tsubaki*, swollen by the centuries to a height and bulk undreamed of in Western gardens. And through it, the Japanese couple had been speaking to their gods. Their faces, as they stood and bowed again before leaving, were radiant with the certainty that they were in the presence of the divine.

Why had the couple chosen a camellia, above all other trees? The apparent explanation is interesting.

For many centuries, before a fashionable tide of Western influence rolled inexorably over the exquisite countryside of Japan, the native *tsubaki* or 'tree with shining leaves', held a special place in Japanese thought and society. It was a tenet of the native animist religion, *Shintō*, 'the Way of the Gods', that those same gods in spirit form made the flowers of the *tsubaki* their home when on an earthly transmigration.

Plantings of the *tsubaki* were an essential feature of temple gardens, graveyards and other areas associated with the religious life of the community — any place where the presence or approval of the gods might be sought, or be advisable.

Today, with a renewed world interest in camellias of every type, many old temple compounds have proved happy hunting grounds for forgotten camellia varieties, more of which are being rediscovered and resuscitated year by year.

The divine aspect of the camellia's history can have had nothing to do with its modern popularity. Let us rather say that the plant's natural beauty of form and flower led both to its association with the worship of bygone centuries, and its appeal to gardeners of today.

What other flower, whose only real home is a group of small Asian islands, could have crossed oceans to become the object of so much adoration from millions of devotees on every continent of the globe?

Or can we sense the old gods smiling up there, among the swirling clouds of *Fuji San*, Japan's sacred mountain?

AN EXPLANATION

The total number of named camellia varieties grown and described at one time or another is estimated to be as high as 20,000. This book can consider only a small percentage: those which have some historical significance; those which have become universally popular; and those which have become the newsmakers in today's considerable world of camellias and camellians.

Through our text and pictures we are able to introduce rare and beautiful Japanese camellias to the growers of the West — and return the compliment with many examples of the grand and glorious cultivars from the United States, where big is beautiful. Some lovely but less spectacular blooms we show have been treasured in the gardens of Europe and Australia for several centuries. Others are so new they have not been pictured in any other book; some will not even be available at the time of the book's publication, as it may take ten years or more for a new cultivar to reach the stage where it can be distributed.

Not all named camellia varieties have been in cultivation at any one time in the 1,200 years of camellia history, which is a blessing; but because of the camellia's well-known capacity for sporting new varieties, and also the widespread enthusiasm and skill of hybridists, the number continues to grow year by year.

Are all of these cultivars genuinely different, one from another? The answer, quite simply, is no. There is a tremendous amount of duplication, the true extent of which may never be resolved!

Inevitably, given the nature of the genus, and the limited range of colours primarily available in it, the same sports have appeared spontaneously in several different places at several different times. Because of the lack of coloured reference for comparison, these duplicated camellia varieties have been independently named, and independently grown in different countries, and in different parts of the same country, with nobody being any the wiser. Hybridists too, working quite independently of one another, have made the same crosses.

If this book (which contains more colour illustrations of the camellia than any other in a European language in modern times) succeeds in reducing the multiplicity of duplicate camellia names by only half a dozen, then its publication will have been fully justified.

No matter who you are, whether you grow camellias or merely admire them in other people's gardens, we believe you will find this book a revelation.

STIRLING MACOBOY
NEUTRAL BAY, NSW
AUSTRALIA

Paul Jones

THE GENUS CAMELLIA

and its species

Unlike the rose, or the lily or the lotus, the camellia is not mentioned in ancient history. Not in China, not in Japan, not in any European country.

While the lack of Western reference might be explained in terms of Europe's complete ignorance of Asia itself, we cannot plead that same excuse on behalf of the camellia's own homelands. Even there, for all the attention that old books and manuscripts pay to it, the camellia might have sprung into the world fully developed, like some god of old, not much above 1,200 years ago.

Yet as science and common sense both insist that it did not commence growing spontaneously, an explanation must be sought for this apparent oversight or omission.

You will find it most conveniently in the enjoyment of a nice, relaxing cup of tea. For this delightful beverage is prepared from the leaf-buds of the glossy, evergreen shrub known in China and Japan as *cha* — which is the same word the Chinese use for the camellia flower. To our Western botanists, this attractive plant is known as *Camellia sinensis* — the tea plant.

It evolved, together with many of its close relatives, somewhere in the vicinity of Burma's Irrawaddy basin, and spread gradually to the north and east over uncounted millennia. Its leaves were infused with hot water and drunk for perhaps three thousand years before the Western discovery of China and Japan.

Official Chinese history begins the fashion of tea drinking in the reign of the almost legendary Emperor Shen Nung, who may have ruled between 1737 and 1705 BC.

There are many alternative attributions, and romantics will probably prefer, as I do, a more colourful beginning related in Buddhist legend.

According to the Greek-Irish writer Lafcadio Hearn (who retold the tradition in his elegant volume *Some Chinese Ghosts*), there was once a holy ascetic named Bodhidarma who, weakened by exhaustion while attempting to fulfil a vow of eternal meditation, at last fell asleep.

Tortured in his dreams by visions, haunted by a carnal love, he awoke and severed his eyelids with a knife, flinging them away so that he might not sleep, might never dream again. But the Lord Buddha, stirred with compassion by the sacrifice, caused the holy man to fall into a deeper trance.

When at last he stirred, wakened by the singing of the birds, his eyes were no longer lidless, and the severed lids he had flung upon the ground had mysteriously vanished. Instead, where he cast them, a wondrous shrub was growing with dainty leaflets eyelid-shaped, and snowy buds just opening to the east!

At once, through his newly acquired supernatural power, the holy man knew the secret of that newly created plant, and spoke to it, saying: 'Blessed be thou, sweet plant, formed by the spirit of virtuous resolve. Verily, for all time to come, men who drink of thy sap shall find such refreshment that a weariness may never overcome them. Neither shall they know the confusion of drowsiness, nor any desire to slumber in the hour of duty or prayer!'

And so it is today, as the pleasant vapour of tea, created for the refreshment of mankind, perpetually ascends to heaven from all the lands of earth!

Thé, *an elegant nineteenth century print of the tea plant,* Camellia sinensis, *by engraver Lambert.*

Opposite: Camellia chrysantha, *painted especially for this book by Australian Paul Jones, who has been called the greatest living painter of flowers. His skill is evident in this picture, which he created from sketches and written descriptions, without ever having seen the living bloom. Compare it with the photograph on page 15, which arrived some months later from China.*

The word 'tea' itself is an approximation of the Chinese Amoy dialect word *t'e*, and so the beverage was once known in England, and still is in France, as *thé*.

The same word in Cantonese is called *ch'a*, and so the beverage is known in China, Japan, India and Russia — even among the London cockneys for whom (at least until recently) a 'nice cuppa char' was the sovereign elixir.

The first reference to the brew in English is thought to be in a letter dated 27 June 1615, from R. L. Wickham of the East India Company to his agent in Macao. Wickham wrote, 'I pray you buy for me a pot of the best *chaw*'.

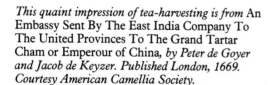

The old port of Macau — 1839. *From a coloured engraving by Auguste Bourget.*

The first shipment of tea may have reached London from this Macao source about 1650, for in 1658 an advertisement appeared in a London newspaper.

It announced with a flourish: 'That excellent, and by all physitians approved China drink, called by the Chineans *Tcha*, by other nations *Tay*, alias *Tee*, is sold at the Sultaness Head Cophee House in Sweetings rents, by the Royal Exchange'.

Charles II's Queen, Catherine of Braganza, became an early convert. It was not long before the garrulous Samuel Pepys (always ready to follow the lead of his betters) reported in his diary for 1660: 'I did send for a cup of *tee* (a China drink) of which I had never drunk before'.

A contemporary Duchess of Bedford, however, set the fashion of drinking it in the afternoon; she had it served with cakes when (to quote her) she had 'a sinking feeling'.

Tea was soon celebrated in art, in literature, in verse as the alternative to strong drink or, as the poet William Cowper put it, 'the cups that cheer but not inebriate'.

Tea became so universally popular that the government saw an opportunity to place a tax on it; an impost that later led to the infamous Boston Tea Party, and indirectly, to the American War of Independence.

And where did all this tea come from? Still from China, and later from the newly established Indian plantations of the East India Company, who had the trading and shipping monopolies between the East and the entire English-speaking world.

It was indeed through the greed of the Company that the Western world began to learn there were *other* camellia species.

Though the story may be apocryphal, it is generally claimed that the first living *Camellia japonica* arrived in London aboard a Company ship in the very earliest years of the eighteenth century; and that as a result, this most perfect of flowers was introduced to Western gardens by accident. The plants had, in fact, been thought to be living specimens of *Camellia sinensis*, the tea plant, obtained by bribing Chinese officials.

This quaint impression of tea-harvesting is from An Embassy Sent By The East India Company To The United Provinces To The Grand Tartar Cham or Emperour of China, *by Peter de Goyer and Jacob de Keyzer. Published London, 1669. Courtesy American Camellia Society.*

The East India Company had hoped to propagate these plants in England for transfer to their Indian and American estates thus, in time, being able to cut out the Chinese profit. But Chinese officials outsmarted the traders and substituted plants of the more decorative *C. japonica*, the leaves of which were useless for tea-making.

The story seems quite likely, but modern scholars say that the company's order was probably misunderstood, as the Chinese then and now make no distinction between the flowering and cropping species of camellia, referring to them all as *ch'a fa* or tea flower. In supplying the more exotically flowering varieties they may merely have meant to be obliging.

We do know that dried specimens of *Camellia japonica* were received from Amoy by London apothecary James Petiver in the late seventeenth century. Petiver published a description of the flower in 1702, under the name *Thea chinensis*. In 1712, the former Dutch East India Company physician Englebert Kaempfer published his *Amoenitatum Exoticarum*, in which appeared descriptions and plates of *C. japonica*, *C. sasanqua* and *C. sinensis*.

Kaempfer had spent time at the Dutch trading station in Nagasaki Bay, and described the *Camellia japonica* as 'Tsubakki', which is basically still the Japanese name.

The great Swedish botanist Linnaeus established the name *Camellia* for the new plants in his *Systema Naturae* of 1735, and confirmed the binomial epithet *Camellia japonica* in his *Species Plantarum* of 1753. He never saw a living specimen, but was working from Kaempfer's notes.

The name *Camellia* was chosen in posthumous recognition of the Far Eastern work of Moravian Jesuit botanist George Joseph Kamel (or Camellus), who had died the year before Linnaeus's birth. Camellus never visited China or Japan, and probably never saw a living *Camellia japonica*, for his work was confined largely to the flora of the Philippines, where they do not grow. But his specimens and notes did contribute greatly to the botanical knowledge of the day.

In light of the recent Japanese discovery of a Jesuit connection with camellias in sixteenth century Japan though (see plate page 26), there does now seem a possibility that Camellus knew of the plant, and may even have described it in a letter lying as yet undiscovered in some private European library. His name, at any rate, will always be associated with the entire genus.

Within thirty years of Camellus's death in Manila, the first *Camellia japonica* was growing in England, where it flowered some time before 1739 in the glasshouses of the enthusiastic amateur Lord Petre, at Thorndon Hall, Essex.

By 1760 a plant of *C. sasanqua* was flourishing in the royal gardens of the King of Naples at Caserta, and the following fifty years saw the introduction of several named *C. japonica* varieties, imported through the East India Company.

Gentleman enthusiasts, hot to be first with any new botanical treasure, paid heavily for the discovery and importation of new camellia species and varieties via the China trade. *Camellia oleifera* was established by 1811, and *C. maliflora* by 1818, while the first *C. reticulata* was brought from Canton in 1820 by Captain Richard Rawes of the East India Company, after whom it was later named.

The horticultural value of the genus was soon established and in 1819, Samuel Curtis published his *Monograph of the Genus Camellia*, the first of many splendid nineteenth century volumes of camellia lore. In it he enthused: 'Just as the dawn is the harbinger of morning, and the sun does not at once reach his meridian glory, so the camellias advance upon us by degrees in beauty ... we cannot but view with admiration the diversity and elegance of this beautiful family of plants, which the all-wise and bountiful hand of God seems to have formed for the delight of mankind...'

By 1829 *C. kissii* and *C. sasanqua* had been introduced, and parallel development was taking place on the Continent. The Abbé Berlèse published several books including a *Monographie du Genre Camellia* in 1838, in which he speculated on the possibility of crossing *C. japonica* with

Above: The Tsubaki of Japan, *an engraving of* Camellia japonica *from Englebert Kaempfer's* Amoenitarum Exoticarum *of 1712. Courtesy The British Library.*

Below: The Swedish botanist Carl Linné (known as Linnaeus), who established the name Camellia in his Systema Naturae *of 1735.*

Camellias, by Clara Maria Pope, from Samuel Curtis's Monograph on the Genus Camellia, *1819.*

other species, including *C. sasanqua*. He considered (rather prematurely as it turned out) that *C. japonica* by itself had already produced all the varieties of which it was capable!

And so other species were sought out and imported: *C. rosaeflora* in 1858, *C. hongkongensis* in 1874, *C. cuspidata* in 1912, *C. saluenensis* in 1924, and *C. taliensis* in 1931. Hybridising experiments began and reached fruition shortly before World War II in England, with the introduction of the *C. X Williamsii* hybrids between *C. japonica* and *C. saluenensis*.

Other species turned up sporadically over the span of a century in the effects of plant hunters of many nationalities, often in the form of dried specimens; sometimes only as a few notes in a botanical description; most recently as photographs.

In all, nearly a hundred species have been recorded to date; some as yet exist only from hearsay, and have not been photographed or propagated.

The climax of research to date has been the confirmation and photography of the almost legendary golden camellia, *Camellia chrysantha*, which is already under propagation both in the United States and in Australia (see plate page 10).

All species of camellia are relatively low evergreen trees and perhaps shrubs, generally with alternate, simple glossy leaves. Their only original habitats are tropical and subtropical Asia, where they grow in partial shade among the evergreen trees of mountainous areas. They are occasionally seen in higher parts of the South-East Asian rainforests, where they enjoy the constant humidity, but are never found in the monsoon areas where deciduous trees lose their leaves in the dry season.

About seventy per cent of the ninety to a hundred species have been found in inland China, on the islands of Hainan and Taiwan, and in the Indo-Chinese peninsula.

One species only has so far been discovered away from mainland Asia and the offshore islands, and that is *C. lanceolata*, which makes its home in mountainous areas throughout the Philippines and many of the Indonesian islands.

The flowers of these many species are by no means all as large and spectacular as those of *C. japonica* and *C. reticulata*. Some are less than a centimetre in diameter, and many are plain white. Others have a perfume, which many of the spectacular cultivars do not, and are much used by hybridisers endeavouring to perfect fragrant camellia cultivars (see page 190).

Generally, the different species have several factors in common. In wild varieties there are usually five or more sepals, and five to nine petals (though sometimes there may appear to be only three, since the calyx is of an intermediate type). The flower petals are normally fused into a single unit, and may even be attached to the outer stamens so that the entire flower falls in one piece, leaving only the ovaries and pistils attached to a short stem. There will be three or five pistils, attached to three or five seed cells in the ovary. The fruit is almost spherical and when ripe, splits into three or five sections to release the large seeds, leaving its central stem and core attached to the plant. The seed capsule is thick and woody, and when dry, hard.

Some camellias previously thought to be species have subsequently turned out to be interspecific hybrids, because in many areas, several species grow together in a mixed stand, where they have hybridised naturally over the centuries. As blooms of the individual species become available for chromosome count, these natural hybrids are being identified by Western taxonomists.

Of the estimated ninety to a hundred camellia species, forty-five species have found their way into cultivation. These, including the wild forms of those already popular in the West through cultivars, are listed below.

Individual cultivars of the species *C. japonica*, *C. reticulata* and *C. sasanqua*, together with their interspecific hybrids, are dealt with in separate chapters.

C. amplexicaulis

Found only in some temple gardens of Vietnam, *C. amplexicaulis* may yet turn out to be an ancient hybrid between species unknown. It is a 1 m (3 ft) shrub with large oblong leaves and velvety-textured purple flowers about 7.5 cm (3 in) across.

C. assimilis

Like several other camellia species found in the Hong Kong area, *C. assimilis* is so limited in its geographical range that some botanists have wondered whether it is a local hybrid. Tall and shrubby, it has narrow red-green leaves and small single white flowers. It has proved a useful container plant, blooming mid season.

C. brevistyla

A slender tree about 8 m (26 ft) high, *C. brevistyla* has been found only in Taiwan. The leaves are small and elliptical, the flowers miniature and white.

C. caudata

A small tree growing to about 7 m (23 ft), *C. caudata* is widely distributed through South-East Asia, and also grows in north-east India, Taiwan, Hainan and other islands. Leaves are long, sharply pointed and serrate. Flowers are white, single and about 2 cm (¾ in) in diameter, borne at leaf axils. It is a charming plant, blooming mid season.

C. chrysantha

The current sensation of the camellia world, *C. chrysantha* is a shrub growing from 2 to 5 m (6 to 16 ft) in height, occurring naturally in China's Guangxi province. It has magnificent, dark green quilted leaves, reminiscent of *C. granthamiana*. The flowers, borne in leaf axils, are 5 to 6 cm (2 to 2½ in) in diameter and have eight to ten petals. The big news is that the flowers (which bloom throughout winter) are a pure golden yellow. Camellia societies in all countries are caught up in a race to grow this extraordinary plant to flowering size, and to discover its compatibility for hybridisation. It is hoped that it foreshadows a whole new spectrum of colour in garden camellias, including yellow, orange, apricot and peach. For the lucky grower, the seeds of this plant may well prove to be the golden apples of legend. Several varieties of sub-species have already been reported.

C. connata

A tree of 8 m (26 ft) and more in height, *C. connata* is already growing in the West, but there is no news of its being of great use in hybridisation. It comes from Thailand, and has white, single flowers 2.5 cm (1 in) in diameter, and oblong leaves with a blunt apex.

C. crapnelliana

Not much grown in the United States, *C. crapnelliana* is doing well in several Australian gardens. It is another of the curious species known only from a single tree, discovered in Hong Kong in 1904. This original tree has now disappeared, but its scions are flourishing. It is known to grow 7 m (23 ft) in height, and has smooth, finely-toothed elliptical leaves 17.5 × 5 cm (7 × 2 in). The wavy-petalled white flowers are medium-sized (about 7.5 cm/3 in in diameter) and bloom mid season. They are strikingly centred with a glowing boss of orange stamens.

C. cuspidata

A shrub from south-west China, *C. cuspidata* grows only 3 m (10 ft) in height, and has pointed, wavy, brown-tinged leaves. The flat, white flowers are single, about 3 cm (1⅛ in) in diameter and have widely flared golden stamens reminiscent of a Higo camellia (see pp. 133–41). *C. cuspidata* blooms mid season, and makes an ideal container plant.

C. drupifera (see C. oleifera)

C. dubia   FRAGRANT

Growing to 3 m (10 ft), *C. dubia* is a shrubby camellia from south-east China. Leaves are sharply pointed, and vary in size from 3.5 to 7 cm (1¼ to 2¾ in). The single blooms are quite delightful: 2.5 cm (1 in) across, varying from white to pink, and very fragrant.

C. euryoides (see C. maliflora)

C. fraterna   FRAGRANT

A dainty shrub from central China, *C. fraterna* may reach 5 m (16 ft) in height; its pointed-elliptic leaves are tinted a greyish-green with black-

Camellia caudata

Camellia chrysantha   Kunming Botanical Institute

Camellia crapnelliana   Photo by John Riddle

Camellia cuspidata

Camellia fraterna

Camellia granthamiana

Camellia heterophylla Barbara Hillier

Camellia hongkongensis

tipped serrations. Charming single 2.5 cm (1 in) flowers have few stamens and are white, occasionally tinged lilac. They bloom in clusters at mid season and are mildly fragrant. A useful tub plant.

C. furfuracea
FRAGRANT

Found only on Hainan island and in small areas of Vietnam, *C. furfuracea* is a shrubby plant of about 3 m (10 ft). Its leaves are large, and fragrant white flowers appear (generally in pairs) at branch terminals.

C. granthamiana

One of the great rarities of the 'camellia world, the resplendent *C. granthamiana* was once known only from a single plant discovered in 1955 on a sheltered hillside of Hong Kong's New Territories. Probably a hybrid of several native varieties, it has propagated well and is now flourishing in other countries. It is a small tree of 3 m (10 ft), wonderfully decked with dark serrated 20 × 4 cm (8 × 1½ in) leaves, deeply impressed with veins. The eight-petalled flowers, borne at terminals, are white and almost 15 cm (6 in) in diameter. They open early in the season and have attractive drooping golden stamens. New plants of *C. granthamiana* have recently been discovered on Hong Kong island itself.

C. heterophylla

C. heterophylla also may be a hybrid of other wild species (probably including *C. reticulata*), and is known from a single plant found in a temple garden in Yunnan. It is a 2 m (7 ft) shrub with dark leaves, which are pointed and serrated. The crimson flowers are single, more than 10 cm (4 in) in diameter and borne terminally. Several hybrids have been raised, notably *Barbara Hillier*, which blooms mid season.

C. hiemalis (Cold Camellia)

C. hiemalis is unknown in the wild, but is most likely (from chromosome counts) to be a natural hybrid of several strains of *C. japonica* and *C. sasanqua*. It most closely resembles the latter, but blooms throughout winter. *C. hiemalis* cultivars vary greatly and will be found listed with the sasanquas on page 168.

C. hongkongensis

Found only on Hong Kong island and its New Territories, *C. hongkongensis* is a slender tree, at times reaching 10 m (33 ft). The dark shining leaves are leathery and pointed, and measure 12.5 × 4 cm (5 × 1½ in). The light crimson flowers are trumpet shaped with a velvety reverse texture. They bloom mid season.

C. indochinensis

Not a great deal of study has been done on this small camellia, native to many areas of North Vietnam. It has broad, elliptic leaves and small white flowers. It has not yet been used in hybridisation.

C. irrawadiensis

(syn: *C. sinensis Var. Irrawadiensis*) Now believed to be a sub-species of the tea plant *(C. sinensis)*, *C. irrawadiensis* is a slender, branched shrub growing to 7 m (23 ft), with roughly elliptical light green leaves. It is native to Burma, and bears white single blooms mid season.

C. japonica (Bush Camellia)

In the wild, *C. japonica* is a most variable plant from small shrub size to 15 m (50 ft) or more. Flowers vary in size, colour and style, generally with five or six petals. Colour is generally red, but white and many shades of pink are known, probably as a result of natural hybridisation. Varieties of the species are found in Japan, eastern China, Korea and Okinawa, blooming at any time during the season. An extensive colour dictionary of cultivars begins on page 62.

C. japonica Var. Macrocarpa (Apple Camellia)

A collectors item, this subspecies of *C. japonica* is found in Okinawa and bears large red apple-sized fruits.

C. japonica Var. Rusticana (Snow Camellia)

Native only to mountainous areas of north-west Japan, the *Snow Camellia* *(C. japonica Var. Rusticana)* has adapted to a shrubby, many-trunked habit, sometimes with almost horizontal growth. Flowers are often semi-double to double and are found in all forms known in the garden camellia range. Hybrids of *C. rusticana* often have furry stems and other minor botanical details that distinguish them from the true japonicas, but generally the two species are hopelessly intertwined in cultivated varieties.

Cultivars of *C. rusticana* are illustrated with the japonicas, beginning on page 62.

C. kissi
FRAGRANT

Most variable according to its area of growth, *C. kissi* may range from shrub size to a tree of 13 m (43 ft) or more. It is found naturally from north-east India right through to southern China and the island of Hainan. The narrow-elliptic leaves are 11 × 3.5 cm (4½ × 1¼ in) and are serrulate at the tips. The small white flowers are single and bloom mid to late season. They are often fragrant.

C. lanceolata

The most tropical of all natural camellia species, *C. lanceolata* is found throughout Indonesia and mountainous areas of the Philippines. It is a tree, growing to 9 m (30 ft), has long, elliptic leaves 14.5 × 6 cm (5¾ × 2½ in). The white flowers are single and 2.5 cm (1 in) in diameter. Because its growth area is isolated, *C. lanceolata* has not intercrossed with other species.

C. lutchuensis
FRAGRANT

Most sweetly fragrant of the natural camellia species, *C. lutchuensis* is found only in the southern Japanese islands, including Okinawa. It is a 3 m (10 ft) shrub, with small pointed 4 × 2 cm (1½ × ¾ in) leaves, often red-tipped when young. The dainty white blooms, borne singly or in clusters at leaf axils, have pink-stained outer petals and are delicately perfumed. *C. lutchuensis* is used in most fragrance-hybridising programmes, but also makes a charming container specimen.

C. maliflora

(syn: *C. euryoides*) Found in a very limited area of central China, *C. maliflora* is probably a natural hybrid of *C. saluenensis* X *C. cuspidata*. It is a bushy 5 m (16 ft) shrub with pale green foliage. The small flowers, opening mid season, are semi-double, soft pink with a rose-red margin, often with petaloids.

C. miyagii
FRAGRANT

(syn: *C. sasanqua Var. Miyagii*) Now considered a local variant of the Japanese *C. sasanqua*, *C. miyagii* is found only in Okinawa. It is a shrub of tall, bushy growth, with mildly serrated 6 × 3 cm (2¼ × 1⅛ in) leaves. The single notched-petal blooms are white, and similar to those of the sasanqua, though smaller. They bloom mid season.

C. nokoensis

From Taiwan, this small tree species of camellia grows to 8 m (26 ft), and bears sharply pointed leaves and tiny white flowers of an almost triangular appearance. These open at leaf axils.

C. oleifera
FRAGRANT

(syn: *C. drupifera*) Known for many years as *C. drupifera* this charming small tree is found from north India through Burma and southern China to all of South-East Asia and nearby islands. Reaching 7 m (23 ft) in height, it bears elliptic pointed leaves, and charming fragrant white flowers with long twisted petals. It is popular with species collectors, and blooms early.

C. parvifolia

Found only on the island of Hainan, this small shrubby camellia has large leaves measuring 14 × 3.5 cm (5½ × 1¼ in), and very small white flowers. It is grown by a small number of enthusiasts.

C. pitardii

Several varieties of *C. pitardii* have been discovered, all native to southern China. They differ mostly in chromosome count and minor botanical details. Small trees growing to 7 m (23 ft), they have heavily veined serrulate leaves about 10 × 3.5 cm (4 × 1¼ in). Their dainty single flowers vary from rose-pink to white in colouring, and open mid season. They are slightly over 5 cm (2 in) in diameter. *C. pitardii Var. Yunnanica* has been much used in hybridising.

C. reticulata (wild form)

The simple, single form of *C. reticulata* is probably the parent of all the cultivated ornamental forms seen today. It occurs naturally in the forests of southern China, at altitudes varying from 2,000 to 3,000 m (6,500 to 10,000 ft). It is an open-branched tree of up to 16 m (52 ft) or more, with the broad, elliptic, heavily reticulated leaves we know from

Camellia japonica

Camellia lutchuensis

Camellia oleifera

Camellia rosaeflora

Camellia salicifolia

Camellia saluenensis

Camellia sasanqua

Camellia sinensis

the hybrid species. The rose-coloured blooms are about 7.5 cm (3 in) in diameter. Blooming time is mid to late season. Reticulata cultivars and hybrids with reticulata parentage are described and illustrated beginning on page 142. (Wild form photo page 145)

C. rosaeflora

(syn: *C. rosiflora*) The popular, pink-flowered miniature *Camellia rosaeflora* is another mystery species, there being no record of its having been discovered in the wild. It has occurred spontaneously both in Ceylon and England, and is believed to be a natural hybrid of the tea plant *C. sinensis*, with some other species. It grows to a small spreading tree, with weeping branchlets and often variegated foliage. The leaves are 8 × 2.5 cm (3 × 1 in). Small rose-pink single flowers appear at leaf axils. It is already a popular container plant.

C. rusticana (see *C. japonica Var. Rusticana*)

C. salicifolia (Willowleaf Camellia)   FRAGRANT

A shrubby small tree from Hong Kong and Taiwan, with a markedly weeping habit, *C. salicifolia* is noted for slender (10 × 2.5 cm/4 × 1 in) willow-like leaves that open pale pink, and fade through bronze to apple-green. These have a slightly furry appearance. The six-petalled white flowers are pleasantly fragrant, and bloom mid to late season.

C. saluenensis (Saluen Camellia)

C. saluenensis, which is found in several forms in the Yunnan area of southern China, is cold-resistant and one parent of all the X *Williamsii* hybrids. It is a small shrub growing to 5 m (16 ft) in height, with narrow elliptic leaves of 4.5 × 2 cm (1¾ × ¾ in). The flower colour (from white to deep rose) is most variable, suggesting (together with its chromosome count) that the species is itself a series of ancient natural hybrids. The blooms are about 5 cm (2 in) wide, and open mid to late season.

C. sasanqua   FRAGRANT

The original species of *C. sasanqua* is a small densely foliaged tree of 5 m (16 ft) or more from southern Japan and the Ryukyu Islands. Leaves are small, pointed and leathery (5.5 × 2.5 cm/2¼ × 1 in). Flowers are white, single and lightly fragrant, blooming in autumn. Sasanqua cultivars are listed and described commencing on page 168.

C. semiserrata

The growth habits of this eastern Chinese species are unknown as it exists only in herbarium specimens. The probability is strong, however, that it is a parent of many popular camellia hybrids. Its leaves are 15 × 6 cm (6 × 2½ in) and the open single flowers are red and more than 6 cm (2½ in) in diameter.

C. sinensis (Tea Plant)

The first known camellia species in the West, and the most important species in commerce, *C. sinensis* is the plant we know as tea. It is found naturally over a wide range from India, through China, to some islands of the western Pacific, and is variable in form, from a small shrub to a 17 m (56 ft) tree in Assam. The leaves too, scale from 10 × 4 cm to 22.5 × 7.5 cm (4 × 1½ in to 8¾ × 3 in). The small white flowers (occasionally pink) have cupped or reflexed petals surrounding a flared boss of gold stamens. All varieties bloom early.

C. szechuanensis

A shrub from southern central China, *C. szechuanensis* may reach 4 m (13 ft) in height, and has narrow leathery leaves. The white flowers appear at terminals only, and are approximately 6 cm (2½ in) in diameter. This plant may prove useful in future hybridisation programmes.

C. taliensis

Several varieties of *C. taliensis* are known to collectors. In the wild, it is a small tree up to 7 m (23 ft), from southern China. The elliptical leaves have rounded apices, and the white flowers appear in clusters of three at leaf axils. They bloom mid season, and have widely flared fluted petals.

C. tenufolia

(syn: *C. tenuiflora*) Possibly a subspecies of *C. sasanqua*, *C. tenufolia* has been found only in Taiwan. It has smaller foliage and smaller white flowers than the sasanqua, and growth is quite pendulous.

C. transarisanensis

A slender, small tree of some 4 m (13 ft) in height, *C. transarisanensis* has been found only in Taiwan, but is now in cultivation. Its slightly reflexed leaves are 4.5 × 1.5 cm (1¾ × ½ in), toothed and with blunted apices. The small white flowers appearing in clusters at leaf axils strongly resemble orange blossom. Their outer petals are marked bright red.

S. transnokoensis

Also from Taiwan, *C. transnokoensis* is already a popular garden specimen, with slender arching branches. Narrow tapering leaves and exquisite white flowers appear in clusters. These are about 2 cm (¾ in) in diameter, with a long cylinder of white, gold-tipped stamens. *C. transnokoensis* blooms mid season.

C. tsaii   FRAGRANT

Found naturally in Yunnan, Burma and Vietnam, *C. tsaii* is a delightful small tree which grows to 10 m (33 ft). Growth is spreading to pendulous, with shining wavy-edged leaves approximately 9.5 × 3 cm (3¾ × 1⅛ in). The small white flowers, flushed with pink on outer petals, are borne in profusion at leaf axils, and open mid season.

C. vernalis (Spring Sasanqua)

Probably not a species as such. Known varieties of *C. vernalis* seem to possess characteristics of both sasanqua and japonica species. Their chromosome count is variable, a sure sign that these are complicated hybrids, probably of natural origin. They are usually listed with the sasanqua cultivars, a practice followed in this book. See page 168.

C. wabisuke

Considered a separate species by the Japanese, the varieties of *C. wabisuke* suggest plants of widely different origins. But all have the same style of flower: small, thimble-like, in a variety of colours. *C. wabisuke TAROKAJA* is the best-known of these simple single flowers, which are greatly admired by devotees of the tea ceremony. The wabisukes flower mid season.

C. yuhsienensis   FRAGRANT

This recently described species was named by Dr Hu Hsen-Hsu of the Institute of Botany, Beijing, in April 1965. It is allied to *C. oleifera*, and like it, is grown in Hunan Province as an edible oil crop. *C. yuhsienensis* grows to 2 m (6½ ft), has greyish smooth bark, and elliptic leaves to 10 cm (4 in) long, with serrulate margins. The flowers, measuring up to 6 cm (2½ in) across, are white, single and quite fragrant. Because of the large bloom and pleasant perfume, this species will be of considerable assistance to the plant breeder. Only recently available to the West.

Camellia taliensis

Camellia transnokoensis

Camellia tsaii

Camellia wabisuke Var.

NAN SHAN CH'A
SOUTH-MOUNTAIN
TEA

The Camellia in China

Although the camellia is associated primarily with Japanese culture, there is little doubt that many of the cultivars in today's gardens have a mainland origin — in the distant centuries before some great ice age distorted the face of Asia, and cut the Japanese archipelago off from China and Korea.

Scientists have in fact found fossil remains of an early ancestor plant which has been named *Camellia proto-japonica*, and have theorised from its structure that it is descended from plants of the magnolia family from southern China.

Both the Japanese species *C. sasanqua* and *C. hiemalis* have close relatives on the coastal islands of Hainan and Taiwan, while wild mainland varieties of *C. sasanqua* were described in a 1688 volume *The Flower Mirror* by Chen Hao-zi.

The principal Japanese species *C. japonica*, however, seems closely related only to *C. reticulata* and *C. saluenensis* from the mountains of China's deep south, an area from which Japan was separated for millennia by a vast blanket of ice.

The species itself has never been discovered growing in the wild on the Chinese mainland, although curiously enough, all cultivars of *C. japonica* brought to the West before about 1890 were imported from China, generally through the southern treaty ports of Canton and Macao. All were double blooms, in the Chinese taste, bearing little or no resemblance to the japonicas grown in Japan. They bear much evidence of extensive hybridisation, and are largely sterile.

These early cultivars were always believed to be descended from original plants imported from Japan, perhaps as early as the eighth century. But now there is a new possibility.

Writing in the *1979 American Camellia Society Yearbook*, Huang Teh-ling, a retired botanist from the Shanghai Arboretum, claims that there are many plants of what is apparently a *C. japonica* subspecies growing wild in Sichuan province (formerly Szechuan). This is to the north of Yunnan, exactly where one might expect to find a bridging species between the camellias of southern China and those of Korea and Japan.

He has studied these plants personally, and describes them as having leaves of a rounder shape and smoother texture, and blooms of an incomplete double style more closely resembling the cultivars exported from China to Europe two centuries ago, than they do the popular Japanese varieties.

Huang further claims that later tests proved that up to seventy-five per cent of the so-called japonica cultivars in the large Shanghai Arboretum were more closely related to the wild Chinese species than to the Japanese, which accounted for only ten to fifteen per cent of the collection.

Huang suggests that it is the natural form of these native Chinese camellias which has exerted a direct influence over the aesthetic judgement of Chinese growers ever since.

Single blooms with conspicuous stamens are regarded by the Chinese as the height of vulgarity, and discarded when they occur in seedlings,

This recently issued set of stamps from the People's Republic of China, was devoted to the camellias of Yunnan. Photo Ray Joyce.

Opposite: This exquisite scroll, painted on silk, was created in the T'ang Dynasty, seventh-tenth century AD. It shows pheasants, with camellias and other winter flowers, and is a copy of the original in the Palace Museum, Taipei. From the author's collection. Photo Ray Joyce.

A modern Chinese brush-painting on silk shows a finch with scarlet camellia blossoms. Photo Ray Joyce.

in complete opposition to the Japanese taste. Huang regrets only that the beautiful double camellias of Sichuan are useless for hybridisation because of their sterility, so that developments can be expected only through sporting (see page 52).

He observes that in spite of a history of cultivation going back to the twelfth century and even further, less than 200 camellia varieties are grown in China. He describes some of these, including a precious green cultivar known as *Green Pearl*, which is today found only in a single temple at Wenchow, in Chekiang province.

As observed earlier, the ancient Chinese made little distinction between the cultivated tea plant and purely ornamental camellia species. The flowering camellias were known as 'wild tea' or 'south-mountain tea' *(Nan Shan ch'a)*, and are first mentioned in a book *Summary of Herbs*, published during the Sui Dynasty in 590 AD. This book also mentions the rumoured existence of a yellow camellia.

A volume of 863 AD is more specific. It notes that 'mountain-tea resembles the sea-stone-pomegranate. It originates from Kwansi, and is also found in Sichuan.' The combination of the three characters sea-stone-pomegranate seems to have been invented to describe the Japanese camellias when they were first imported to China. In other words, it was a plant that bore fruit that looked like a pomegranate, but had a stone (as opposed to the pomegranate's small seeds) and came from over the sea. This is an almost perfect description of *C. japonica Var. Macrocarpa*, which is found only in the extreme south of the japonica range, in Japan's Ryukyu Islands at their closest approach to the Asian mainland. It could not have applied to the japonica cultivars grown in the south, which were sterile and bore no fruit.

The 863 AD quotation definitely suggests that the Japanese camellias were known in the northern centres of Chinese civilisation even before the native Chinese species. That would appear to be the key to a cryptic line in an early seventh century poem, 'Celebration at the Eastern Room': 'While the sea-pomegranate has flowered and been forgotten, the mountain cherry has not yet fallen'; an indication that even then, camellias were being cultivated in China.

This is borne out by the appearance of the camellia as an occasional subject in Chinese art during the southern T'ang Dynasty, which began in 618 and ended when the country fell apart into a number of states in 906 AD.

Professor Yü of the Yunnan Botanical Institute in Kunming has stated that no less than nineteen varieties of *C. reticulata* alone have been known and grown in China since about 900 AD and that very old trees still exist in Kunming. This has recently been confirmed by Western botanists, who say that in the gardens of the Hsishan temple there is an ancient specimen of *SHIZITOU (Lion's Head)*, which was planted over 300 years ago and is now about 17 metres (56 feet) high, with a trunk some 50 centimetres (20 inches) in diameter.

When the reticulata varieties imported from Yunnan in 1948 first flowered, one of them, *SONGZILIN*, proved to be identical to the earlier import *Robert Fortune*, brought to England by John Parks in 1842.

We know that Parks never travelled away from the southern treaty ports of China, and therefore the camellia he introduced must have been brought over 1,600 kilometres (1,000 miles) from mountainous Yunnan to the nurseries of Macao or Canton. This is a staggering journey for a living plant, for it could only have been made by river barge down China's great interior waterways.

While this is still a common route for many goods from the Chinese interior, the return journey is far slower and more difficult, being all uphill through a variety of locks and long portages. It is unlikely that such time and labour would have been expended in the 'carrying of coals to Newcastle' — or in this case, taking to the mountains less spectacular coastal varieties of a plant that already grew there.

This may be one reason why the extraordinary *reticulata X japonica* hybrids developed in the West since 1948 have no counterpart in China.

The fertile single and semi-double japonicas were not grown in southern China or in Yunnan, and the reticulatas themselves were not grown in the centre and north of China where the Chinese Empire and civilisation developed. There, only the japonica camellias had been known; and it was centuries before the *Nan Shan ch'a* or camellias from the southern mountains appeared in cultivation outside their native territory. This was probably in the seventeenth century, at about the same time that the first reticulata is recorded in Japan as *TŌ TSUBAKI*, the 'Chinese Camellia'.

The camellia really became sufficiently established for conservative Chinese artisans to use as a theme during the northern Ming Dynasty (1368–1644) when it appeared in scrolls, in carved and inlaid lacquer, and ultimately in porcelain decoration, though it was never widely used in the latter.

This red lacquer box and cover was carved in the early fifteenth century with a perfectly balanced design of camellias and foliage. Photo by courtesy of the Victoria and Albert Museum, London.

Themes in porcelain decoration were inclined to be symbolic, and the camellia seems to have had no particular symbolism in Chinese culture, being thought of as purely decorative.

An educated Chinese who visited Japan during the late Ming period at the invitation of the Tokugawa Shōgun is said to have praised the camellias in Edo (modern Tokyo) by saying 'these mountain tea flowers are more beautiful and varied than those of China'.

He apparently did not realise that the blooms might have been native to the country he was visiting, for he seemed genuinely astonished that they could have bettered the Chinese standard.

It seems, however, that away from the cloistered life in monasteries, temples and palaces, the Chinese at grass-roots level were not as a general rule aware of the camellia flower. Even in modern times it is not held in the same esteem as the peony, poppy, plum blossom, peach and pomegranate as a theme in decorative art.

On several recent visits to Hong Kong and Macao, I found no awareness of it among the official Chinese bookshops and libraries, nor among art dealers, few of whom recognised it even from the Chinese characters and illustrations that I carried with me.

Fewer still had ever seen it used in art, though I did locate the magnificent Coromandel screen of the Ching period which is used on the endpapers of this book. Even that is obviously influenced by Japanese design, and was probably made for the Japanese market.

Beyond some small silk paintings, and modern copies of Ching period plant pots, there was very little available in comparison with the shops in major Japanese centres, where the variety of camellia material is limited only by the weight of one's purse.

Nevertheless, what little is available from Chinese sources is quite charming, and makes pleasant decoration. I was particularly attracted by a recently issued set of Chinese stamps, depicting rare camellia species from the southern mountains.

Camellias and wild ducks, portion of a carved Coromandel lacquer screen of the Ch'ing period, finished in gold leaf. A larger illustration of the screen is used as the end papers to the book. Author's collection.

So it is obviously to the Yunnan area that one must go to find the camellia accorded status in everyday life and art. There, it is the floral emblem of an entire province, and holds the same place in the people's hearts as do the kumquat and the peach in other parts of China. Because it blooms at the time of the lunar New Year (February-March), it is often exchanged by friends as a New Year's gift, symbolising prosperity and long life. Potted reticulatas are seen in many courtyards, and may even be included in marriage dowries.

Now it seems that the discovery of new camellia species on the Chinese mainland has far to go beyond the reticulatas. The recent importations of golden *C. chrysantha* and perfumed *C. yuhsienensis* (referred to elsewhere in this book) show that there are still great botanical opportunities in co-operation between the West and China.

TSUBAKI
The Camellia in Japan

While the camellia plays no part in ancient Japanese written history, its influence can be felt strongly in legend and in tradition.

At Ise, the Grand Shrine of the creator-goddess Amaterasu Omikami (ancestress of the present Imperial family) is sheltered deep in a wood of camellia trees. And in mythology, it is recorded that when her brother, the divine Prince Susanō-ō married the Princess Inada Hime no Mikoto, a camellia tree was planted to celebrate the occasion. In the centuries since, the crossing branches of that particular tree, at Yaegaki shrine, have actually grown together (perhaps aided by some discreet inarched grafting) so that their perfect union has come to symbolise the marital bliss not only of the Imperial ancestors, but of lovers throughout the land, whose happiness can be sealed by the magic of the camellia.

From these earliest times on, there has been an intimate connection between the Imperial family who claim descent from these gods, and the flower of the *tsubaki*.

At first, the ancient Chinese custom of sweeping out the bad spirits at New Year was borrowed, substituting a branch of flowering camellia for the traditional branch of flowering peach.

NISHI NO KYŌ, *a lost japonica cultivar depicted in the manuscript* Chinka Zufu, *c.1700. From the Japanese Imperial Household Collection.*

LOWALOSEIAOSANCTISSOSACRAMETO

S·PIGNATIVS · S·PFRANCISCVS
SOCIETATISIESVS · XAVERIVS·
S·MATTHIAS· S·LVCIA

This became, in time, a ceremony performed at the Imperial palace each January, when a wand of camellia wood was used to exorcise evil spirits. This tradition continues to the present day at the Kamigamo shrine in Kyōtō, and the Ōmiwa Shrine at Nara. In the Shōsō-in repository of the Todai-ji temple is displayed a five-coloured wand made of gold and silver, reputedly used by the Empress-wife of Emperor Koken as she exorcised evil spirits at the opening of the Todai-ji in 752 AD.

The oldest *written* record of the camellia is in the *Kojiki* (712 AD) where there are two poems attributed to an empress who was wife both to the Emperors Nitoku and Yuraku. One relates how the shining beauty of the camellia leaves reflects the glory of the Emperor, the other how the colourful blooms seem to praise him. No wonder she was a survivor in the court circles of the day!

Both *Nihon Shoki* (720 AD) and *Bungo Fudoki* (around 740 AD) tell that a savage tribe in the Bungo district was conquered in 83 AD by the twelfth Emperor Keikō (or Keigyō), using weapons made from the wood of the camellia tree. This traditional story is often cited in support of the belief that the camellia has powers to chastise the bad and to banish evil.

A camellia rod was part of a Buddhist priest's attire right up to the Edo period.

All of these ancient records refer to the wild, red-flowered *Camellia japonica* that grows throughout the length and breadth of the Japanese islands, from the mountains to the sea. The first suggestion that it might be found in any other form is a notation that a rare white camellia was presented to the Emperor Temmu (673–686 AD).

Camellias were used in many ways in court ceremonials throughout the Nara and Heian periods. *Enkishiki*, a book of 927 AD, in detailing court regulations and ceremonies of the early Heian period, frequently mentions the use of camellia oil and camellia branches.

The *Shoku Nihongi* (796 AD) relates how Japanese ambassadors to the Chinese courts of the Sui and T'ang dynasties, brought gifts of oil made from the seeds of the camellia. This was considered to have healing powers and was welcomed by the Chinese emperors.

Museum collections show us exquisite furniture and porcelain patterned with camellia blooms in many colours, court robes and brocades woven with different camellia designs — even coats of arms (*mon*) in which camellia blooms and leaves have been distorted into a formal pattern.

At the Sentō Palace, at the Katsura Detached Palace and many famous temples and nunneries in Kyōtō, we can see camellias that were traditionally planted by Imperial personalities of the past, and have been tended lovingly to this day.

Camellias were not, of course, grown to any extent by the common people, but an ordinary man might hope to make a fortune by the discovery of some new or particularly spectacular variety growing wild. (Then, as now, some camellia varieties threw sports and produced variant seedlings indiscriminately.) It was not realised that a totally new kind of flower was the result, not of intervention by the gods, but rather of spontaneous hybridisation among the several camellia species native to the Japanese islands, and often growing in close association.

A sufficiently interesting new camellia variety might be offered to a temple, or to the nobility — even to the Imperial household — and a high price paid for its acquisition. It would then be presented to some important shrine, with great spiritual reward to the donor. Imperial history is rich in accounts of prices paid for particular camellia plants by certain emperors.

The great nobility, too, flaunted a real or pretended association with Imperial descent by a real or pretended passion for the beautiful flower, while poems in the *Manyōshū (Collection of a Myriad Leaves)* clearly indicate the love and affection held for the camellia by the literati of this period. One poem, the 'Otomonoyakamochi', describes not only the beauty of camellias in the wild, but also as garden subjects. This is the first mention of cultivation.

For the common folk, far removed from scenes of courtly splendour

ICHIMAI KAWARI, *an unusual japonica cultivar depicted on a nineteenth century Japanese screen painting, is no longer cultivated. However, paper flowers of a virtually identical pattern are used at the Todai-ji Temple, Nara, in certain Buddhist ceremonies. Courtesy Yoshiaki Andoh.*

The Virgin with a white camellia, *a detail from the painting shown on the opposite page.*

Opposite: Fifteen Mysteries of Maria, *a Jesuit Mandala painted before the end of the sixteenth century in Japan, and shortly to be designated a national treasure. Also known as* The Virgin with a White Camellia. *Photo courtesy of Kyōtō University.*

and the great gardens of the nobility, the camellia was a plant of many practical uses. Its red flowers were used in dyeing, its tough wood in weaving and the making of many tools and agricultural implements. The oil from the nuts or seeds was an ingredient of food, medicine and cosmetics. It gave the people light in the darkness and heat in the cold months of winter.

And then, quite suddenly, in about 1000 AD, all references to the camellia in Japanese literature disappear. It seems probable that with the introduction of cheaper sesame oil and jute oil, the camellia was no longer of commercial or practical interest to the peasantry. Without this incentive to seek out trees in remote parts of the country, new varieties were no longer discovered to stimulate the jaded senses of the nobility.

The first camellia craze had, quite simply, done its dash.

This exquisite fragment of an antique silk fabric in a camellia pattern was exhibited at the 1980 Japan Congress of the International Camellia Society.

The flower was to stay out of favour until the Muromachi period of 1333–1568, when it began, slowly, to make a comeback as a popular landscaping plant in naturalistic Japanese gardens of all sizes. It joined the pine, plum, azalea, bamboo, maple and flowering cherry in creating some of the most memorable gardens of history. Many of the most beautiful of these Muromachi landscape creations were totally destroyed in the civil wars which wracked Japan during this period, but in Kyōtō there are still some camellia trees up to 400 years old which fortuitously escaped destruction during the many sackings of the city.

The camellia played a particularly strong part in gardens designed for the enjoyment of the tea ceremony, which first came into popularity at about this time.

Detail of the camellia pattern on an antique Japanese kimono, or robe. It was probably worn at court, or by a popular geisha.

The ceremony, which sprang into being as a reaction against the seemingly endless, jingoistic war games of the day is a minor offshoot of the non-violent Zen Buddhist teachings. It highlights enjoyment of the more beautiful, simple aspects of everyday life. The ceremony takes place, ideally, in a small garden tea-house, carefully constructed to suggest refined poverty, and is inevitably reminiscent of the rustic fantasies of Marie Antoinette and her court on the eve of the French Revolution.

The tea-house must be built simply of natural materials in subdued colours, and is furnished with flowers, Buddhist texts and a minimum of aesthetically pleasing utensils in which the tea is brewed and enjoyed. This is done with a great deal of ritualised etiquette on the part of all participants, and leads to a mellow mood of relaxation and communion with nature.

Simple single camellia blooms soon became an essential part of the ceremony in winter months, symbolising longevity, friendship, elegance and harmony. When the camellia variety now called *TAROKAJA* was introduced at this time, it was first named as *URAKU*, after Uraku-sai, a warrior and famous master of the tea ceremony.

It was against this curious background of ritualised war games on the one hand, and play-domesticity on the other, that a significant event passed almost unnoticed on the southern island of Kyūshū. In 1543, a Portuguese vessel was driven ashore in a storm near Nagasaki.

This was the West's first contact with the Japanese on their home territory, and was followed in 1549 by the arrival of a group of Jesuit missionaries under the leadership of Navarrese Francis Xavier. Xavier had met some Japanese traders far away from home in Malacca, and from conversation with them, and with returned Portuguese seamen, felt that the populous archipelago first referred to by Marco Polo as Zipangu offered great possibilities for conversion to Christ. He spent over two years in Japan, visiting many cities and the court of the Shōgun himself, winning converts from all classes before he left to continue his mission in China, where he died in 1552.

This early introduction of the Christian faith to Japan was not to last out the century, at least in public. The missionaries soon made important enemies among the priests of Japan's native religions, and persecutions began shortly after the new faith was proscribed.

A remarkable and very beautiful souvenir of the period has recently come to light in Japan. It is a work of art that shows not only the impact of the mission in Japan itself, but also highlights the camellia as a subject for Western art, a full two centuries earlier than its introduction to Europe.

It is a hanging scroll or mandala measuring 74 × 61.15 centimetres (29 × 25½ inches), and known as the *Fifteen Mysteries of Maria*, which research has proven to be painted before the end of the sixteenth century. It was found in the attic of a farmer's house in the mountainous village of Sendaiji in the Takatsuki area of Osaka. Takatsuki was governed in the late sixteenth century by Ukon Takayama, a local Daimyo who embraced Christianity along with his peasantry. He was exiled to the Philippines later, after refusing to renounce his religion, and it is believed the painting had been safeguarded ever since by the local people as a focus of their secret faith.

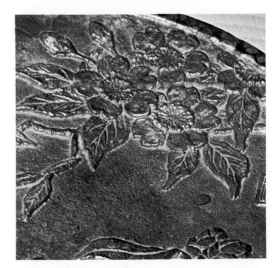
Old Japanese mirrors were traditionally of polished bronze, with heavily decorated reverses. Here, a camellia pattern was used.

This charming four-footed lacquer tray of the Edo period (1600–1853) is inlaid with pewter, silver and gold, and illustrates camellias and narcissus, a popular early spring combination. Author's collection. Photo Ray Joyce.

The scroll, which is illustrated on page 26, includes a portrait of the Virgin Mary holding the infant Jesus and a white camellia. This appears to be by a Western hand (perhaps one of the Jesuits), as does the accompanying portrait of Francis Xavier himself, which may quite possibly be a study from life. The two portraits are surrounded by fifteen scenes from the lives of the Holy Family. These, to judge by their features, were painted by Japanese students of the mission.

The white camellia in the hand of Mary is unique both in East and West, and may well be the sole painting of the subject in the world. The picture is now in the care of Kyōto University, and has been designated an important cultural object in Japan.

Another important relic of the period is a stone memorial to the Christian martyrs of Nagasaki (still the centre of the Christian faith in Japan). Its design includes some exquisitely carved camellias, indicating that the bloom had now become a symbol to the Christians as well.

To the Buddhists, it already symbolised the serenity of their paradise; in Shintō it was regarded as the earthly incarnation of the gods themselves; now to the Christians, it personified the purity of Virgin and Child.

Camellias in a courtyard garden of the Old Imperial Palace, Kyōtō.

Surely this was a monopoly on symbolism for one simple flower?

The adoption of the camellia by all three religions was accompanied by an increase in its popularity among the everyday folk. As the prosperity of the merchant classes increased following the civil wars, many of them established pleasure gardens of their own in which the camellia was seen in profusion.

And with the establishment of the military dictatorship at Edo (modern Tokyo), new gardens were created there. The second Shōgun, Hidetaka, had many beautiful camellia specimens planted in the grounds of his Edo Castle (now the Imperial Palace).

The camellia had now come to mean many things to people in all strata of Japanese society. Even the samurai, or military caste, became absorbed in the raising of its flowers in the periods between wars, though they endowed them with a different mystique. These medieval warriors saw in the hardy camellia a war-like spirit, and admired it as a symbol of fair play and purity of purpose — a sort of Holy Grail. It is found decorating armour and weapons of the period, while one of the most highly admired varieties was the one we now call *Tricolor*, whose three tints were understood to symbolise the ruling Tokugawa family, the commander-in-chief of the army, and the city of Edo itself.

Modern porcelain plaque of camellias and wistaria, photographed at the Arita Porcelain Works, Kyūshū. Photo Ray Joyce.

With interest in the flower at a new height in all levels of society, it was inevitable that books on the subject would soon appear. The first of these (that we know of) was the *Kadan Kōmoku* of 1664. It includes the first catalogue of camellia varieties — sixty-six of them, including the Chinese *Camellia reticulata* which was introduced at this time, and is described under the name *SATSUMA KURENAI* or *Satsuma Crimson*.

This was soon topped in 1694, when the Ito clan, a family of nurserymen who worked in the horticultural service of the Shōgun, published the famous *Kadan Chinkin Shō* or *Summary of Flowering Plants and Ivy* which contained no less than 230 camellia varieties.

But it seems that the Imperial family was to have the last word. After World War II there was a rumour in Japanese camellia circles that the Imperial collection included a book with even more paintings and varieties than the *Kadan Chinkin Shō* (which had probably been sponsored by the rival Shōgun). The Imperial book was finally located in 1961 by

Dr Takeshi Watanabe, who published extracts from it in a Kyōtō garden magazine between the years 1963 and 1965. Neither its authors nor its origin can be verified precisely, but art experts say the style of painting suggests it was painted some time before the middle of the Edo period (1600–1853) with a probable date of *c*. 1700. From the fact that it contains 720 different drawings of 618 camellia varieties (there are some duplications) it is assumed that the book attempts to portray all known varieties of camellia up to the date of its creation.

Above: Ancient clipped hedges of Camellia japonica *at the entry of Kyōtō's Silver Pavilion, Ginkakuji.*

Left: Popular Japanese camellia cultivars tend to be simpler in form than Western favourites. A selection of blooms from the Herbal Garden of the Takeda Chemical Industries Company.

The superb colour, and the minute detail of the accompanying descriptions, means that it is possible to identify some of the blooms in today's gardens.

The book's probable origin is in the reign of the Emperor Gōsai, who is stated in an old document to have been so fond of the camellia that he had all its varieties painted by the leading court artists of the day. Unfortunately, when the news became known, he was presented with so many new and rare plants that the folios of wonderful sketches multiplied beyond all reason. He was then obliged to put a stop to the project.

With the co-operation of the Imperial Household Agency, this dazzling volume was reproduced in facsimile by a Japanese publishing company in 1969.

Perhaps the loss of the Emperor's patronage caused interest in camellias to decline; or perhaps the market was already saturated. But by the time the Meiji restoration of 1868 came around, the popularity of the camellia was at a low ebb again, to judge by its lack of mention in garden publications of the day.

The Ito family of nurserymen published one last catalogue, in which the number of available camellias had shrunk to 199 varieties, classified by flower type, season and leaf differences. This is the last record we have of what was grown in the nineteenth century, for the city of Tokyo, already expanding with the onset of industrialisation, soon spread all over the old outer suburbs, obliterating the camellia nurseries from the city.

What few specimens remained of the old Tokyo varieties were moved out to the Saitama prefecture, where many of them were rediscovered at the nursery of Minagawa Jisuke during a new upsurge of interest that followed the conclusion of the Pacific War in 1945.

This saw history repeating the lessons of the Muromachi and Edo periods, when a generation of war and devastation was immediately followed by renewed interest in life's simple pleasures — and particularly in the flowers of the *tsubaki*, the tree with shining leaves.

A decorative crackle-glazed porcelain bowl of camellia design photographed at the Arita Porcelain Showroom.

Right: Camellia patterns are still popular on the wares of all Japanese porcelain manufacturers. Here are examples of modern Imari and Kutani ware. Photo Ray Joyce.

Mon, the family crests that are the equivalent to European coats of arms, frequently feature stylised botanical patterns. Here is one in a camellia design.

The recently reborn camellia hobby received a much-needed boost on 5 June 1945, when a new native species was discovered and identified. It was at first called *Camellia rusticana*, though it has subsequently been downgraded to *Camellia japonica Var. Rusticana*.

This subspecies is confined exclusively to mountainous areas of Japan's north-west on the island of Honshū. The reason it was overlooked for so many centuries seems to be that it grows only above the level of general habitation, and has small flowers.

Due to a shortage of paper in post-war Japan, the news of its discovery was not published until 1947, when it caused a great deal of excitement, and much comment from botanists and gardeners. Camellias are not really cold-hardy, and the discovery of a species that bloomed above the snowline was at first thought to augur the possibility of breeding a whole new range of cold-resistant camellias.

Research showed that *C. rusticana* (or the *Snow Camellia*, as it had come to be known) was no more cold-hardy than the japonicas, but had achieved a remarkable adaptation to its environment.

The bush is very low, even flat, with a number of small flexible trunks instead of the japonica's one. It usually grows under deciduous trees, so that it gets some sun in winter. The flatness and flexibility enables it to resist the weight of the snow, and under the snow layer, during winter, temperatures are higher than in the open air.

The flowers, which are borne at branch terminals, actually break through the snow to open. There are many minor differences between the *Snow Camellia* and the japonica, including the fact that the leaves and many other parts of the plant are covered with fine hair, just like many of the camellia species of inland China. Research has shown that *C. rusticana's* range is far wider than previously thought, and that it is in fact one parent of many popular cultivars, which are of an intermediate type. Some of those are identical to wild varieties. Semi-double and even double rusticanas have been discovered growing naturally, and some of them are now seen in the West. Several are illustrated in the japonica dictionary of this book, beginning on page 68.

The camellia cultivars grown in Japan are the oldest in the world. They have been selected and reselected over more than a thousand years, and largely reflect the cultural preferences of the local people in their form, colour and foliage.

As many were confined to particular areas or even particular temples, and were not in general distribution until very recent times, quite distinctive varieties are often found on different islands or in different areas of the country.

There is some confusion over names, because in the days of the Shōguns entire collections were sometimes seized, transported from one part of the country to another and often renamed. As in the West, much effort is being expended by camellia lovers to establish synonyms and verify the original varietal names. This is not always easy, because flowers can vary considerably as the result of their adaptation to regional soils and microclimates.

In the Kanto area of which Tokyo is the centre, the uniquely Japanese taste for variegated leaves and flowers developed, and was first noted in the book *Golden Leaf Anthology of Trees and Plants* by Mizuno Tadaaki (1829).

In the Chūbu area surrounding Nagoya, the taste was for simple leaves and small single flowers suitable for use in the tea ceremony. In these camellias, the stamens have become distorted into a form of petaloid so that flowers are usually sterile.

The best-loved camellias of Kyōtō and other cities in the Kansai area are generally conservative in style, as befits the atmosphere of a city rich with more than a thousand years of tradition. Until recently, few of the Kansai camellias had varietal names. Instead, they were known by the name of the temple in which they grew, with a resulting confusion in nomenclature which is still being sorted out.

The specialised Higo camellias of Kyūshū are dealt with later in this book, beginning on page 133.

Finally, Japan has the wabisuke camellias, which are classed as a species of their own by most taxonomists (as in this book). Small, single and bell-shaped, they are almost completely sterile because of the atrophy of their stamens and pistils. Where do they fit in? One recurrent theory states that they were brought to Japan after the Japanese invasion of Korea in the late sixteenth century. The story may be true because they are definitely more closely related to the Chinese camellia species than to the Japanese.

The wabisukes, of which there are several colours, have so far not been located in the wild and would seem to be a cross between two distantly related species.

Today, with the rediscovery of so many wonderful old flowers, the camellia is once again enjoying the fruits of popularity in Japan. There is a Japan Camellia Society (Nihon Tsubaki Kyōkai) founded in 1953, which together with many smaller regional groups holds regular shows and promotes exhibitions. New camellia discoveries are actually big news to the national magazines and newspapers.

The prestigious National Museum at Tokyo has published a volume on the camellia as a theme in Japanese arts and crafts, and it is possible to buy a variety of camellia-patterned goods of many kinds.

In a couple of short shopping sprees during a recent visit, I discovered fabrics and fans, decorative porcelain and cooking utensils, wood carvings and lacquer, screens and scrolls, enamels, cosmetics and boxes.

Could any other flower provide so wide a choice?

An old camellia tree at the Silver Pavilion, Ginkakuji, Kyōtō.

Camellias of various colours are frequently used on hand-painted folding fans. Here are two modern examples purchased cheaply at Kyōtō. Photo Ray Joyce.

THE CHINESE ROSE
The Camellia in Europe

Marco Polo.

Below: Bella di Firenze, *an early nineteenth century cultivar from Verschaffelt's* Nouvelle Iconographie des Camellias, *1848. It appears in all respects identical to the mysterious Japanese cultivar* ORANDA KŌ, *recently rediscovered in Spain.*

It would be risky even to guess when the first European eyes were gladdened by the sight of a camellia in bloom, for we know little of the early contacts between East and West.

Roman merchants certainly made sporadic visits to the Asian empires, though so far as we know, only in the vicinity of the trading ports of south India, Ceylon (Sri Lanka), and Siam (Thailand), where their coins and artefacts have been found. Before them, Alexander the Great halted his armies on the very brink of China's camellia country, and left cultural influences that were reflected in the arts of Asia for many centuries.

Marco Polo and his party were the first civilian travellers actually to visit the heartland of the Chinese empire, arriving early in 1275. But if they saw camellias, they made no mention of them when they returned to Venice twenty years later.

It is almost certainly to some unnamed Portuguese sailor that the honour of the first sighting belongs, for their trade contacts with China began in 1516, and their colonial city of Macao in China is the oldest European outpost on the mainland of Asia, established in 1557. But even before that, Portuguese maritime history was rich in Asian contacts, the city of Malacca having been captured in 1511, and adventurous merchants landing in Japan as early as 1543.

Portuguese sea captains and merchants were alive to every commercial possibility, but if they made any reports on the value of tea or camellia oil, these have not come to light. It may be that their records, along with almost all other official Portuguese maritime memorabilia, were destroyed in the great earthquake that flung Lisbon into the sea in the early eighteenth century.

It is certainly to be imagined that they must have become aware of the gorgeously flowering camellia, and that their report on the plant lies waiting only to be discovered, perhaps in some hard-to-read document in Latin among the papers of a private Iberian library, or even in the Vatican.

Did they attempt to transport the plants back to their homeland? Probably, in spite of the rigours of a year's journey by sea. And it is even possible that they succeeded. There are some very old camellia plants in Portugal and Spain whose history has never been satisfactorily explained. One at least is of a Japanese variety, *ORANDA KŌ*, that was never recorded as being imported to Europe, and of which there is no other known specimen on the continent. Two other large camellia trees in the garden of the Conde de Campo Bello near Oporto, have a combined spread of over 117 square metres (140 square yards). Again, there is no explanation of their presence and no record of their age. But the Conde's garden was first planted in the early sixteenth century.

If the history of camellias growing in the gardens of southern Europe is largely unknown, the story of their introduction to England and the more northerly states is quite well documented.

The first actual reference to the flower appears to be in an article on 'Far Eastern and Indian Plants', published in Dresden in 1682 by Gerhach Meister, a German who had visited Japan. We can only assume he was travelling under the aegis of the Dutch East India Company, who had been trading regularly with the Japanese islands.

Also in the late seventeenth century, the British East India Company had commenced a regular trade with China through the southern port of Amoy, where an early resident was the Scottish physician James Cunningham. Cunningham's interest in herbal medicine led him to prepare a number of dried specimens of useful Asiatic plants. These ultimately found their way into the hands of London apothecary James Petiver, and among them was a single red *Camellia japonica*, collected on the island of Chūsan. Petiver published a description and a sketch of this plant in a publication with the unlikely name of *Gazophylacii Naturae & Artis* in 1702. Petiver's extensive collection of natural history specimens was ultimately acquired by Sir Hans Sloane, whose larger accumulation became the nucleus of the British Museum.

Petiver's sketch was followed only ten years later by Englebert Kaempfer's professional detailed drawings of the camellia species *japonica*, *sinensis* and *sasanqua*, one of which is reproduced in our opening chapter. Kaempfer's drawings were all made from live specimens during his protracted stay at Deshima in Nagasaki Bay, where he was physician to the

The first, though fanciful, European colour impression of a camellia with the peacock pheasant of China, from A Natural History of Birds *by George E. Edwards, 1745. Courtesy of the American Camellia Society.*

Left: The Departure of Marco Polo for Cathay, *from an illustrated manuscript in the Bodleian Library, Oxford.*

Dutch East India Company's base. Kaempfer also named and described a number of Japanese camellia varieties, some of which are grown today.

As already noted in the chapter on the camellia species, a plant of *Camellia japonica* was actually raised to flowering size in the Essex greenhouses of Lord Petre, though where it came from is still a mystery. This bloom was described in 1745 by English naturalist George Edwards in the following words: 'The flower here figured ... is called the *Chinese Rose*; it blows broader than a Rose, and is of a red Rose colour with the stems (*sic!*) in the middle of a yellow or gold colour. The green leaves were stiff, firm and smooth, like those of Evergreens.' The variety is unnamed and unrecognisable in Edwards's rather fantastic painting, though it is said to have been the single wild red japonica species. Propagations from this same plant and its seedlings were the only camellias in England for over fifty years. A more detailed and accurate painting of one of them blooming in a hothouse appears in *Curtis's Botanical Magazine* of 1788. This apparently stimulated a great deal of interest, for the varieties *Alba Plena* and *Variegata* were imported shortly after, in 1792, by Captain Connor of the British East India Company. These first two cultivated varieties seen in the West were joined in 1794 by *Rubra Plena* and *Carnea*, and in 1806 by *Incarnata*, also known as *Lady Hume's Blush*. A flood of additional varieties arrived over the next quarter of a century, including of course the first specimen of *C. reticulata* in 1820.

It must be emphasised that all of these camellias came from China, through the ports of Amoy and Macao — none from Japan itself, which was closed to Western trade at this time. All of them, with the exception of Lord Petre's single red japonica, were in the Chinese taste; that is to say, peony form to fully double. It was still a while before single-flowered seedlings in various colours were propagated in England itself. A single white camellia is shown for the first time in Samuel Curtis's *Monograph of the Genus Camellia* of 1819, and is described in the *Botanical Register* for the same year as having been raised from seed.

Above: The Flower Market, *an 1822 print of the Paris institution where, among other things, potted camellias sold for 2,600 francs, a small fortune in those days. Courtesy American Camellia Society.*

Right: Part of an early gold leaf and paper screen from southern Japan, showing sixteenth century Portuguese trading vessels at Nagasaki.

Other early arrivals from China were named *Anemoniflora*, *Peoniflora* and *Myrtiflora* from distinguishing characteristics of their blooms, and by the early 1820s there were enough seedbearing plants in cultivation to make a commercial camellia nursery a practical proposition. This was opened by Alfred Chandler at Vauxhall on London's South Bank. Chandler introduced his namesake bloom *Chandleri* in 1825, and the lovely *Elegans*, ancestor of so many of today's most beautiful cultivars in 1831.

By the early 1830s the fame of the beautiful new flower had spread not only all over England, but to the continent as well, where it was soon discovered that they could be grown in the open air, as opposed to glasshouses, and set seed freely. They soon became popular garden plants in Spain, Portugal, southern France and in Italy, where the first japonica is believed to have flowered in 1794, in the Firenze garden of Count Leopold Galli.

As many new varieties appeared within a few years, they were celebrated in paintings by the French artist Redouté, in his exquisite volume *Les Camélias*, and in a series of unpublished sketches commissioned by the Italian doctor Luigi Sacco, who by 1830 had accumulated no less than 12,000 camellia plants from many sources! These may have stimulated the wealthy Italian Abbé Lorenzo Berlèse to devote himself to the study and propagation of the genus, in the course of which he built up the most extensive collection of cultivars seen outside of Asia.

In 1837, he published his famous *Monographie du Genre Camélia*, describing 282 varieties of the flower in detail, with a rather effusive system of quality rating which consisted largely of the words *Superbe! Magnifique!* and *Trés Belle!* Proof of the existence of a sort of *folie des camélias* lies in the fact that he was obliged to issue a second edition in 1840, with the number of blooms described increased to 508. Between 1841 and 1843 he brought his efforts to a triumphant climax with a series of three magnificent volumes, *Iconographie du Genre Camélia*, containing 300 colour plates as well!

By the 1840s and 1850s the camellia craze was at an all-time peak, with new varieties or 'perfections' being bred and propagated on every hand.

At 'Trentham', the Duke of Sutherland's palace in the English Midlands, an entire avenue of them was planted under glass.

At the Duke of Devonshire's 'Chatsworth' in Derbyshire, two specimens of *Captain Rawes* and an *Alba Plena* were planted in 1840 in a great glass case designed by Joseph Paxton, who was later to create the huge Crystal Palace for the Great Exhibition of 1851. This case was more than 10 metres (33 feet) long and 8 metres (26 feet) high, built against a south-facing wall; the camellias planted in it are still alive, and flourishing to a height of 8 metres (26 feet) with around 1,000 lovely blooms a season.

Even Queen Victoria mentions the new craze in correspondence from Osborne (March 1845) to one of her innumerable European relatives: 'If we have no mountains to boast of, we have the sea, which is ever enjoyable, and we have Camellias . . .'

Still a hungry public cried out for more and more new varieties. In 1850, the Belgian nursery firm of Bailmann was able to issue a catalogue containing more than 700 cultivars, and in 1848 his rival Ambroise Verschaffelt began the publication of a massive twelve-year series of volumes under the title *Nouvelle Iconographie des Camellias*. This was ultimately to include 623 colour plates, all collectors items today for the camellia lover. The plates were accompanied by a highly coloured text designed to appeal to the eager amateur. Here is a sample:

The Camellia, by the elegance of its aspect, the persistency of its beautiful foliage, the amplitude and the brilliant colouring of its blossoms, has won the favour of all lovers of beautiful plants. It reigns today almost as a despot in every collection, of which it is the principal ornament. It has recreated the lover of flowers most surfeited with horticultural pleasures; the ladies seek it to add to their adornment: its blossoms of the most dazzling white, the brightest pink, the most splendid red, or variegated with these different colours, accompany or animate their complexion in the most charming manner. No bouquet will do without a Camellia, no flower painting without it. The Camellia, in a word, is indispensable for everything, everywhere!

One of the most popular cultivars introduced at this period was named *Donckelarii* after M. Doncklaar, Director of the Royal Gardens at Ghent.

In Germany, in Italy, in France, the excitement was the same. New plants were snatched almost from under the noses of nurserymen by a hungry aristocracy, and found their way into palace conservatories in Vienna, Budapest, the Balkans and St Petersburg.

The camellia had come to be associated with an age of formal elegance. Its cool and serene beauty were much in tune with the studied poise of the nineteenth century dandy and the fashionable debutante.

But aristocratic fashions have a habit of spreading to 'less desirable'

Contessa Lavinia Maggi, *from Verschaffelt's* Nouvelle Iconographie *of 1848. It is still a popular and widely grown cultivar.*

Borzone's coloured engraving of the cultivar Planipetalea, *from Vanhoutte's volume,* Flore des Serres, *a famous camellia volume of the mid nineteenth century.*

Camellia japonica Donckelarii, *from an old Belgian illustration.*

New Zealand soprano Kiri te Kanawa as the doomed Lady of the Camellias in Verdi's La Traviata, *a role she has made her own. She has also had a camellia named after her (see reticulata dictionary).*

classes, and the Chinese Rose had become sick. The worm in its bud was revealed by popular novelist Alexandre Dumas Fils, whose story *La Dame aux Camélias* of 1848 caused a scandal. It was the tale of a lovely, doomed, lady of pleasure who signified her availability by wearing white camellia blossoms for twenty-five days of the month, red for the other five. The novel became a popular play, then an opera, *La Traviata* by Verdi, premiered in Venice in 1853. That signified the beginning of the end of the craze, at least in upper circles. English writer Sacheverell Sitwell singles out for special comment several hybrid camellias which were introduced at this time: 'One wonders why and by whom, the Second Empire Camellias were raised. They are far removed from the atmosphere of Chopin ... these striped flowers have as their analogy more the music of Gounod ... *Countess Lavinia Maggi* and *Princess Bacciochi* must remain the favourites of any collection of striped camellias. They are lovely in themselves, and in their association with a forgotten world of luxury and fashion.'

The great camellia madness lasted until about 1870, after which time the flower fell from popular favour, and did not regain its place for over half a century.

It is difficult to understand why the camellia should have suffered eclipse at this time, particularly as new and very beautiful varieties had just become available for the first time from Japan itself.

Perhaps too much attention had been focused on it as a greenhouse plant, beyond the range of all but the moneyed classes. Or perhaps it was the rise of a materialistic new industrial age, more concerned with Mammon than Flora.

Fortunately, the crash was not accompanied by the wholesale destruction of plants which occurred in Japan about the same time. The plants themselves (in Europe) waited eagerly in the wings for their inevitable opportunity to make a comeback, while their propagators made ends meet by switching to other plant genera, and exporting many of their choice camellia creations to areas where the craze had not abated. Records of European nurseries such as Guichard of Nantes, and Seidel of Dresden show sales at this time to such faraway places as Argentina, Chile, Uruguay and Costa Rica; the growing of choice blooms continued unabated in Italy, Portugal and the United States.

The stimulus for the camellia's comeback, in Britain at least, was not to come for more than sixty years. And then it arrived by post, among the wealth of seeds despatched by Englishman George Forrest from his plant-hunting expeditions in the far west of China.

But that is another story, and belongs in the chapter on the camellia hybrids, beginning on page 181.

JAPONICAS
The Camellia in America

by Milton H. Brown

A soft spring breeze wafts the scent of magnolias through the cross-halls of a lovely southern mansion. You can hear the rustling of crinoline skirts as the Southern Belles are waltzed by finely dressed young gentlemen. There are the older gentlemen in white suits, rocking on the porch; they are sipping bourbon and talking about the crops. The Belles are wearing dark red japonicas; the older folks are looking down the lane and, even in the moonlight, seeing the large japonica bushes in full bloom.

In our dreams, in our romantic fiction, the camellia will forever be associated with the plantation life of the old Confederacy. But life is reality, and the reality is that japonicas came into America in, of all places, Hoboken, New Jersey! This was in 1797 or 1798, when a single red was imported by John Stevens. It was first referred to in 1835 by botanist M. P. Wilder, who wrote what he had been told at first hand by Michael Floy, a nurseryman in Bowery Village of New York City: that in July 1800, Floy had brought over with him from England 'a plant of the Double White for John Stevens, Esq, of Hoboken, New Jersey, who had two or three years previously imported the Single Red'. This white imported by Floy was *C. japonica Alba Plena*.

For a time (more than a century, in fact) these plants and their descendants were known in the United States simply as 'japonicas', in much the same way as Australians refer to the flowering quince, *Chaenomeles*, as a 'japonica'.

Things change slowly, and though more and more Americans are now using the name *Camellia japonica* (along with *Camellia reticulata* and *Camellia sasanqua*), throughout much of the Southland, even in the 1980s, you can still hear people refer affectionately to their 'japonicas'.

It is reported that the first importation of processed tea was by the Dutch into New York in 1650. But despite a regular sea trade between Europe and North America, the introduction of the camellia itself seems to have been delayed for quite some time.

As might be expected, the first species of the genus *Camellia* to enter the United States was the tea plant *(Camellia sinensis)*. Seeds were first sent to Savannah, Georgia to be planted in the famous Trust Gardens; this was in 1744, according to Francis Moore, who made his report that year after returning to England. The seeds were sent from the East Indies and, according to Moore, 'though great Care was taken, did not grow'. According to the US Patent Office's Report of 1857, living tea plants came to Georgia in 1772. They were growing on Skidaway Island, near Savannah before 1805 according to another report. But tea-growing in Georgia was ultimately a failure because of insufficient capital and other mitigating circumstances such as the malaria hazard of the Savannah region. In 1813 an apparently more serious effort was made to grow tea in the Charleston, South Carolina nursery of Philippe Noisette. This attempt lasted longer, but tea did not flourish in South Carolina either.

Other nurserymen began importing and raising camellia plants from seed, thus obtaining new varieties. The first camellia listing in the United States was probably that in the catalogue of William Prince's Linnaean Botanic Garden, Flushing, New York, in 1822, in which he listed 17 varieties, one of them *Lady Banks' Tea Leaved Sasanqua*. Also in New

Milton Brown, of Fort Valley, Georgia, is one of the most knowledgeable figures in camellia circles, where he is affectionately known as 'Brownie'. As Executive Secretary of the American Camellia Society, and Editor of its quarterly Journal, his influence is widely felt not only in America, but all over the camellia world. In February 1980, he led a group of American camellia enthusiasts on a pioneering visit to the People's Republic of China.

York, the nursery of Thomas Hogg and his son added to camellia history when they issued a catalogue in 1835 listing 39 varieties of camellias. Others in New York at that time who helped popularise camellia growing were Noel J. Becar, who originated the famous *Brooklynia* and *A. J. Downing*; Thomas Dunlap; D. Boll, who originated *George Washington*, *Henry Clay* and others; and Grant Thoburn.

Needless to say, the fame of these exotic plants soon spread outwards from New York City. H. Harold Hume's *Camellias in America* gives accurate details of this early history:

Formal camellia gardens at the headquarters of the American Camellia Society, Massee Lane, Georgia. Courtesy Milton Brown.

Camellias at Japanese teahouse, Descanso Gardens, California.

Much attention was given to camellias as greenhouse plants in the Boston area during the early years of their culture in America. Varieties from China that came first to Europe and varieties originated in Europe were imported as soon as available. Seedlings also were raised in an effort to secure new and different sorts, while plants and flowers were produced for nursery and florist trade. Much was done and successfully done to popularize them. From this distance in time it appears that the place camellias came to occupy in the area was due mainly to the interest and efforts of a small group of amateur and professional plantsmen, among whom Marshall P. Wilder, C. M. Hovey, Samuel Sweetster, and Col. Thomas H. Perkins were noteworthy; to the Massachusetts Horticultural Society; and to *The American Gardener's Magazine and Register*, later *The Magazine of Horticulture*. The society at its meetings and above all through its exhibitions large and small brought the camellia before the general public, while the magazine supplied information on varieties and culture for the guidance of growers . . .

Records of the Massachusetts Horticultural Society show that in 1829 the Society offered a premium of $3.00 for the greatest number and finest kinds of blooms of *Camellia japonica*. Interest grew rapidly and camellias became an important feature of the Society's exhibitions; and in 1939 the Society established a separate camellia show, held annually. The 152nd exhibition of camellias in Boston was held in March 1981.

Philadelphia, too, soon became a centre for camellias. It is estimated that between 1840 and 1850 more plants were produced there than in any other city in the United States. From its greenhouses, camellias were sold locally and in surrounding cities, shipped to Europe, and furnished for planting in southern gardens. The Pennsylvania Horticultural Society took a leading part in advancing the culture of camellias. Active, too, were nurseryman Robert Buist, who brought out several editions of *The American Flower Garden Directory* in which he gave liberal space to camellias; James B. Smith; and David Landreth. In April 1829, three varieties of camellia were shown in the Philadelphia Horticultural Society Show, and in April 1830 twelve were shown. Various others were also very active in this area; for example, John Sherwood had in his greenhouses some 20,000 plants during the 1847-1848 season.

In the southern United States some of the old camellias were direct imports from Europe; but according to Hume, most came from greenhouses in cities of the Atlantic seaboard from Washington, DC northward. Large collections of camellias were soon to be part of the plantation life of Charleston, Savannah, Wilmington, Mobile, New Orleans and parts of Mississippi. Ralph Peer has written, 'It was probably in the 1830s that the wonderful camellia collections of Magnolia Gardens and Middleton Place, in the Charleston area, were first planted. Both of these Gardens contain many camellia plants more than 100 years old.'

A camellia-strewn pathway at Middleton Place, Charleston, South Carolina. Courtesy Milton Brown.

The camellia pioneer of the West was James L. L. F. Warren who went from Boston to Sacramento in 1850, the year California became a state. He sent back to Boston for plants, including camellias, and seed which arrived aboard SS *Panama* on 3 February 1852. According to A. E. Morrison, a founding member of the American Camellia Society, these plants were advertised for sale in the *Sacramento Union* on February 7th. Mr Warren predicted in 1853, 'This truly magnificent plant, unsurpassed in loveliness, will ere long become acclimated with us to form our pride as an ornamental tree in our garden'. Sacramento was named 'Camellia City' in 1910, held its first camellia show in 1924, and has held one annually since that date. Camellias soon spread throughout California and top growers and research people were to be found in both northern and southern California. Camellias then also went 'up the coast' to Washington and Oregon.

Magnolia Gardens, Charleston, South Carolina. Courtesy Milton Brown.

Interest in camellias, which had waned following the Civil War and the Reconstruction, took on new life soon after the turn of the twentieth century. Once more Japanese shipments reached the West Coast and there are records of shipments of camellias from Germany, Belgium and France to the eastern seaboard. There were consecutive annual camellia shows held in the 1930s in Georgia, Virginia, California, Alabama, Florida, Texas, Louisiana and Massachusetts. The Azalea and Camellia Society of America was formed in 1932 with officers from Georgia, California, Florida, Louisiana and Massachusetts. Its first *Yearbook* in 1933 had a section on azaleas and one on camellias, the latter including a writeup on seven species and descriptions of 102 camellia varieties whose names commenced with the letters 'A' and 'B' of the alphabet. This pioneer organisation later became known as the Camellia Society of America and its 1939 *Yearbook* had descriptions of 177 varieties beginning with the letter 'C'. It also included sections on camellia culture, early 'Show Reports', and descriptions of 11 additional species. On 29 March 1946 the Camellia Society of America merged its organisation with the American Camellia Society which had been incorporated on 24 October 1945.

A well-grown bush of the fragrant cultivar Kramer's Supreme, *at the home of camellia enthusiast Willard F. Goertz, San Marino, California.*

The American Camellia Society rapidly became known as the national camellia organisation and was largely responsible for the increased interest in camellias throughout the country. Its membership has grown

Popular American cultivar Glen 40 *in the North Walk at San Marino's magnificent Huntington Gardens.*

California's famed Descanso Gardens, near Pasadena, are landscaped with camellias. Here, a superb, scarlet, formal double drops its blooms in a running stream.

to over 5,200 in 44 states and 22 foreign countries. Since 1940 many other local, regional and a few state camellia societies have been formed, and have done much to increase interest in camellias through meetings, shows and publications. The publications of the American Camellia Society, among others, are respected worldwide because of their content: a balanced mixture of serious research, simple yet detailed articles on growing and showing camellias, reports on shows and listing of show dates. They also feature colour pictures of new and old varieties, details of the business and fun of the national meetings, and other miscellaneous articles of interest to camellia enthusiasts, including the regular listing of new camellia registrations.

In the early 1960s, many organisations, horticultural and otherwise, experienced a drop in recruitment interest due to the general tightening of the economy. Memberships in most — if not all — camellia societies suffered. Then along came an increase in 'the good things of life' that put money into boats, travel and hobbies of all kinds. Today, 'the greening of America' is growing at an all time rate, yet camellia enthusiasm must once again be engendered in the hearts and minds of the young people building or buying new homes.

With the introduction into America in 1980 of the species *Camellia chrysantha*, a colour revolution in camellias will soon be upon us and we will have large camellias in scintillating shades of peach, apricot and orange. After all, it was only after the introduction of a small wild yellow *Rosa foetida* from Persia 100 years ago that the colour range of roses was able to extend beyond red, pink and white. The introduction of the wild yellow *Paeonia lutea* from China (where it had been known since the 1660s) gave us the lovely shades in peony hybrids now grown in America and elsewhere.

In addition to the colour breakthrough, we will be expecting an increase in fragrance now that *Camellia yuhsienensis* has arrived. This species, too, was introduced into America in 1980. Through these, and other newly introduced species, we can also hope for improvements in cold-hardiness and heat tolerance.

CAMELLIA GARDENS IN AMERICA

From the stovehouses and conservatories and orangeries of New York and New England, camellias found their way down to the port cities along the East Coast of America. Some of the first camellias to be grown out-of-doors in the gardens of this country were probably planted in the Charleston area. There, two gardens in particular stand out because of their splendid camellia plantings — though they are diametrically opposed in style. The first is Magnolia Gardens, a romantic exercise in soft, natural landscaping, which has been in the hands of the same family since 1676; and nearby, the formalised gardens of Middleton Place, dating back to 1741.

I couldn't begin to mention all the gardens that specialise in camellias, but will name a few that might titillate some readers to take a camellia tour. Many greenhouses in the Boston area; Longwood Gardens in Pennsylvania; and Planting Fields Arboretum on Long Island are attractively planted with camellia collections. The National Arboretum, since the 1940s, has had camellias planted in a most natural way under tall evergreens. It was the plantings here that convinced us that another old wives' tale was just that. *Camellia sasanquas* are not, in fact, hardier than *Camellia japonica* as had so long been believed by growers in the South.

The depression years found the late Fred Huette developing the world-famous Norfolk Gardens where camellias are planted casually along trails and are, indeed, one of the highlights of this garden along with the azaleas. Public gardens with camellias exist in such cities as Manteo and Wilmington, North Carolina and, as already mentioned, South Carolina has Middleton Place and Magnolia Gardens near Charleston. Our own American Camellia Society headquarters near Fort Valley, Georgia has both formal and informal plantings of camellias within ten acres of gardens. The main street of Marshallville, Georgia is lined with lovely camellia trees 30 or more years old. There are plantings both in greenhouses and out-of-doors at Callaway Gardens near Warm Springs, Georgia.

Many gardens along the Gulf Coast that highlight camellias in their plantings are also well worth visiting. They include Maclay Gardens in Tallahassee, Florida; Bellingrath Gardens near Mobile, Alabama; and Live Oak Gardens near Baton Rouge, Louisiana. When visiting the West Coast, you must see the extensive camellia collection at the museum and art gallery of Huntington Gardens near Los Angeles. The camellia high-light of California is the City of Sacramento, itself known as the City of Camellias. Camellias first came to Sacramento in the year that Califor-nia became a state, and are a feature on the large grounds of the Capitol, in public plantings, along highways and around buildings. The very famous Camellia Festival each March presents a camellia parade with floats decorated with camellia petals, similar to the Pasadena Rose Parade which is held each New Year's Day. Camellias are also planted in many public parks elsewhere in California and in some public places in Washington and Oregon.

Along a camellia trail at Descánso Gardens, La Cañada, California.

Camellias are no longer just for the palaces of the grandees of China and Japan, or even for the wealthy plantations and large public gardens of America. They may still be called 'japonicas' in the former tenant houses throughout the southern states, though most of us are fancier now and call them *Camellia japonica, C. reticulata, C. chrysantha* and such. Camellias are well within the price range, and indeed often less expensive than new varieties of other exotic plants such as *Hemerocallis*, orchids and iris. They can be and are grown singly in small cottages or con-dominiums, but flourish just as well as in the mass plantings of landscape gardens of large houses.

Left: Beneath the shade of valley oak trees, a fine bush of Australian cultivar Great Eastern, *at No. 1 Camellia Lane, the northern California home of hybridist David Feathers.*

The American Gardener's Magazine for January 1835 contains an article by botanist M. P. Wilder that expresses perfectly why camellias have been so well thought of in America for such a long time. Mr Wilder wrote:

> In the whole range of splendid exotics which have been introduced into this country, there are few, if any, that combine so much elegance and beauty, either as it regards the dark, shining *evergreen* of their foliage, or the dazzling brilliancy of their flowers, as those constituting the natural order Camelliae. At all seasons of the year it is unrivalled for the richness of its foliage, but in the dreary months of winter, when almost all the attractions of the floral king-dom are wrapt in slumber, it stands forth with peculiar splendor, displaying its blossoms of varied hue, and reigning at once the pride and glory . . .

ASPASIA AND OTHERS
The Camellia in Australia and New Zealand

by Eben Gowrie Waterhouse

The arrival of Camellias in Australia was heralded in these engaging terms: 'I wish much to convey to you the *Camellia japonica*, the most magnificent flowering shrub that has ever been introduced to this country. The flower, which is red as the rose or white as driven snow, is the most perfectly beautiful that can be imagined. Mr Gibbs says he will send some plants and thinks they will flourish in the open in New South Wales.' This is an extract from a letter written from London on May 30, 1821, by John Macarthur Junior, to his sister Elizabeth in New South Wales, where her brothers James and William were administering their father's estate at Camden Park.

The plants duly arrived from England in February, 1831.* The names recorded in William's notebook are *Japonica, Welbankiana,* Double White, *Carnea* or Buff, *Anemoniflora* or Waratah, and *Myrtifolia.* The double white is *Alba Plena,* which John had described to his sister as 'white as driven snow'; and 'red as the rose' would be *Camellia japonica.*

It is interesting to note that the *Anemoniflora* sent in 1831 still survives at Camden Park. It was used by William as a seed parent. In 1845, he wrote to C. Loddiges and Son, Nurserymen in London: 'We have raised four or five hundred seedlings chiefly from seeds produced by the old *C. anemoniflora* or Waratah Camellia. As this never has any anthers of its own we are in the practice of fertilizing its blossoms with the pollen of such other sorts as we can procure. Our largest plant of camellia has been planted out rather more than nine years. It is of regular pyramidal form perfectly clothed with branches from the ground upwards and nearly twelve feet high.'

Macarthur named sixty-nine of the seedlings he raised. He issued printed catalogues of camellias, grapes, olives and other plants in 1843, 1845, 1850 and 1857 and despatched many plants to nurserymen and private growers in New South Wales, Victoria, Tasmania and South Australia. Camden Park was thus the first great source of supply of camellias within Australia.

The late Professor Waterhouse, a linguist by profession, was also one of the world's foremost authorities on the camellia. He raised and named many popular varieties, founded Sydney's famous Camellia Grove Nursery, and was President of the International Camellia Society. He was an authority on the history and nomenclature of early camellia cultivars. This introduction to the history of the flower in Australasia is adapted, with permission of his family and the publishers, principally from material in his two volumes Camellia Quest *and* The Magic of Camellias, *the latter written with Norman Sparnon. The books are both now collectors items.*

THE CAMDEN PARK SEEDLINGS

The following is a list of the Camden Park seedlings described by Sir William Macarthur. They are copied in their order from the notebook (date 1852?) in the Mitchell Library.

1/50 *Aspasia*	13/50 *Proserpine*	25/50 *Euterpe*
2/50 *Imogen*	14/50 *Hermione*	26/50 *Gulnare*
3/50 *Ianthe*	15/50 *Clymene*	27/50 *Medora*
4/50 *Miranda*	16/50 *Medea*	28/50 *Helena*
5/50 *Iras*	17/50 *Vesta*	29/50 *Clio*
6/50 *Dido*	18/50 *Euphrasia*	30/50 *Althea*
7/50 *Perdita*	19/50 *Cleopatra*	31/50 *Armida*
8/50 *Circe*	20/50 ————	32/51 *Isabel*
9/50 *Cassandra*	21/50 *Rowena*	33/51 *Calliope*
10/50 *Bellona*	22/50 ————	34/51 *Volumnia*
11/50 *Pyrrha*	23/50 *Clara*	35/51 *Portia*
12/50 *Marina*	24/50 *Myra*	36/51 *Calpurnia*

Opposite: The summer house at 'Eryldene', Sydney home of the late Professor E. G. Waterhouse, author of this chapter. The house and garden are now in care of a Trust, and open to the public on many occasions throughout the year. Photo Douglass Baglin. Courtesy Eryldene Trust.

* On SS *Sovereign.*

Below: An aerial view of Camden Park, the historic home of the Macarthur family, near Camden, NSW. It was here that the first camellias in Australia were planted in 1831. Photo Douglass Baglin.

Bottom: Cleopatra, No. 19 of the seedlings raised at Camden Park by Sir William Macarthur. It was first listed in 1850, and is still grown today.

37/51 *Beatrice*	48/52 *Hermia*	59/52 *Metella*
38/51 *Annette*	49/52 *Pallas*	60/52 *Rosaline*
39/51 *Virginia*	50/52 *Sylvia*	61/52 *Corah*
40/51 *Tamora*	51/52 *Francisca*	62/52 *Desdemona*
41/51 *Juno*	52/52 *Paulina*	63/52 *Fenella*
42/51 *Hero*	53/52 *Celia*	64/52 *Timandra*
43/51 *Marcia*	54/52 *Hippolyta*	65/52 *Juliet*
44/51 *Julia*	55/52 *Valeria*	66/52 *Octavia*
45/52 *Leila*	56/52 *Heloise*	67/52 *Viola*
46/52 *Phrynia*	57/52 *Lavinia*	68/52 *Dante*
47/52 *Olivia*	58/52 *Marianna*	69/52 *Rosalind*

Each Camellia name in the above list is preceded by two numbers. The second number seems to indicate the year of its flowering. 20/50 and 22/50 are left blank. Probably these two Camellias had not yet flowered.

Of the first seventeen Camellias in the list, plants of all except *Medea* (16/50) are recorded in the Sales Books as having been distributed. After that only *Cleopatra, Myra, Euterpe, Gulnare, Medora, Clio, Isabel* and *Calliope* appear in the sales records until 1856, when the records cease.

Some may still be at Camden Park, and further study may succeed in identifying them, but they do not seem to have been distributed.

Later nurserymen made further importations from Europe, and as many as 172 of the varieties illustrated and described by Verschaffelt appear in one or other of our early Australian nurserymen's catalogues.

MICHAEL GUILFOYLE'S SEEDLINGS
Michael Guilfoyle's 'Exotic Nursery' was situated at New South Head Road, Double Bay, and he must have had many Camellias before 1856.

For on July 11th of that year, at the Camellia Show held at the Royal Hotel, Sydney, when nearly 2,000 Camellias were exhibited for competition, it was Guilfoyle who carried off the honours ... 'Foremost in every arrangement for competition and in every prize awarded to Camellias we must name Mr. Guilfoyle'. (*Sydney Morning Herald*, July 14th, 1856.)

M. Guilfoyle & Sons catalogue for 1866 lists 95 varieties of Camellias without description and states that he has 'a continual succession of new and beautiful sorts. Our plants are grown perfectly hardy. All are grafted. We never increase by layers.' The Camden Park Camellias which were being offered at this time were all increased by layers and never by graft-

Below: Jouvan, *a beautifully coloured formal double camellia first listed by Australian grower Guilfoyle in 1866.*

ing, according to a statement by Sir William Macarthur. As layered plants require more attention until they are established, losses must have occurred, and it would seem that Guilfoyle is here turning this fact to his own advantage. Included in Guilfoyle's 95 Camellias (1866) are *Helenor, Tabbs, Wrightii, Jouvan* and *Xanthus*. These, together with *Edith, Lady Bowen, Lady Young, Metallica, Miss Murray, Mrs Fairfax* and *Mrs Mort* are mentioned by Taylor and Sangster in their 1877 catalogue as being 'superior seedlings raised by Michael Guilfoyle'. A number of those mentioned are still in the nursery trade.

Left: The old camellias at Milton Park, former country home of the Hordern family, near Bowral, NSW were planted before the First World War. The garden is now owned by the American King Ranch, and is open to the public each spring.

SHEPHERD'S SEEDLINGS

At this stage the nurseryman T. W. Shepherd began to play an increasingly important part in the importation, propagation and distribution of Camellias in Australia. In 1851, Shepherd offered 32 Camellia varieties; in 1875, 73; and in 1885, 144. In 1862, Shepherd & Co issued the following select list:

Azurea: The flower is of the largest size, paeony shaped, the colour is a dark or metallic purple,* and is perhaps the nearest approach to a blue that has yet occurred in the tribe.

Leviathan: Its flower is perhaps the largest known, measuring from six to eight inches in diameter. Colour rosy scarlet, belongs to the paeony flowering class, flowers late.

Speciosissima: Flowers brilliant scarlet, paeony shaped and unusually elevated in the centre.

Shepherdii: Rose, large and double.

Chats: Brilliant rich rose, free bloomer.

Below: Anemone form bloom Speciosissima *was originated in Australia by pioneer grower T. W. Shepherd in the mid nineteenth century.*

* Currently described as dark red, anemone form.

SHEATHER'S SEEDLINGS

Silas Sheather was employed at Camden Park. We do not yet know at what date or for how long. He was probably associated with the production of Sir William Macarthur's later seedlings. He left Camden Park and established his Camellia Grove Nursery at Parramatta. His was thus the third 'Camellia Grove' Nursery. The only printed record we have of him is an advertisement of his in Fuller's *Sydney Handbook for 1877*, page 123:

CAMELLIA GROVE, PARRAMATTA.
A spot of beauty — and a beautiful spot.

Above: Helenor, *a striped camellia from Australian Silas Sheather is still popular more than a century after its introduction.*

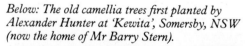

Below: The old camellia trees first planted by Alexander Hunter at 'Kewita', Somersby, NSW (now the home of Mr Barry Stern).

One of the principal sights of the town and district is, without doubt, Sheather's Camellia Grove. As the name implies, here may be seen in all the glory of perfection that Queen among flowers, the Camellia. S. Sheather's attention having been devoted to the cultivation of Camellias for the last thirty years, he has now one of the largest and the most recherché collections in the world. The following names are all in stock, a large number of which are S.S.'s own introduction.

Prince Frederick William, Harriet Beecher Sheather, Mrs Wright, Napoleon, Astarte, St George, Coronation, Leda, Sheatheri, Sulphureus, Dryade, Princess Louise, Cup of Beauty, Bonomiana, Incarnata, Minnie Warren, Alba Plena, Fimbriata Alba, Imbricata Alba, Lady Belmore, Mrs Delissa, Storeyii, La Pace, Helenor, Candidissima, Myrtifolia, Jubilee, Jenny Lind, Miniata, Mrs Mort, Henri Favre, Bergoma, Countess of Orkney, Lady Bowen, Countess Calina, Countess of Derby, Wrightii, Euterpe, Carlotta Papudoff, Paolina Maggi, Charles Albert, Alba Altissima, Princess Mary, Tricolor, Virginia Franco, Imbricata, Venus de Medicis, Dionysia Poniatowski, Picta, Vesta, Woodsii, Aspasia, Variegata Plena, Pressi, Queen Victoria, Nitida, Blanda.

Note the address, Silas Sheather, Camellia Grove, Parramatta, and George St. Markets. Sydney.

The Camellias in his list not previously recorded by other nurserymen are *Prince Frederick William, Harriet Beecher Sheather, Mrs Wright, Astarte, St. George, Sheatheri, Sulphureus, Princess Louise, Minnie Warren, Lady Belmore, Mrs Delissa*. It is certain that some, if not all of these were Sheather's seedlings. All of them, except the last, appear in later nursery lists, and the two first are outstanding varieties still well known and widely distributed today.

THE ALEXANDER HUNTER SEEDLINGS

Alexander Hunter, who had served his apprenticeship as nurseryman with Shepherd and Co. at their Chatsworth Nursery at Rooty Hill, established a nursery of his own about 1870 in Liverpool Road, Ashfield. Here he grew a large number of Camellias and called his nursery 'Camellia Grove'. It was the second nursery of that name. For Robert Henderson, who died in 1865, had conducted a nursery at Camellia Grove, Newtown.

Hunter kept a notebook in which he entered the names of his Camellias in 1872 and again in 1877, but he does not appear to have published a catalogue.

In 1884, Alexander Hunter left his Ashfield nursery to become the pioneer citrus grower at Somersby, on Mangrove Mountain, about ten miles from Gosford, where he selected a large area of virgin land. He took with him a number of Camellias and amongst them a few unnamed seedlings of his own raising. These he heeled in close together, intending to plant them out later. This he never found time to do. Today, four of these seedlings can still be seen growing together, forming a dense group of about 20 feet high and 22 feet through, and covered each season with a profusion of beautiful blooms.

In 1920, Alexander Hunter retired, selling his property to Mr G. C. Linton, who still* resides at Somersby. Mr Linton, who in the meantime has planted a fine collection of Camellias, named the Hunter seedlings and arranged for them to be propagated. Names and descriptions were published for the first time in Messrs Hazlewood Bros. catalogue in 1941.

Alexander Hunter: Semi-double crimson, with a cluster of golden stamens lighting up the background of the petals.

Constance: Semi-double deep rose, veined crimson, surrounding prominent stamens of rich yellow.

Jean Lyne: Semi-double white with pink stripes, while the centre petals and stamens form a pleasing effect.

Edith Linton: Semi-double silvery pink. In this variety the stamens and centre petals are intermingled.

Ruth Kemp: Semi-double light rose. Flowers of medium size with a prominent cluster of central stems (*sic!*).

THE LINTON SEEDLINGS

After acquiring the property from Alexander Hunter, Mr Linton became interested in Camellias and planted out some of the seedlings obtained from the large Alexander Hunter group, and named one of them *G. C. Linton*. This is a refined, semi-double bloom of bright red, with central stamens. Another is a beautiful, large, informal double, pure white, rose-like Camellia opening out and showing a cluster of lovely golden stamens. This the author propagated and named *Virginal*. It was first listed and described by Camellia Grove, St. Ives, in 1945.

THE WATERHOUSE SEEDLINGS

Professor Waterhouse himself raised some hundreds of camellia seedlings, many of them, according to his notes, from seeds sent him by Mr Linton from his Alexander Hunter group. Among these, he named and described the following:

Waverley (1944): Semi-double red, wavy petals, decorative. This showy variety has from nine to fifteen round and beautifully undulating petals and a central cluster of golden stamens.

Somersby (1945): Double deep red, with golden stamens. The colour of this beautiful camellia pales somewhat when fully open.

Adrian Feint (1947): A large, decorative semi-double white, with vivid crimson stripes. Its beautiful large buds are also most attractive.

The origin of several other seedlings the Professor raised and named about this time is not so certain. These include (again in his own words):

Trumpeter: Very large scarlet single of trumpet form ... first listed by Camellia Grove, St. Ives, 1946.

Beverley Caffin: Large, semi-double white, with carmine flakes. Fragrant. Probably a seedling from *Jean Lyne*. First listed by Camellia Grove, St. Ives, in 1945. This Camellia tends to throw an occasional rose sport *(Beverley Caffin Rosea).*

Lilian Pitts: This charming variety is one of the earliest to flower ... it is a semi-double, with ten or eleven outer rounded petals, two-thirds of the petals being pure white, with vivid streaks and suffusions of cerise-carmine, the other petals being completely or almost completely cerise-carmine. Among the central stamens are several smaller petals white or carmine. The flowers vary slightly, but are all very charming and decorative. ... Listed by Camellia Grove, St. Ives, 1946. This Camellia occasionally throws a sport completely carmine *(Lilian Pitts Rosea).*

Subsequent to the publication of his book Camellia Quest *in 1950, Professor Waterhouse achieved great success with a series of seedlings and hybrids from a plant of* Camellia saluenensis *in the garden of his own home, 'Eryldene', at Gordon, NSW. Named and propagated by him, these went on to world popularity, and will always be associated with his name. How they came about was described by him in an issue of the now defunct* Bulletin *of the Northern California Camellia Society. He wrote under the heading 'Some Saluenensis Seedlings and Hybrids':*

Jean Lyne, *an Alexander Hunter seedling from 'Kewita', was propagated by his successor, G. C. Linton after 1920.*

Lilian Pitts, *a spectacular striped japonica seedling, was propagated by the late Professor Waterhouse.*

* This comment was made in 1950. Mr Linton's property 'Kewita' was later inherited by his relative Keith Brushfield, after whom the *Brushfield's Yellow* camellia was named. 'Kewita' was purchased from Colonel Humphries in 1979 by Mr Barry Stern, and is occasionally open to the public.

My plant of *saluenensis* was imported from Scott, of Merriott, Somerset in 1938. It was planted in a bed in the vicinity of a number of *C. japonica* and flowered each year. From the beginning it showed a tendency to 'die back'. In 1945 it flowered profusely and set seed. In 1946, the plant died, but in the meantime, twenty-two seedlings had sprung up beneath it and were potted up as I did not wish to lose the species which was at the time, as far as I knew, the only *saluenensis* in Australia. But as the seedlings grew I was struck by a certain variation in their foliage which in no case was exactly like that of the parent *saluenensis*.

Above: The pink hybrid camellia E. G. Waterhouse, *raised by, and named for, the late great camellian.*

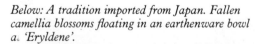

Right: Classic columns frame a garden view at 'Eryldene', the late Professor Waterhouse's garden at Gordon, NSW. Courtesy Eryldene Trust. Photo Douglass Baglin.

Below: A tradition imported from Japan. Fallen camellia blossoms floating in an earthenware bowl at 'Eryldene'.

In 1954 three of them produced flowers, and it was evident that cross pollination had occurred in my garden and without my intervention. One of the three, *E. G. Waterhouse*, was a complete formal double, beautifully imbricated. Another, *Lady Gowrie*, a large semi-double upwards of five inches in diameter, with about twenty petals and a narrow dense cylinder of slender stamens. The tall petals are very deeply and beautifully notched at the apex, forming two lobes. Colour fuchsine-pink. *Lady Gowrie* bears a certain resemblance to *Donation* but is yet quite distinct. It bears flowers freely on rather pendulous branches. *Margaret Waterhouse* is a semi-double with three rows of petals and a diameter of four inches. Its colour is amaranth-rose. It is of vigorous and erect habit. It is very floriferous, bearing blooms of a simple charm over a period of three months.

All twenty-two seedlings have now flowered. Ten are singles, ten semi-doubles and two are complete formal doubles. All of them inherit the characteristic saluenensis colour, ranging from amaranth-rose to fuchsine-pink. With the exception of *E. G. Waterhouse*, the foliage favours *saluenensis* rather than *japonica*.

Of the ten singles, six bear flowers of no merit, but *Ellamine* is an outstanding single upwards of four inches in diameter. Colour fuchsine-pink. The blooms are extremely showy, not only on the plant but when they fall to the ground.

Of the semi-doubles not mentioned *Bowen Bryant* is deeper in colour than the others, very floriferous and an extremely vigorous grower.

E. G. Waterhouse and *Shocking Pink* seem to be the first fully double *Williamsii* hybrids to be reported. The former has yielded a variegated form with about 90% white from a grafted plant. The latter is the deepest in colour of the present batch of seedlings. There can be no doubt that *saluenensis* crosses very readily with *japonica* and that the future holds great promise for those who cross-pollinate these two species.

Professor Waterhouse concluded his introduction to the history of the camellia in Australasia as follows:

Camellias were highly prized in Australia until towards the close of the nineteenth century. Thereafter they began to decline rapidly in favour, their names became confused and forgotten, plants were neglected and died, and by the nineteen-twenties only a very few of the old, standard varieties were offered for sale. In 1925 a leading Sydney nursery listed only *Alba Plena* and *Fimbriata*!

A generation grew up who did not know Camellias. But a revival was on the way. Camellia shows in three successive years, 1939-1941, drew large and enthusiastic crowds, and nurserymen made haste to propagate plants to meet the growing demand. By 1952, the revival was Australia-wide, and the Australian Camellia Research Society was formed with branches in various states.

Today, annual Camellia shows are held in the capital cities and in many local areas. Camellias are now grown more extensively in Australia than ever before.

Lady Gowrie, *a delicately coloured* X Williamsii *hybrid camellia, developed by Professor Waterhouse at 'Eryldene'.*

CAMELLIAS IN NEW ZEALAND

We know Camellias must have reached New Zealand before 1843*, for they are mentioned by R. Stokes, of Wellington, in the New Zealand Journal of that year in a list of various plants he had obtained mostly from Sydney, Australia. And it is possible that some of the surviving old plants on mission stations may have been planted before that date. But we have traced no published list of Camellia names in New Zealand earlier than that given in Alfred Ludlam's pamphlet published at Dunedin in 1865, *Essay on the Cultivation and Acclimatization of Trees and Plants.* Ludlam had arrived in New Zealand in 1840, and acquired the farm 'Newry', at Waiwhetu in the Hutt Valley. He mentions having seen Camellias in New South Wales, and it is not unlikely that he obtained his plants from Macarthur at Camden Park since Macarthur's catalogues contain all the seventeen varieties listed by Ludlam.

In 1870, the *Gardener's Chronicle of New Zealand* contained an article by F. Wakefield stating that Ludlam had about eighty varieties 'which probably were never equalled in the open air in the finest gardens in Europe'. Another keen horticulturalist, Thomas Mason (known as 'Quaker Mason') who had arrived in Wellington in 1841, had beautiful botanical gardens of twelve acres in the Lower Hutt with sixty Camellia varieties, but we have no record of their names.

It is surprising how many old Camellia plants can be found here and there in New Zealand today. At Gordonton, there is a Camellia tree forty feet in height and thirty-three feet broad. New Zealand, especially the North Island, possesses one of the finest climates in the world for Camellias. They flourish almost without attention and grow into trees. These camellias are being investigated by the New Zealand Camellia Society, a very active body with branches in various parts of New Zealand. A national convention and Camellia show is held each year, and an attractive and informative Camellia *Bulletin* is published.

New Zealand has introduced the finest varieties from all parts of the world, and some outstanding hybrid Camellias have been produced by Dr Brian Doak, Mr Les Jury and Colonel Tom Durrant.

A superbly grown bush of Yunnan reticulata ZHANGJIA CHA (Chang's Temple), *in the garden of Colonel Tom Durrant at Tirau, New Zealand. The deep, volcanic soil grows amazing camellias. Photo Tom Savige.*

* The first camellia in New Zealand may have been planted in 1834 at the inland mission of Mangapouri on the banks of the Puniu River.

SPORTING IN CAMELLIAS
Genetic Evolution

by Thomas J. Savige

In certain families of plants, the appearance of a part of the plant with different physical characteristics from the rest is not uncommon. Where the colour of the blooms is affected, this becomes particularly obvious. Such changes are known as mutants or 'sports'. They are more apparent in cultivated species. This is probably because, under natural conditions, many would be eliminated by virtue of a low survival factor, whereas in cultivation they are maintained by various methods of vegetative propagation because of their beauty or unusual form. The twisted filbert and variegated *Agonis flexuosa* are examples of this.

Amongst camellia species, *Camellia japonica* and its hybrids are particularly noted for their sporting propensity and many hundreds of horticultural varieties have been obtained by propagating these variations. Oddly enough, the other species of camellia rarely show evidence of sporting; only a few examples are reported for *C. sasanqua* and none at all for *C. reticulata* (except virus-induced variegations).

The reasons for sporting or mutating lie deep within the living organism and are part of its evolutionary and inheritance mechanism. It is thought that the present garden forms of *C. japonica*, because they are the product of endless inter-crossing and outcrossing, over the centuries during which they have been cultivated, have accumulated a very high genetic variance. Much of this remains potential unless released by the effect of environment on selection. Unfortunately, there is also a considerable genetic load of disadvantageous variations which may be released by recombinations.

The growth of a plant involves continuing cell reproduction. The reproduction of a cell by division involves chromosome division. Whenever a chromosome divides, there are produced two daughter chromosomes with similar genes. Genes arise only from genes, and heredity is due to accurate gene reproduction. However, when a gene copy varies from the original, a gene mutation has occurred. Likewise, the chromosomes may be changed by the loss or rearrangement of component genes. This is known as a chromosomal mutation.

Gene mutations on their own generally cause less change than the chromosomal mutations; in fact, many are so small they go unnoticed.

When mutations occur in the seed a mutant individual is produced. When they occur in the growing part of a plant, they are referred to as a somatic mutation or 'bud sport'. It is by vegetatively propagating from this bud sport that new horticultural varieties are produced. The most common form is a colour change in the flowers. This is followed by change of flower form, change of petal edge, change of leaf edge, leaf variegation and change of leaf form. Some of these changes appear to be linked.

In considering colour change, variegation caused by virus is not included; only the changes considered to be caused by modification of the heredity factors.

The most common colour changes occur to the white-flowered varieties with some colour. These may vary from the faintest pink spot on one petal, to being variegated, striped or spotted with colour. Generally, a sport with a wholly pink colour will appear first, then one with a deep pink or red colour. The groups of sports based on the original varieties of *Paolina Maggi, Mathotiana Alba* and *Contessa Lavinia Maggi* are well-

Mr Savige, of Wirlinga, New South Wales, has taken over the research work of the late Professor E. G. Waterhouse in bringing order out of the chaos of international camellia nomenclature. He is President of the International Camellia Society, and has recently returned from a study visit to Yunnan.

Opposite: A typical sporting camellia is the old favourite, Paolina Maggi, *first shown in 1855. The single deep pink stripe on occasional petals has developed into a fully pale pink bloom in its sport* Mrs H. Boyce, *and even further to an almost crimson self-coloured sport in* Kallista.

C. M. WILSON

ELEGANS SUPREME

HAWAII

FRANCINE

known examples. It will usually be found that the terminal sport (that with the deepest colour) is the most stable, rarely reverting or modifying, while the intermediate sport will often produce reversions to the parent form.

Subsidiary colour forms that sometimes appear include striped forms and forms with paler coloured petal edges. On the more versatile sporting camellias, there have been forms with coloured petal edges and white centres, the 'picotee' coloured, and a wide range of colour variations. Certain camellias have proved very unstable as far as colour forms are concerned. Examples are those based on the parent cultivars *Aspasia*, *Elegans*, *Betty Sheffield* and *HIKARU GENJI*.

Fimbriation of petal edges has been one of the most admired mutations, exemplified by the ancient Chinese variety *Fimbriata* (the fimbriated sport of *Alba Plena*). We find fimbriations on *Hawaii* from the *Elegans* group; *Fred Sander* from the *Tricolor* group; *Ville de Nantes* from the *Donckelarii* group, and many others.

Change of form also occurred with fimbriation when *Hawaii* took a peony form in mutating from *C. M. Wilson*. *Lady Kay* is a peony form sport of *Ville de Nantes* but retains the fimbriation. Mutation of form is generally away from the regular to the irregular, such as *Mrs Hooper Connell*, a peony sport of the regular *Alba Plena*. The examples of *Hawaii* and *Lady Kay* have been mentioned. In many of these 'form' sports, the foliage is affected. Both *Hawaii* and *Kona* in the *Elegans* complex have leaves that are of less substance and smaller average size than the parent, while *Elegans Supreme* has deeper leaf serrations and heavier texture.

The fimbriations of sports such as *Hugh Kennedy* (sport of *The Czar*) and *Guilio Nuccio Fimbriated* are of a different type, inasmuch as the flower is smaller and the petal texture thicker and coarser. At the same time, the leaves are more leathery, thickened and rugose with obscure serrations. Some of the effects of this form of leaf mutation are evident on one type of leaf variegation. *Benten* is a good example, the periphery of the leaf being distorted and pulled in wherever the variegation nears the edge.

Inasmuch as petals are basically modified leaves, certain genetic groups exercise an overall control on form, so that when mutations occur within these groups both petal and leaf are affected.

Thus there are apparently three types of mutations that include fimbriations:
1. Straight fimbriation without other change.
2. Fimbriation linked with accompanying change of flower form.
3. Fimbriation linked with accompanying change of leaf form.

The mutation of leaf variation comes in two forms:
1. The blurred, irregular type of variegation, as on *Benten*, often with white and pewter streaking.
2. The clearer, more defined and regular variegations, as on *Francois Wiot* and *Benten Kagura*, where the colour of the variegation tends towards gold with more definite margins.

In Japan, a considerable number of camellia varieties have variegated leaves, but it is not possible, with the information available, to indicate those caused by bud sports. In general, however, most varieties of plants with variegated foliage (other than virus-induced) are of somatic origin stemming from such bud sports. Examples are common amongst the maples and conifers and, from observation, this seems true of camellias.

Little is yet known about what actually triggers spontaneous mutation. While the actual mutation may be random, from an evolutionary point of view mutational frequency seems to increase with environmental pressure. As far as camellia bud sports are concerned, there are a number of cases arising from adjacent tissue damage. It is usually found that heavy pruning of varieties arising from a somatic variation causes the re-appearance of the parent variety. In this case, the cell structure at the growth points has re-established its earlier genetic construction.

Bud sports occur with varying degrees of stability. Those of the terminal red colour, such as *Otahuhu Beauty*, are the most stable of all.

On the other extreme, the writer has twice apparently successfully grafted a fully double form which occurred on his *Debutante*. Each time the resultant plant produced *Debutante* blooms only. Such transient modifications are probably caused by the distribution and concentrations of growth control hormones and auxins and cannot be considered mutations.

Probably the most famous sporting complex of all is that headed by the old Chandler seedling *Elegans*. This variety was first reported in the 'Transactions of the Horticultural Society of London' in February 1831: '*Elegans* – raised by Chandler from the *Waratah*. Free growth. The flowers are a delicate rose, 3½ in. to 4 in. [9 to 10 centimetres] in diameter.'

It is next listed in the *Horticultural Register* Vol. 1, 1831–32: '*Elegans* – another seedling raised by Chandler, at the same time as *Woodsii* (1826). This is a handsome plant with flowers large and well made, and a different red to that of the *Woodsii*, nor do they appear to sport so much.'

Famous last words! There is hardly another camellia which has produced the range of sports, both in colour and form, as have stemmed from this still popular old variety. In America the original is known as *Elegans (Chandler)*; in other countries, simply as *Elegans*, which is its priority name. Following is a list of varieties arising by mutation starting from the original clone:

ASPASIA

ELEGANS: Pink, anemone form.

SPORTS

— *Elegans Miniata:* Light lavender-pink, medium size, anemone form.
— *Elegans Supreme:* Rose pink with deep petal serration.
— *C. M. Wilson:* Light pink, edged white.
— *Hawaii:* Pale pink, fimbriated, peony form.
— *Kona:* Greenish-white, fimbriated, peony form.
— *Shiro Chan:* White with light basal pink.
— *Snow Chan:* White, anemone form.
— *Elegans Splendor:* Light pink, edged white. Deep petal serration.
— *Elegans Champagne:* White with cream-yellow centre petaloids.
— *Francine:* Pink variegated white, anemone form.

LADY LOCH

SPORTS

— *Barbara Woodroof:* Light orchid-pink outer, cream-white centre petaloids.
— *Elegans Supreme Variegated:* Variegated form.
— *C. M. Wilson Variegated:* Variegated form.

The most famous Australian sporting camellia is *Aspasia*:

ASPASIA: White to cream with some rose streaks. Peony form.

SPORTS

— *Lady Loch:* Light pink, veined deeper pink, edged white.
— *Can Can:* Pale pink with darker veining and petal edges.
— *Otahuhu Beauty:* Rose-red, peony form.
— *Camden Park:* Rose-red with white blotches.
— *Strawberry Blonde:* Light salmon-pink, speckled deep pink.
— *Glamour Girl:* Light salmon-pink, veined and marked deep pink.
— *Margaret Davis:* White to cream with rose-red splashes and edge bright rose-red.
— *Just Sue:* Light cyclamen-pink, edged bright rose.
— *Jean Clere:* Bright rose-red with band of white around petal edge.

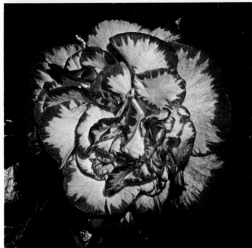
MARGARET DAVIS

In the above list, the cultivars are shown as sports of the particular variety from which they are obtained by the originator. However, it is quite usual, for example, to see *Otahuhu Beauty* on plants of *Can Can* or *Lady Loch*, and *Can Can* on plants of *Strawberry Blonde*.

JEAN CLERE

A famous Japanese camellia, *HIKARU GENJI*, heads another sporting family:

HIKARU GENJI: Semi-double pink, margined white, with some deep pink streaks running through to petal edge.

SPORTS

- *The Mikado:* As above, without the streaks.
- *Look Away:* Deep pink centre, wide white border.
- *Quaintance:* Soft pink with lines of deep pink.
- *Colonial Lady:* White with deep pink streaks.
- *Orchid Pink:* Light pink, darker pink margins.
- *Spring Sonnet:* Pink fading to white in centre.
- *BENI BOTAN:* Deep rose-pink.
- *Beauty of Holland:* Rose-pink, spotted white.

光源氏

紅牡丹

The lovely Japanese cultivar HIKARU GENJI (above) is also the parent of a large number of sports, of which BENI BOTAN (right) is the best known.

The most famous group of sports from the USA stems from *Betty Sheffield*:

BETTY SHEFFIELD: White, striped and blotched pink, loose peony form.

- *Betty Sheffield Blush:* Light pink, marked deep pink.
- *Betty Sheffield Silver:* Blush-pink bordered white, silver sheen.
- *Betty Sheffield Pink Heart:* Blush-pink with deep pink centre, white edge.

SPORTS

- *Betty Sheffield Supreme:* White with deep pink border.
- *Betty Sheffield Blush Supreme:* Blush-pink with wide edge of deep pink.
- *Betty Sheffield Coral:* Coral-pink.
- *Betty Sheffield Dawn:* Pale dawn pink.
- *Betty Sheffield Dream:* Pale pink.
- *Betty Sheffield Pink:* Deep pink.
- *Betty Sheffield Pink Variegated:* Deep pink, spotted white.
- *Betty Sheffield Pink Chiffon:* Light pink with orchid tones.
- *Blond Betty:* Peach-pink.
- *Funny Face Betty:* Pale pink merging into deep pink.
- *Lucky Seven:* Red.

All the variations of *Betty Sheffield* in the above list are of colour only, many of them proving most unstable with a tendency to sport on to the solid pink and red. It is even difficult to maintain a good form of the most desired variety, *Betty Sheffield Supreme;* invasion of the *Betty Sheffield Pink* sport in particular must be ruthlessly cut out.

Other sporting camellias of interest include the old Japanese variety *EZO NISHIKI*, which, under its Western name of *Tricolor*, produced the fimbriated mutants *Fred Sander, Cinderella* and *Dainty*. Another old Japanese variety *OTOME SHIBORI* produced the varieties *Sweetheart, Mother of Pearl, Huntington Pink* and *SHIRO OTOME*.

The American variety *Tomorrow* has produced some beautiful sports, one of particular interest being *Queen of Tomorrow*, which has thick-textured foliage and modified petals. This is reported to be the result of a colchicine-induced mutation.

Mathotiana (United States) has also produced a whole group of sports, including the fimbriate *Flowerwood*, the scarlet semi-double *Sultana* and the red peony form *Mathotiana Supreme*.

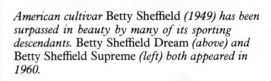

American cultivar Betty Sheffield *(1949) has been surpassed in beauty by many of its sporting descendants.* Betty Sheffield Dream *(above) and* Betty Sheffield Supreme *(left) both appeared in 1960.*

If a sport is located on a camellia, it should first be checked as to whether this is identical or not to any existing sport. If not, and if it is desired to propagate it, prune back the growth of the branch to force development of the sporting point. Always endeavour to leave one or more growth buds on the parent plant in case the first graft fails.

There is a suggestion that the various sports occur at certain time intervals after the production of the original seedling. We often find the same sport first occurring everywhere at about the same time. For example, we have *Aspasia* first grown about 1853, then the *Lady Loch* sport occurring about 1890, *Otahuhu Beauty* about 1911, *Strawberry Blonde* 1949, *Can Can* 1961, *Margaret Davis* 1962, *Jean Clere* 1969 and finally, *Just Sue* in 1971.

Many of these sports were also located in areas other than the place of origin, about the same time or shortly after. All plants of one variety are but vegetative extensions of, and hence part of, the original seedling, so something like this might be expected.

However, seedlings have been observed which produced both the light pink and deep pink sports, together with the basic white variety on first time of flowering.

So keep an eye open for flowers that are different on your camellias. Who knows when another sport to match *Elegans Splendor* or *Tomorrow Park Hill* will appear?

WHAT CAMELLIA IS THAT?

The classification and identification of camellia cultivars. Their nomenclature, size, form and colour

羽衣

Delicate Japanese cultivar HAGOROMO *(which translates as 'feathered robe'), was for many years known in Western gardens as* Magnoliiflora.

The popular semi-double camellia Lady Clare *is now correctly known as* AKASHIGATA, *its original Japanese name.* 明石潟

In the last quarter century, a great deal of work has been undertaken by a number of different camellia bodies in an effort to straighten out the thorny question of international identification and nomenclature. The aim is to establish one, and one only, valid name for each cultivated camellia variety, thus reducing the unwieldy accumulation of names to a more manageable size.

It is probable that national and local pride, and also personal feelings, will sometimes be hurt as this activity proceeds, but there can be no real doubt as to its value.

Nomenclature committees of the American Camellia Society, the Australian Camellia Research Society, the International Camellia Society, the New Zealand Camellia Society and the Southern California Camellia Society have all agreed that the first validly published name for each variety or cultivar must have priority. They have ruled that *valid* publication consists of a listing of name, accompanied by a description and/or illustration sufficient to identify the variety. This must be in a dated (at least as to year), printed (or similarly duplicated) publication which is (or has been) available to the public. This may include horticultural books and magazines, nursery or trade catalogues and publications of horticultural societies, and applies in all languages.

Because of the origin of the camellia species, it has been agreed also to accept names first published in other than Roman characters. This means that the old Chinese and Japanese names have priority (where they were published) over other more recent Western names, so that many older imported cultivars have reverted to their original names, which were often quite euphonious and are charming in translation. *Lady Clare* becomes again *AKASHI GATA*, *Tinsie* becomes *BOKUHAN*, *Magnoliiflora* becomes *HAGOROMO*, to give only three examples of the hundreds of camellias that were named and known in Japan for centuries before they were imported to the West. When there are linguistic or other difficulties, however, these Japanese names may be used in translation, except in the case of personal names.

The Chinese names (particularly of the reticulata varieties) pose more of a problem, since many of them are quite unpronounceable to other nationalities, and in any case translate more as a description of the flower than as a true name in the Western sense. For example, *MAYE YINHONG* means *Reticulate Leaf Spinel Pink*, and *LIUYE YINHONG* means *Willow Leaf Spinel Pink*.

In these cases, it is allowable (and customary) to give the camellia a new Western name containing an allusion to the Chinese original; for instance, the last-named *LIUYE YINHONG* became *Willow Wand*.

These Chinese names, incidentally, consisting of four words, would be considered too long for modern nomenclature, where one or two words only is the rule, with a maximum of three.

Modern camellia names should also be in a modern language, whether as a personal name or some other word, and *not* Latinised to form a pseudoscientific word which might be confused as a species, for example, *Anemoniflora* or *Chandleri*, two names of nineteenth century cultivars.

One name must not be used for plants of two or more species (for example, not for both a japonica and a sasanqua). There are already examples of this among many of the old Japanese cultivars.

Where a camellia has sported one variety only, the name of that sport should include the name of the camellia on which it appeared (for example, *Finlandia* and *Finlandia Variegated*). Where many different sports appear from one original however, this is not obligatory as it may become quite confusing. The many sports of *Carter's Sunburst* are a good example.

It is no longer customary to include in names forms of address which might become confused. Therefore, in any future names, modes of address like Miss, Mrs, Ms, Mr, M. Mme, Sr, and Sra are out. Official titles such as Dr, General, Duke, Queen and Professor are still in.

In describing the many cultivars in this book, I have followed the rule of priority nomenclature. I have also used the traditional forms in describing colour, size and style of bloom and flowering period (though these will require some further explanation), and form or habit of growth where this is important or unusual.

Colour, alas, is subjective. Apart from the statistical fact that more than twelve per cent of the male population in the West is completely colour-blind, the colour of many camellias (particularly the reds) may vary according to soil composition, whether the camellia is planted in sun or shade, and many other factors. In this case, colour photographs speak more accurately than any words. Those in this book have all been carefully balanced to the original flowers *as I have seen them*; but while photographing camellias on both sides of the Pacific as well as in Japan, I noticed considerable variation among specimens of the same cultivar. For instance, the beautiful *Guilio Nuccio* is generally more of a vivid scarlet in Sydney than the 'coral rose-pink' by which it is described in the USA, and which it appeared to be in pictures taken at the Nuccio Nursery.

Above: Carter's Sunburst*'s many descendants all have names including that of the original, but this is now considered bad nomenclatural practice. Here is* Carter's Sunburst Pink.

This chart gives a clear indication of the wide variation in sizes among camellia cultivars accepted for show judging:

1. Miniature
2. Small
3. Medium
4. Medium Large
5. Large
6. Very large

1   2 3 4 5   6

加茂本阿弥

A typical single camellia, KAMO HON AMI.

Ellen Sampson *is a popular semi-double bloom.*

Speciosissima, *an old-time anemone form bloom.*

Flowering period is also a problem, and we can only generalise it as early, mid or late season, without specifying the month.

Early would mean March to June in the southern hemisphere, October to January in the northern. Mid season would mean June to August in the southern hemisphere, January to March in the north. Late season would be August to October in the southern hemisphere, March to May in the northern hemisphere. But here I am, writing this piece in Sydney in November, and several of my camellias *(Drama Girl, Leonard Messel* and *Paolina Maggi)* are still flowering, proving that the camellia season may vary according to the climate.

But there are other factors as well. An early summer means early bud formation; a late autumn may mean sasanquas begin flowering later than usual; a hard winter may mean a delayed spring blooming. Then again, the farther you are from the equator, the later each variety may bloom. Seasonal camellia shows normally work their way north in the northern hemisphere, south in the southern. We cannot hope to suggest precisely when a given cultivar will flower in your garden, or even in your area; or whether it will do well there in the first place. Nearby camellia growers and nurserymen are your best reference for this.

Whatever we do, camellias will flower better and look better when the spring weather remains cool; late-blooming varieties should be planted where they will receive a good degree of shade at the time they are in peak display. Wherever possible, pale coloured cultivars (especially whites) should be planted where they will never receive early morning sun, as it burns the flowers while evaporating the dew on them. Nor do white cultivars fare well with the burning westerly sun of late afternoon on them.

Size is something we can be specific about. The chart on page 59 clearly shows the great variation in camellia sizes. Each written entry gives the average size of bloom on that variety. Remember, however, that we must assume the cultivar is being properly grown in a soil and a climate it enjoys. I would personally have classified *Nuccio's Gem,* from my own garden, merely as a medium-sized camellia of perhaps 8 centimetres (3 inches) diameter, had I not seen it in northern California at a full 11 centimetres (4½ inches) — definitely large. Poor soil and a harsh climate will reduce flower size; over-fertilisation, heavy disbudding and chemical treatment may increase it.

The camellia size classifications used in this book are those accepted internationally for show judging. These are (with their approximate metric conversions):

MINIATURE: 2½ inches or less (6.5 centimetres or less)
SMALL: 2½–3 inches (6.5–8 centimetres)
MEDIUM: 3–3½ inches (8–9 centimetres)
MEDIUM LARGE: 3½–4 inches (9–10 centimetres)
LARGE: 4–5 inches (10–13 centimetres)
VERY LARGE: over 5 inches (over 13 centimetres)

In doubtful cases, we describe size in terms of a range, for example, medium to large. This scale applies to all japonica, reticulata and non-reticulata hybrids. Most species and many sasanqua cultivars are well below the smallest classification in size.

It would be wonderful if each camellia could be illustrated in actual size, but space limitations make this impossible. As a general rule, however, sasanqua and miniature blooms are shown natural size; japonica, Higo and hybrid blooms half natural size; while the scale of the gigantic reticulata blooms is suggested by a selection of illustrations close to size, though other reticulatas must be limited to smaller reproduction.

The classification of **flower form or style** is quite straightforward, although all flowers do not always obey the rules at all times. Some varieties are noticeably variable from one bloom to another. Where possible, this is noted in the relevant entry.

The accepted classification of camellia flowers divides the whole group into the six illustrated types. These types are:

SINGLE
From five to eight petals in one row, and a prominent display of stamens and pistil, which may include petaloids. The petals may be loose, regular or irregular. This type of camellia is most highly appreciated in Japan. Examples: *AKEBONO, Amabilis, KAMO HON AMI*, most sasanquas and Higos.

SEMI-DOUBLE
Two or more rows of large outer petals (nine or more petals) surrounding a prominent stamen display; again, sometimes with petaloids. The petals may be regular, irregular or loose; may overlap heavily, or may be set in several rows to give a charming 'hose-in-hose' effect. Examples: *AKASHIGATA, Ellen Sampson, Grand Slam, HAGOROMO, HIKARU GENJI, The Czar* and most of the *Williamsii* hybrids.

ANEMONE FORM
One or more rows of large outer petals, either flat or undulating. The centre is a variable convex mass of petaloids and stamens. Examples: *Edelweiss, Elegans, Speciosissima*.

PEONY FORM or INFORMAL DOUBLE
A deep, rounded flower of the following forms:
(a) *Loose peony form* — loose petals which may be irregular, sometimes intermingled with petaloids and stamens at the centre. Examples: *ARAJISHI, Vedrine*.
(b) *Full peony form* — a domed mass either of mixed, irregular petals, petaloids and stamens; or irregular petals and petaloids without stamens. Examples: *Aspasia, Debutante, Georgia Rouse, Lady Loch*.

ROSE FORM DOUBLE
Petals imbricated or overlapped as in a formal double, but finally opening to reveal a spectacular stamen display in a concave centre. Examples: *Elizabeth Dowd Silver, Glen 40, Mathotiana*.

FORMAL DOUBLE
Many rows of petals fully overlapped in symmetrical form, usually with a cone of tightly furled petals in the centre. Sometimes this may open petal by petal to reveal no stamens at all, and hence the flower is sterile. Sometimes the petals are arranged in layers to give a hexagonal appearance; in other cultivars they form a perfect spiral. Petals may be flat, cupped or recurved. The formal double camellia was the most valued form in China, and later, in nineteenth century Europe, where it was known in camellia circles as a 'perfection'. Examples: *Alba Plena, Blushing Beauty, Commendatore Betti* (hexagonal), *Nuccio's Gem* (spiral).

You will also come across occasional cultivars described as lily or tulip shaped, in which the generally long petals open only partially into the bell shape of a lily or a tulip. Some of these blooms are very beautiful indeed, and much sought after by connoisseurs, but there are not enough of them to form a separate class. They are usually single or semi-double.

Among the older, rarer Japanese cultivars, there are some very extraordinary flowers indeed, including triple-decker blooms. But these are not likely to concern the average camellia hobbyist, who may indeed never see them.

The camellia cultivars described and illustrated in this book are divided among chapters, each devoted to the cultivars of a particular species or style. The cultivars of *Camellia japonica* follow immediately, after which you will find the miniature japonica cultivars, and the wonderful Higo cultivars from Kumamoto province on the island of Kyūshū.

The reticulata cultivars and camellias with reticulata parentage form the next chapter, followed by the autumn-flowering sasanquas, including a few cultivars of the species *hiemalis* and *vernalis*. Hybrid camellias, including crosses of all species except reticulata, form the final major group.

Additional cultivar illustrations will also be found in other chapters, and in the introductions to dictionary sections. These are, of course, cross-referenced to their relevant descriptions elsewhere in the book.

ARAJISHI, *a famous peony form flower.* 荒獅子

Roseform double Elizabeth Dowd Silver.

A perfect formal double, Commendatore Betti.

CAMELLIA JAPONICA

Including cultivars of the sub-species
C. japonica Var. Rusticana,
with notes on cultivation

The most popular species of camellia in cultivation is *C. japonica*, in its myriad variations. It has been grown more widely, and for a longer period of time than any other species. It accounts, perhaps, for more than three-quarters of the total number of camellia cultivars grown everywhere in the world.

The japonicas are easy to grow in any mild winter climate, though they will endure occasional drops in temperature down to freezing point. However, neither they, nor any other camellia species, are recommended outdoor plants for any area where heavy frost or winter snows are the rule. In borderline areas, they can be grown with considerable success in the shelter of a shade or lath house, or under the protection of evergreen trees.

The culture of japonica camellias is basically an understanding and reproduction of their native habitat, where they are commonly found on the slopes and in the valleys of evergreen forests. Here they receive shade and shelter from summer sun and from winter's storms. The atmosphere is generally humid all year, the soil perfectly drained, containing a great deal of gravel or sand, and covered with rotting leaf debris.

Most camellias in Western gardens are grown in coastal areas, though not necessarily within sight of the sea. An individual plant is best positioned (in the southern hemisphere) within an arc stretching from the south-east, through the south to the south-western side of a building, fence, tree or other protection. Northern hemisphere growers merely substitute north for south in the previous sentence, and plant accordingly. Your camellias should receive no more than half the sun on a summer's day, and only afternoon sun (if any) in the winter flowering months. Morning sun during the blooming period tends to mark the flowers badly by evaporating overnight dew or precipitation on the buds and petals, particularly those of pale coloured varieties.

Camellias are also sensitive to excess wind, robbing surface roots of nearby trees and alkaline soil, including drainage from lime-enriched beds nearby. They are not fussy about soil depth, but should not be planted any closer than 2 metres (6 feet) apart from one another.

Where a large number of camellias is grown, and the ideal shelter of trees or buildings is not available in the open garden, they can be grown to perfection in tubs which can be moved about seasonally — or alternatively, collected together in the shelter of a shade house or fernery. This is an ideal solution for hot, dry, inland areas.

Closer to the sea itself, camellias are best grown in the lee of quicker growing trees or large shrubberies, where they'll be protected from salt-laden wind. Even then, regular watering of the foliage is advisable to prevent the accumulation of burning salt film on leaves and buds. This watering is best done in the evening.

Camellia japonica is a large plant — actually a small tree — and may grow in time to 7 metres (21 feet) in height in a suitable position. Generally however, it looks and flowers better when pruned to a more compact shape — no more than 3 metres (9 feet) high and across. Never plant japonicas closer than 1 metre (3 feet) to a wall, fence or driveway, or an ugly, lop-sided plant will result in later years. The only exception

This superbly trained group of camellias is planted in an amazingly narrow bed along the side of a California home.

Opposite: Clark Hubbs, *a dazzling scarlet cultivar from California, is typical of modern American camellia cultivars. It has fringed petals.*

to this (and an attractive one where the space is not available) is to espalier the camellia, or train it to a two dimensional shape, attached to the wall or fence.

When camellias must be planted in the vicinity of heavily rooted trees, it may be advisable to trench out past the camellia roots from time to time to keep the tree's roots at bay. Deeper tree roots are rarely a problem, for camellias are essentially surface rooters. They do however resent undue competition from heavy plantings of ground cover, or even lawn and other grasses. It is far wiser to leave the ground bare for a radius of several feet around each bush.

Right: Specimen camellias and azaleas are protected from summer heat in the dappled shade of a lath house. Garden of enthusiast W. F. Goertz. Photo Willard Goertz.

A decorative display of cut camellia blooms in the bowl of a Spanish wall fountain.

Planting Japonica camellias are far more tolerant of variation in soil acidity than *Azaleas*. While preferring a soil of about pH6 reading (slightly more acid than neutral, which gives a pH7 reading) they will also do well enough when the soil is *slightly* alkaline. Growers in areas where the natural soil reading is above pH8 would be wise to lower the alkalinity chemically, or raise their camellias in tubs of special, acid mix.

The ideal soil composition is a rich, light loam, well enriched with humus in the form of rotted leaf mould or peat moss. Heavy soils should be lightened by the addition of coarse bush or river sand — over-sandy soils need an extra ration of peat to prevent their draining too freely.

The necessity for good drainage can scarcely be overstressed. If the camellia cannot be planted on a slight slope, it will be safer planted with the nursery soil line slightly above the surrounding garden level. Dig a hole at least double the width of the root ball, and half as deep again. Mix the soil you have removed with the peat and compost and/or sand. Tip a portion of this mixture back in the hole and stamp it firm.

Thoroughly water the plant in its nursery container, slide or tip it out and place in position. Tease out any roots that were tending to travel around the perimeter of the nursery root ball, then fill the hole surrounding the new plant, and firm with your boot. Experienced growers often use the leftover soil to form a small dam about 45 cm (18 in) out from the trunk. This need only be 7.5 cm (3 in) high, but will make sure that any water your camellia does get is thriftily used and does not flow away.

After planting, dribble the hose into the saucer-shaped depression you have made, and fill it several times. Remember to water regularly until

Densely flowering camellias such as colourful Glen 40 *can be planted to form a magnificent hedge along a side boundary.*

the camellia has settled into its new home. Planting can take place any time from early autumn to late spring — but never in the hot months.

After Care Regular camellia maintenance is minimal when compared to the requirements of other shrubs. A single annual dressing of cow manure and well-decayed compost in early spring is sufficient feeding for the year, and acts as a good mulch during the hotter weather. An additional feeding with soluble, liquid fertiliser is sometimes given in autumn, using it either at the manufacturer's recommended strength or below, and only *after* watering the plant.

Do not dig or cultivate around camellias — remember they are surface rooters. Merely weed regularly, and remove the old mulch each spring, replacing it with fresh manure and compost.

Watering should be done regularly, but infrequently. One deep, weekly soaking is preferable to a daily sprinkle. Watering should be heaviest in summer, autumn and in winter, if the season is a dry one. It can generally be tapered off in spring. Do not water the plant itself when it is in bloom, only the root area below.

Pruning of camellias is rarely necessary if the flowers are picked regularly, but older trees can be rejuvenated if all branches are taken back to the thickness of a pencil before the rush of new spring foliage appears. *Very* large trees can be given an additional pruning to shape in summer or autumn. Generally this pruning, which results in the loss of many flower buds, will improve the size and texture of the blooms.

A typical fruit of Camellia japonica. *The hard skin will soon split to reveal several seeds from which new plants can easily be raised.*

Pests are few, the worst of them being various leaf-eating caterpillars which revel in the soft growth of new spring foliage. A thorough spraying with arsenate of lead in early spring will put an end to their activities, and the remaining whitish residue will gradually be washed away by rain. Leaf-sucking pests such as aphids, mites and thrip can often be despatched with a blast from the hose, but thorough spraying with a systemic poison is more permanent. Ask your local nurseryman to recommend one. Scale of several types may be found under the leaves, but can generally be prevented with an annual spring spraying with dilute white oil in water — remember to spray *under* the foliage where the scale appears.

Below: Camellias make ideal container plants. Here is Dixie Knight, *planted in an Italian terracotta urn, and pruned to columnar shape.*

Above: To the Japanese, an exquisite sight — the ground carpeted with fallen camellia blooms. To the American grower it is more of a nightmare, suggesting the ravages of the dreaded camellia flower blight.

Above right: A perfectly espaliered specimen of the fragrant japonica cultivar Kramer's Supreme *at the home of Mr and Mrs Charles O'Malley.*

Principal diseases are root rot, and camellia flower blight, which fortunately seems to be confined to parts of North America.

Root rot is caused by *Phytophthora cinnamomi*, a fungus found in continuously wet soil. It is more easily prevented than cured, by paying proper attention to soil drainage before planting. If the rot does occur later (signalled by wilting, listless foliage) the only possible step is to move the plant to an area where the soil has been thoroughly fumigated or drenched with one of several products on the market. (Again, your local nurseryman is your best source of advice.) The ultimate cure is to destroy the plant, which is unlikely to recover completely.

No cure has yet been found for the dreaded camellia flower blight, caused by a fungus named *Sclerotinia camelliae*. Its ravages can be minimised by meticulous attention to hygiene, however. The blight-causing blooms must be picked up daily and destroyed by fire, together with any affected flowers still on the plant. The plant itself can be thoroughly saturated before and after the blooming period with a good fungicide, the mulch surrounding it carefully swept away and destroyed. In that way, it is possible to break the blight's breeding cycle.

Tub culture Growing camellias in containers has become very popular in recent years, and has many advantages when garden space is limited, or when soil or climatic conditions are adverse. Potted camellias make splendid specimens on terraces or patios, as doorway features, or even as accents in the open garden. They can be moved out to brighten bare spots in winter, and taken back to some sheltered corner during the summer months. Provided the drainage is ample, and the camellias are tubbed in well aerated soil mix, the plants will thrive with little attention for many years.

A minimum container diameter of 40 cm (16 in) is recommended, and if the collection is large, the containers are best purchased to a uniform design.

At least 5 cm (2 in) of drainage material should be placed in each container, graduating from pieces of broken flower pot through coarse pebbles to fine gravel. This will be topped up either by a soil mix containing plenty of peat, or a mixture of 75 per cent pure peat and 25 per cent coarse sand. Such a mixture will drain well, but retain adequate moisture. Do not assume that the plant is drying out just because the surface seems dry. Poke a finger well in, and if there's the least sign of damp, postpone the watering. More tubbed camellias die from drowning than any other cause!

Above: A hanging pot of the old favourite Elegans (Chandler) *in the garden of California camellian Ken Hallstone.*

Left: Japonica Ellen Sampson *in full bloom on the author's terrace.*

In the dictionary sections that follow, all camellia cultivars are listed under all known synonyms, with cross reference to the valid name under which they are described. The valid name headings include the year in which the cultivar was first described or introduced. All entries include the country of origination, and in many cases, where known, the name of the original grower.

Some entries contain a deal of interesting historical information, both on the camellia cultivar itself, and about the person or place after which it was named. Throughout the book, where a camellia is reported to be fragrant, this is noted at the top of the relevant cultivar entry.

Japanese names are pronounced with equal stress on each syllable. The vowels are short, as in c*a*t, g*e*t, s*i*t, r*o*t, m*u*ck, except where they bear a horizontal accent, in which case they become as in l*a*rd, h*ee*d, tr*ie*d, r*oa*d, cr*u*de.

A few simple Japanese words used often in camellia nomenclature are: NO, meaning of or from; NISHIKI = brocade or pattern; SHIBORI = striped; BENI = red, KURO = black; SHIRO = white; DAI = large; KO = small; SHIN = new.

Japonicas

ADOLPHE AUDUSSON VARIEGATED

AKASHIGATA　明石潟

AKEBONO　曙

ALBA PLENA

ADA WILSON (see ROSEA SUPERBA)

ADMIRAL NIMITZ (see KISHŪ TSUKASA)

ADOLPHE (see ADOLPHE AUDUSSON)

ADOLPHE AUDUSSON 1877
(syn: *Adolphe, Audrey Hopfer*) A famous French camellia released in 1877, *Adolphe Audusson* has had many nomenclatural problems since that date. But Audrey must bow to Adolphe in the matter of priority. It is a large, semi-double bloom of glowing dark red, and a great favourite for over a century. It blooms mid season.

ADOLPHE AUDUSSON VARIEGATED
(syn: *F. M. Uyematsu*) A boldly variegated sport of the previous variety, *Adolphe Audusson Variegated* is in all other respects identical to its parent.

AKA DAIKAGURA (see BENI DAIKAGURA)

AKASHIGATA (Akashi Bay) 1877
(syn: *Empress, Lady Clare, Nellie Bly*) Imported to the United Kingdom from Japan in 1877, when it was named *Lady Clare*, the beautiful *AKASHIGATA* can be traced back only ten years earlier under its Japanese name, but is probably older. A fast-growing camellia of wide weeping growth, it blooms early and freely. The foliage is dark green, long, pointed and serrated. The large semi-double blooms have a crêpelike texture, are a delicate carmine-rose, and may have matching petaloids. (See also photo p. 58)

AKEBONO (Dawn) 1948
(syn: *Betty, SHIN AKEBONO* [US], *Valentine*) One of the simplest and most perfect of Japanese cultivars, *AKEBONO* was introduced from Japan to the West only in 1948. It has a medium-sized, generally single bloom of slightly cupped form, and tinted palest pink. *AKEBONO* blooms mid season, but is a beautiful plant any time of the year. In the United States, it is known as *SHIN AKEBONO*, due to confusion with a different, but identically named camellia introduced in 1937.

ALBA FIMBRIATA (see FIMBRIATA)

ALBA PLENA 1792
One of the oldest camellias in cultivation, and very slow in growth, *Alba Plena* is recognisable in Chinese manuscripts as far back as the Sung Dynasty, when it was known as *TA PAI (Great White)*. It gained its present name in 1792, when it was imported by a Captain Connor of the British East India Company, and thus became the first double camellia seen in the West. The bloom to which all other doubles are compared, it is a medium-sized formal double flower of porcelain white, with a hundred or more petals, and blooms very early. Few camellias are so widely grown.

ALBERTII 1841
(syn: *Prince Albert*) Named for Prince Albert of Saxe-Coburg-Gotha in the year following his marriage to England's Queen Victoria, this is a lovely, old-fashioned camellia of medium size and full, ruffled peony form. A romantic blush-pink in colour, it is lavishly striped in carmine and white, and blooms mid season. It was imported from China, where it doubtless has an older name.

ALEXANDER HUNTER c. 1870
This dark crimson single camellia, with occasional petaloids, was raised in Sydney by pioneer grower Alexander Hunter in the 1870s, but not named until 1941, long after his death. It is of medium size, and flowers very early.

ALICE SLACK (see BLOOD OF CHINA)

ALISON LEIGH WOODROOF 1955
Shading from blush to a deep glowing pink at petal edges, *Alison Leigh Woodroof* is a 1955 introduction. Small in size, semi-double, and flowering mid season, it is very popular with devotees of the boutonniere-size camellia.

ALLEN'S PINK (see TRIUMPHANS)

ALOHA (see ARAJISHI)

ALPINE GLOW 1959
A fine semi-double bloom of glowing cerise-red, *Alpine Glow* was introduced by hybridist Caesar Breschini. The irregularly fluted petals are slightly reflexed, fully revealing a central boss of cream stamens. Medium in size, it blooms mid season.

ALTA GAVIN 1962
Often seen in United States shows, *Alta Gavin's* popularity seems limited to the continent where it was first grown, in Louisiana. It is a semi-double bloom of medium to large size, and with white petals shading deep pink at the flower's perimeter. Blooms mid to late season.

AMA NO KAWA (Milky Way) 1877
Dating back to 1877 in Japan, the brilliant *AMA NO KAWA* was unveiled to the West in 1930. It is a large semi-double white camellia, with incurved, crêped petals. Mid season is its flowering peak.

AMABILIS 1893
(syn: *Mrs Frances Saunders, White Poppy*) Medium-sized *Amabilis* is a useful white single camellia for mid season. Rather resembling a Higo camellia (which see) it has a heavy boss of stamens, and is of flat form. It was introduced by Japan's Yokohama Nurseries in 1893, but the local name is not recorded.

AMIGO 1962
Admirers of the small camellia fall in love at first sight with *Amigo*. The normal-sized bush produces masses of small anemone-form blooms in deep coral-rose, on each of which a coronet of golden stamens surrounds a central mass of coral

ALEXANDER HUNTER

ALTA GAVIN

petaloids, often striped rose. Blooms mid season.

ANEMONIFLORA 1806

(syn: *Honeycomb, Mrs Sol Runyon, Waratah*) This very old camellia of semi-double anemone form and medium size was imported from China in 1806 to London's Kew Gardens. It would seem to have a close resemblance to *Great Eastern*, both from the style of its flower and from its coloration: glowing crimson-red with radially streaked central petals. *Anemoniflora* has acquired many invalid names. Blooms mid season.

ANEMONIFLORA ALBA 1825

(syn: *Waratah White, White Anemone*) No longer in great popularity, this 1825 cultivar from Chandler of Vauxhall, England, is still found in many older gardens. Its anemone form flowers are similar in style to the previous entry, but of plain white.

ANGEL 1953

(syn: *Candlelight*) This large white camellia of semi-double form varies from others of its type in the profusion of fluted, notched petals and the faint golden glow of its cupped centre. It was developed in California in 1953, and blooms mid season.

ANGEL (see also BENTEN)

ANGELICA (see GOVERNOR MOUTON)

ANITA 1940

A medium-sized semi-double bloom of most unusual shape, *Anita* was released in 1940. An open lily form flower, *Anita* has slender pale pink petals, radially striped and flecked with carmine. It blooms mid season on a bush of strong, compact growth.

ANN SOTHERN 1960

Earl Hudson of California must have shared my enthusiasm when he named this lovely camellia after actress *Ann Sothern*. It is delicate, rather fluffy, and with petals of ample proportion that shade from Venetian pink to a centre of porcelain-white. Large in size and semi-double, it can produce occasional petaloids. *Ann Sothern* blooms mid season.

APACHE (see RED GIANT)

ARABIAN NIGHTS 1958

The only feature connecting this beautiful camellia with the Arabian Nights' entertainments seems to be the colour, which is described as Oriental pink. It is a large semi-double bloom with ruffled, reflexed petals tinted in many variations of pink. Blooms in mid season. It is a creation of Pasadena's McCaskill Gardens.

ARAJISHI (Restive Lion) 1877

(syn: *Aloha*, BENI ARAJISHI, *Callie*) All red and ruffled like the young lion in traditional

AMIGO

ANEMONIFLORA

ANGEL

ANITA

ANN SOTHERN

ARAJISHI

荒獅子

Japonicas

Japanese Noh Plays, *ARAJISHI* is one of the showiest camellias in any catalogue. It can be traced back to 1877 in Japan, and was exported to the West in 1891. It is often described as a dark salmon-rose, but I prefer to think of it as a gorgeous red. It is fully peony form, with gold stamens flashing among a profusion of frilled petaloids. The bush is full of vigour, blooming mid season. (See also photo p. 61)

ARAJISHI VARIEGATED
Similar in form and habit to the previous camellia, *ARAJISHI VARIEGATED* splashes the red blooms with white.

ARNALDO DA BRESCIA
(see FRA ARNALDO DA BRESCIA)

ARRABELLA 1949
(syn: *Donna Kaye*) *Arrabella* has been declared the priority name for this showy bloom, which opens orange-red buds and fades them to a glowing salmon. It is medium in size and semi-double, with petals precociously notched and ruffled. The plant bursts into bloom mid to late season.

ASPASIA 1850
(syn: *Flore Celeste, Paeoniaeflora*) One of the great sporting camellias, Australian cultivar *Aspasia* first bloomed in the garden of Camden Park, New South Wales in the 1840s, where it was named by William Macarthur. The original plant is still to be seen there, and its scions bloom right around the world, though in the USA under the name *Paeoniaeflora*. *Aspasia* itself is a fine camellia, although its principal claim to fame may well be an inherent genetic instability. At least half a dozen other superior camellias (of similar form but different coloration) have appeared as sports on plants of its descendants (see *Margaret Davis*). The original *Aspasia* is a medium-sized informal double camellia of peony form. The ruffled petals are creamy white with the odd streak or line of carmine-pink. An earlier red camellia named *Aspasia* appears in old catalogues. (Photo p. 55)

ASPASIA (US) 1853
(see EMPEROR OF RUSSIA VARIEGATED)

ASPASIA ROSEA (see OTAHUHU BEAUTY)

ASPASIA VARIEGATA (see CAMDEN PARK)

AUDREY HOPFER (see ADOLPHE AUDUSSON)

AUNT JETTY (see GOVERNOR MOUTON)

AURORA BOREALIS
(see FINLANDIA VARIEGATED)

AUSTRALIS 1951
A 1951 production of Camellia Grove Nursery, New South Wales, *Australis* is an open peony form bloom of medium size. The colour of its mid season flowers is brilliant rose-red, and they open to display a dazzling array of golden stamens.

AVE MARIA 1956
Not many modern Italian camellias go on to world success, but the charming *Ave Maria* is an exception. Released by grower Breschini in 1956, it is a small to medium formal double of pale silver-pink. Very like *USU OTOME* but with a shorter flowering season.

BADGEN'S BEAUTY (see PINK PEARL)

BALLET DANCER 1960
American collectors describe this as a 'sweet pea' type camellia, in which the colouring shades gradually from an overall creamy-pink to a brilliant coral at petal edges. Beyond that it is a medium-sized flower of full peony form, with mixed petals and petaloids. Early to commence flowering, late to finish, it is a valuable bushy plant for any collection.

BAMBINO 1959
Similar in colouring to *Amigo*, *Bambino* is another small japonica. Coral rose-pink and perfectly anemone form, it has notched petals surrounding a mass of central petaloids with lighter tips. Blooming mid season.

BANDAI 1964
A charming camellia imported by California's Nuccio Nurseries in 1964, *BANDAI* is a cultivar of the japonica subspecies *C. rusticana* or *Snow Camellia*. The bloom is a medium-sized white semi-double with a profusion of notched, pointed petals, and a mid to late season blooming period. The growth is compact with small leaves of brilliant green. Its Japanese origin is not known.

BANDANA OF KYOTO
(see KYŌ KANOKO VARIEGATED)

BARONNE DE BLEICHROEDER (US)
(see OTOME SHIBORI)

BATISTA (see BENI BOTAN)

BEAU HARP VARIEGATED
(see DR JOHN D. BELL)

BEAUTY OF HOLLAND 1938 FRAGRANT
(syn: *C. P. Morgan, Doris Madalia, HIKARU GENJI YOKUMOKU, Princess Lucille*) A superb sport of the japonica *HIKARU GENJI*, *Beauty of Holland* is listed in few catalogues these days, which is hard to understand since it was once so popular. Medium in size, blooming mid season, it is an informal double flower of deep rose-pink, liberally spotted and splotched with white. It was introduced to the United States in 1938.

BELGIUM RED (see ROMANY)

ARRABELLA

BANDAI 万代

BELLA ROMANA 1863

A gorgeous Italian cultivar introduced in 1863, *Bella Romana* is a floral paean to the beautiful women of the city that gave it birth. Medium-sized, rose form double, and blooming mid season, the flowers are a rich light pink, profusely lined and striped in glowing carmine. But alas, it makes little impact among modern collectors, who seem obsessed with size.

BELLE JEANETTE 1851

(syn: *Cleopatra*) As far as can be definitely established, *Belle Jeanette* was first listed in 1851 by French grower Miellez, but Italian camellians are still arguing that it is one of their varieties. However the argument ends, it is a lovely flower — a medium-sized formal double of rose-red flecked white. Bloom peaks mid season.

BELLIFORMIS 1856

Another charmer from the great days of the Italian hybridists, *Belliformis* is everything its name suggests — a beautiful flower of perfect form. Medium-sized formal double in style, it has cupped petals which shade from a deep rose at the flower's heart, and are interspersed with paler petals toward the edges. There are also occasional white markings on this mid season beauty. It was introduced by Florentine grower Charles Luzatti in 1856.

BENI ARAJISHI (see ARAJISHI)

BENI BOTAN c. 1877   FRAGRANT

(syn: *Batista, Harmonious, Herme Pink, Herme Red, HIKARU GENJI AKA, KŌ BOTAN, Majestic, Pink Herme, Pink Jordan's Pride, Powell's Pink, Radiant Glow, Red Herme, Red Jordan's Pride, Rosy Dawn, Wings*) It's fortunate not many camellias acquire the same number of names as this rose-red beauty, or we should soon run out of names. But *BENI BOTAN* has priority; it was known thus at least as far back as 1877, long before the Star Nursery imported it from Japan in 1930. Like its sport parent *HIKARU GENJI*, it is a medium-sized semi-double bloom, flowering mid season. Its upright centre petals are sometimes streaked with white. (Photo p. 56)

BENI DAIKAGURA 1933

(syn: *AKA DAIKAGURA, Daikagura Pink, Daikagura Red, Great Sacred Dance Red, Pink Kagura, Shangri La*) A stunning sport of the old variegated Japanese cultivar *DAIKAGURA* (which see), *BENI DAIKAGURA* is a medium to large peony form camellia that varies in colour from deep pink to rose-red. The petals are notched and fluted and may still show occasional white markings. It dates back to 1933 and was introduced to the United States thereafter.

BENI HASSAKU 1937

(syn: *First Day of 8th Month, HASSAKU*) A charming Japanese cultivar, supremely elegant in its simplicity, *BENI HASSAKU* is a single

BEAUTY OF HOLLAND 光源氏横杢

BELLA ROMANA

BENI DAIKAGURA   紅太神楽

BENI HASSAKU   紅八朔

BETTY SHEFFIELD SUPREME

camellia of rather open flat form, and was introduced by Japanese grower Chugai in 1937. The irregularly sized petals remind one of rose-pink silk. There are both white and variegated sports.

BENI MYŌRENJI (see MYŌRENJI)

BENTEN (Goddess) 1930   FRAGRANT
(syn: *Angel*)   A true camellia novelty, and much favoured by devotees of Japanese flower arrangement, the cultivar *BENTEN* (variously translated as *Goddess* and *Angel*) bears small, single, deep pink flowers that bloom in mid season. The plant's real glory, however, are the brilliantly coloured leaves in which the green is margined with a variable band of creamy-yellow. It was imported to the United States from Japan in 1930, and many growers find it has distinct fragrance.

BESSIE MORSE BELLINGRATH
(see TOKI NO HAGASANE)

BETTY (see AKEBONO)

BETTY FOY SANDERS 1965
An interesting semi-double bloom of flared trumpet shape, *Betty Foy Sanders* flowers early to mid season and is medium in size. The petals are white with irregular red radial markings.

BETTY HOPFER (see TOKI NO HAGASANE)

BETTY SHEFFIELD 1949
A successful camellia introduction of 1949, *Betty Sheffield* has a remarkable history of sporting and has given rise to at least a dozen newer and more spectacular forms in subsequent years. It is a medium to large camellia of loose peony form, with slightly waved petals, flowering mid season. The base colour is white, blotched and striped with both red and pink. The bush is dense and compact.

BETTY SHEFFIELD BLUSH 1958
A popular sport of the preceding variety, *Betty Sheffield Blush* is similar in growth, style and flowering habit, but the blooms are overall pale pink with irregular marks of a deeper shade.

BETTY SHEFFIELD DREAM 1960
This further chapter in the Betty Sheffield story is a completely pale pink flower named *Betty Sheffield Dream*. In all other respects it is identical to the parent plant. (Photo p. 57)

BETTY SHEFFIELD PINK 1957
A Georgia nursery launched *Betty Sheffield Pink* in 1957. It is a self-coloured deep pink sport of the original lady — the style and habit are otherwise the same.

BETTY SHEFFIELD SUPREME 1960
The supreme triumph of the Sheffield series, *Betty Sheffield Supreme* is a large, loose informal

BETTY SHEFFIELD VARIEGATED

BILLIE McCASKILL

double camellia with each petal richly bordered in pink to rose-red in picotee style. There is great variation both in the intensity and width of the border of this superb mid season bloom. (See also photo p. 57)

BETTY SHEFFIELD VARIEGATED 1958
Georgia's Thomasville Nurseries produced this stunning sport. *Betty Sheffield Variegated* is overall deep pink with white markings.

BIG DADDY (see IMPERATOR)

BIG RAINBOW (see ŌNIJI)

BILLIE McCASKILL 1956   FRAGRANT
A 1956 introduction from Pasadena's McCaskill Gardens, *Billie McCaskill* is a vigorous plant that bears medium-sized semi-double blooms of soft pink. These have deeply notched petals, but frequently fail to open fully.

BLACK CAMELLIA (see KURO TSUBAKI)

BLACK DRAGON (see KOKURYŪ)

BLAZE OF GLORY 1965
A spectacular large camellia of loose anemone form, *Blaze of Glory* was introduced in 1965. The blooms are blazing red, and often reveal a hint of gold stamens among deeply fluted and twisted petals. The flowering period spans both early and mid seasons.

BLEICHROEDER (see OTOME SHIBORI)

BLOOD OF CHINA 1928   FRAGRANT
(syn: *Alice Slack, Victor Emmanuel*) A deep salmon-red camellia of medium size and loose peony form, *Blood of China* was a 1928 introduction, and is still popular in cultivation. The blooms vary from semi-double to loose peony form, and open late in the season. Occasional variegation in the central petaloids is to be expected. (Photo p. 190)

BLUSHING BEAUTY 1964
A sweet formal double camellia of medium size, *Blushing Beauty* is widely grown both in Australia and the United States, where it was introduced in 1964. Flowering mid season, the colour shades from a pure white centre to blush-pink outer petals. The plant has an open habit.

BOB HOPE 1972
The nearest achievement yet to a deep black-red, Nuccio's wonderful 1972 cultivar *Bob Hope* has distinct purple-black markings both on the buds and in its irregular petals. It is a large semi-double flower, blooming mid season. *Bob Hope* the flower is well on the way to achieving the international popularity of its namesake.

BOLEN'S PRIDE (see VEDRINE)

BRILLIANT GENJI (see HIKARU GENJI)

BLUSHING BEAUTY

BOB HOPE

BRUSHFIELD'S YELLOW

C. H. HOVEY

C. M. HOVEY

CAMPARI

CAN CAN

CARA MIA

CARLOTTA PAPUDOFF

CARTER'S SUNBURST

Japonicas

BROCADE OF EZO PROVINCE
(see EZO NISHIKI)

BRUSHFIELD'S YELLOW 1968
By no means the truly yellow camellia that
growers have sought so long, *Brushfield's Yellow*
will do until the real thing comes along. It is a
medium-sized anemone form camellia of antique
white, in which the petaloid centre is tinted pale
primrose. It was raised by the late Keith Brushfield of Australia, and since its 1948 introduction
has become a popular novelty plant for container
and open garden.

BUFF (see LADY HUME'S BLUSH)

BURGDORF BEAUTY (see PINK PEARL)

C. H. HOVEY 1878
Introduced in 1878 by C. M. Hovey of Boston,
the old cultivar *C. H. Hovey* is worth seeking out
for its unusual mid season colouring. A medium-
sized formal double bloom of dark red, it has a
strong magenta cast. Most petals are radially
streaked with pinkish-white, the streaks being
widest towards the centre of the bloom.

C. M. HOVEY 1853
(syn: *Colonel Firey, Duc de Devonshire, Firey
King, Solaris, William S. Hastie* [*Mississippi*])
Companion to the previously listed cultivar,
and of even earlier introduction (1853),
C. M. Hovey is named for its propagator, a distinguished American nurseryman. It is a medium-
sized formal double camellia of brilliant
vermilion-red, flowering late in the season. It has
attracted many synonyms and is still widely sold
as *Colonel Firey*.

C. M. WILSON 1949
(syn: *Grace Burkhard, Lucille Ferrell*) This
charming sport of the English *Elegans* (which
see) appeared in the garden of Mrs A. E. Wilson
of Florida in 1949, and was duly named for her
husband. In habit, size and style it is identical
to its sport parent, but the blooms are soft
powder-pink with deeper veining. (Photo p. 54)

C. M. WILSON SPLENDOR
(see ELEGANS SPLENDOR)

C. P. MORGAN (see BEAUTY OF HOLLAND)

CALIFORNIA 1888
(syn: *Durfee Road*) A light rose-red cultivar of
medium, bushy growth, *California* was
introduced to the West in 1888 after importation
from Japan. It is a large semi-double bloom with
broad swirled petals veined in deeper red, and
its lack of current popularity can only be due to
a rush of more recent introductions. It makes a
wonderful mid season display.

*CALIFORNIA DONCKELARII
VARIEGATED* (see MONJUSU)

CALLIE (see ARAJISHI)

CAMDEN PARK 1952
(syn: *Aspasia Variegata*) Less popular than
other sports of the original *Aspasia, Camden Park*
was so named in 1952 after the Macarthur estate
where the original seedling of this remarkable
series was first grown. It is a medium-sized
bloom of rose-red blotched with white and like
the others, flowers mid season.

CAMPARI 1966
The Italian name of this recent US cultivar is
perhaps a nod to the older *Bella Romana*, which
it closely resembles. Light pink, flecked and
striped with crimson and of medium size, *Campari* is more formally double in style than its predecessor. *Campari* also flowers later in the
season.

CAN CAN 1961
A sport of *Lady Loch*, and in the second generation, of *Aspasia, Can Can* is a spectacular Australian cultivar of medium size and peony form.
The colouring is pale pink, the petals ruffled like
a dancer's skirt and finely edged with deep violet-
rose. *Can Can's* centre petals have a flush of gold,
and it blooms mid season.

CANDIDA ELEGANTISSIMA
(see NAGASAKI)

CANDIDISSIMA 1830
(syn: *Louise Centurioni, White Star*) A slow-
growing shrub imported from Japan in 1830 by
the English grower Chandler, *Candidissima* is a
formal double of medium size and absolutely
pure white colouring. Very similar to *Alba Plena*
but blooms late in the season.

CANDLELIGHT (see ANGEL)

CAPTAIN JOHN SUTTER
(see KISHŪ TSUKASA)

CAPTAIN MARTIN'S FAVOURITE   c. 1840
First distributed in South Carolina in the 1840s,
Captain Martin's Favourite is known to have
been imported from Europe, and may be an early
Italian cultivar. It is medium-sized, formal to
rose form double, deep pink splotched white. It
blooms mid season, and though Captain Martin
is long gone, it is still one of the favourite
camellias.

CARA MIA 1960   FRAGRANT
A medium to large semi-double camellia with
golden stamens swirled through a petaloid centre,
Cara Mia is a 1960 introduction from Nuccio
of California. Blooming early to mid season, it
is blush-pink, graduating even lighter towards the
centre.

CARDINAL 1957
A splendid camellia of medium to large full

peony form, *Cardinal* is a true cardinal red, and blooms mid season. It was registered in 1957 by Carters' Camellia Nursery, California.

CARDINAL'S CAP 1961
A small-sized bloom of perfect anemone form, *Cardinal's Cap* blooms mid to late season and is reminiscent of the old-world variety *Speciosissima*. Its colouring is a rich cardinal red, and it would appear to be identical to Japanese *JIKKŌ*, recorded back in 1879.

CARLOTTA PAPUDOFF 1863
What a delightful flower — and what a shame it is not more widely known and grown. *Carlotta Papudoff* is a large, mid to late season camellia introduced by Malenchini of Livorno, Italy in 1863. Beginning life as a formal double, it soon opens out to a froth of ragged, deep rose-pink petals, barred and spotted with white. The growth is open.

CARNIVAL QUEEN 1969
Developed by Nuccio's from a chance seedling, *Carnival Queen* has all the razzle-dazzle of a circus ring. The large blooms surprise with infinite variations from irregular semi-double to full peony form. They are basically white, but with broad unexpected stripes of pale pink and rosered. The show is on mid season.

CAROL COMPTON (see KOKURYŪ)

CARTER'S SUNBURST 1958 FRAGRANT
Another remarkable series of sporting camellias arrived on the scene with the 1958 introduction of *Carter's Sunburst*. The original discovery (a large to very large bloom of semi-double to loose peony form) has waved, high-standing inner petals and petaloids. The colour is soft pink splashed with flecks and stripes of cerise. Blooms are long-lasting and open throughout the camellia season. (See also photo p. 59)

CARTER'S SUNBURST PINK 1964
Similar in most respects to the original, *Carter's Sunburst Pink* is now fixed as a separate variety, self-coloured in deep pink with just a touch of deeper shaded veining at the petal edges. It is considered a prizewinner wherever camellias are grown.

CARTER'S SUNBURST PINK VARIEGATED 1962
This second variation on a theme of *Carter's Sunburst* has an overall colouring of deep pink, with irregular white splotches. It was released by Kramer Bros Nursery of California in 1962.

CARTER'S SUNBURST VARIEGATED
Similar to the original *Carter's Sunburst*, this variation shows a pronounced degree of white variegation.

CASSANDRA 1850
(syn: *Chandlerii Magniflora*)   Among many of

CARTER'S SUNBURST PINK

CASSANDRA

CATHERINE McCOWN

CHAMELEON

Japonicas

the camellia seedlings given classical names by Australian pioneer grower Sir William Macarthur, *Cassandra* has stood the test of time. First flowered at Camden Park in 1850, she is still grown today by real enthusiasts. *Cassandra* is a large red camellia of anemone form, described by Macarthur himself as 'scarlet-crimson, four rows of outer petals, inner petals small and crowded, with a few white amongst ...'. *Cassandra* blooms mid season.

CATHERINE McCOWN 1950
At one stage of its development, the flower of this charming camellia looks quite different in style and shape to any other I have seen. It is registered as medium-sized, semi-double to anemone form; however the anemone petaloids open out to a trumpet shape, very like that of a daffodil. Blooming mid season, it is a 1950 introduction in pale pink.

CATHERINE STIMSON 1964
A strangely coloured camellia indeed is *Catherine Stimson*, an Australian introduction of 1964. Large, semi-double and vigorous, it produces blooms of deep blood-red, with a strong touch of purple at the margins of its rippled petals. Blooms early to mid season.

CELTIC ROSEA (see SEMI-DOUBLE BLUSH)

CHALICE (see HANA FŪKI)

CHAMELEON 1974
A spectacular multi-toned camellia, *Chameleon*, like the small lizard for which it is named, seems to change colour at will. Large and semi-double, it may be any combination of white, pink and rose-red, with speckles and variegations reversing the ground colour. A late bloomer, introduced in California 1974.

CHANDLERI 1825
One of the first and most popular camellia cultivars in the West, *Chandleri* was released by Chandler's Nursery of Vauxhall, England in 1825. A medium-sized bloom of semi-double to anemone form, and blooming mid season, it bears a strong resemblance to the later Australian cultivar *Speciosissima*. Bright red in colour, it has been known to bear occasional white markings.

CHANDLERI ELEGANS
(see ELEGANS)

CHANDLERI ELEGANS PINK
(see ELEGANS)

CHANDLERI ELEGANS PINK
VARIEGATED (see FRANCINE)

CHANDLERI RUBRA (see ELEGANS)

CHANDLERII MAGNIFLORA
(see CASSANDRA)

CHANDLERI

CHARLES HENTY

CHIRI TSUBAKI　　重散椿　　CHÒ CHÒ SAN　　チヨウチヨウサン

CLARK HUBBS

CHARLES HENTY 1967
Raised in Victoria, this large camellia is reminiscent of the Japanese *HIKARU GENJI*. In this case however, the background tone of the semi-double to peony form flower is China pink, shading to a white edge. There is much evidence of deeper veining, and the flowers open mid season.

CHERRY BLOSSOM (see SAKURABA TSUBAKI)

CHERRY-LEAF CAMELLIA
(see SAKURABA TSUBAKI)

CHIRI TSUBAKI
(Scattering Camellia) c. 1550
Known and loved for centuries in Japan, the charming *CHIRI TSUBAKI* or *Scattering Camellia* is a variable flower, often with blooms of pink, white, or pink and white variegation, all on the same tree. It is a semi-double of medium size and mid season bloom, only introduced to the West by Eikichi Satomi of Japan in 1956. Its name is in reference to the shattering habit of mature flowers.

CHŌ CHŌ SAN (Madam Butterfly) 1936
(syn: *Palmerston*)   In bud or freshly opened, the blossoms of *CHŌ CHŌ SAN* have an extraordinary perfection and delicacy; but alas, like Madam Butterfly, the operatic heroine after whom they were named, they are highly vulnerable, and after a short time, they drop. A medium-sized bloom of palest pink, *CHŌ CHŌ SAN* is generally of semi-double concave form, with occasional petaloids. The pale, pointed foliage suggests a relationship to *HAGOROMO*, but the original Japanese name of this variety has been lost. It was re-named by the American nurseryman who imported it in 1936. Blooms in mid season.

CHŌ NO HAGASANE (see HAGOROMO)

CHŌSEN TSUBAKI (Korean Camellia) 1930
The uncommon *CHŌSEN TSUBAKI* was imported via Japan to the United States in 1930. At first thought to be a new species, it has proved to be a local variety of *C. japonica*, which also grows naturally in south-east Korea. It is a large, single, darkish red bloom, rarely opening flat. Blooming period is mid season.

CHRISTMAS BEAUTY 1958
Picturing a single bloom of this most unusual camellia cannot do justice to its startling effect in the garden. For a start, it is a tall, slender plant with weeping branches, rather like a fir tree. Seen in company with other camellias, the dark shining foliage seems to have a reddish tone, setting off to perfection the large semi-double blooms of bright coral. These appear over several months and have a formal 'hose-in-hose' appearance. *Christmas Beauty* also has a variegated form. Both were released in Mississippi in 1958.

CONFLAGRATION

CONTESSA LAVINIA MAGGI

CORROBOREE

COUNTESS OF ORKNEY

Japonicas

CLARK HUBBS 1960
A dazzling scarlet cultivar from Fresno, California, *Clark Hubbs* was registered in 1960. It is a large, full peony form bloom with ruffled fringed petals. As the colour of the mid season blooms is particularly rich, a large plant can make a stunning specimen. (See also photo p. 62)

CLEO WITTE (see VEDRINE)

CLEOPATRA (see BELLE JEANETTE)

CLEOPATRA (MACARTHUR) 1850
The glamorous serpent of the Nile seems to have an irresistible fascination for camellia hybridists, for at least three of them have used *Cleopatra* as a cultivar name. Priority would seem to rest with William Macarthur of Australia, whose *Cleopatra* was first listed in 1850. There is some confusion about its colouring, which was originally described as scarlet-crimson. The camellia grown today is white, striped pink and blooms mid season. (Photo p. 46)

COLLETTII 1843
(syn: *Collettii Maculata, Genevieve de Barbier, Girard Debaillon, Purpliana*) A Belgian variety from 1843, *Collettii* is still widely grown in many parts of the world. It is a small to medium camellia of full peony form, blooming early in the season. The flowers are variable in colour, from nearly solid red to pure white, but in each extreme, variegated with the opposite colour.

COLLETTII MACULATA (see COLLETTII)

COLONEL FIREY (see C. M. HOVEY)

COLONIAL LADY 1938
(syn: *Crystal Lake, Fragrant Striped, White Jordan's Pride*) A 1938 sport of *HIKARU GENJI, Colonial Lady* is a medium-sized semi-double bloom of pure white, striped and flecked with rose-red. It blooms mid season. Originally propagated by McCaskill's of California.

COMMANDER MULROY 1961
A medium-sized formal double camellia, in bloom mid season, *Commander Mulroy* was released in Louisiana in 1961. It is white, with the petals deeply and irregularly edged with red.

COMMENDATORE BFTTI 1872
An 1872 Italian cultivar from grower Boutourlin, *Commendatore Betti* is a medium-sized formal double bloom of deep rose-pink, occasionally blotched with white. The flat mid season flowers have an interesting shape. (Photo p. 61)

COMTESSE WORONZOFF 1858
Also developed in Italy by Boutourlin, the lovely *Comtesse Woronzoff* commemorates some forgotten aristocrat and is a sport of the older *Centifolia Alba*. A large bloom of softest pink, it has reflexed outer petals and is veined and shaded

CRUSSELLE

DAIKAGURA   太神楽   DAUTEL'S SUPREME

DEMI TASSE

carmine. Classed as a formal double, it generally produces flowers of a more rose-like form.

CONFLAGRATION 1945
A curious shade of light vermilion, *Conflagration* is an interesting camellia for colour fans and breeders. It is a large semi-double bloom of irregular shape, the petals much ruffled. *Conflagration* was introduced by Magnolia Gardens of South Carolina in 1945.

CONTESSA LAVINIA MAGGI 1860
Another lovely Italian camellia of the nineteenth century, and perhaps unfamiliar to modern growers, *Contessa Lavinia Maggi* is a medium-sized formal double bloom of palest pink, radially striped with carmine-rose. It was introduced in 1860 and blooms early to mid season. Its several sports include the white-marked *Roi des Belges*. (See also plate p. 37)

COQUETTI (see GLEN 40)

CORAL PINK LOTUS 1955
A most elegant 1955 introduction, *Coral Pink Lotus* is a very large camellia, semi-double and blooming mid season. The outer coral-pink petals are reflexed (like a lotus) and have darker pink veining; the inner petals are lavishly marked with orchid-pink and white. *Coral Pink Lotus* is also cultivated for its low, spreading growth.

CORONATION 1954
Named by McCaskill Gardens of Pasadena in honour of the crowning of Elizabeth II, *Coronation* is a very large semi-double camellia with ruffled, pure white petals and pale lemon-yellow stamens. The plant, a sturdy grower with spreading habit, blooms mid season.

CORROBOREE 1962
A seedling from the old German cultivar *Tricolor (Siebold)*, this startling camellia was introduced in 1962 by E. G. Waterhouse, doyen of Australian camellians. It is medium-sized, semi-double in style, and flowers mid season. The white petals are slashed radially with crimson and cerise stripes and the centre is a simple boss of gold-tipped stamens. A corroboree is an Australian Aboriginal dance ceremony.

COUNTESS OF DERBY 1856
A profusely flowering old-fashioned double camellia of rose to peony form, *Countess of Derby* was first described in England in 1856, but is found in older gardens of the southern hemisphere as well. A mid season bloomer, it varies from pale pink to creamy-white, with glowing carmine stripes.

COUNTESS OF ORKNEY 1847
Similar to many other English camellias of Victorian times, the lovely *Countess of Orkney* is still grown after almost a century and a half. The plant, a compact slow grower, produces in mid season large peony-form blooms of creamy-white, striped with rose-pink. The *Countess* was launched in English society in 1847.

CRESTED SATIN (see MONJUSŪ)

CRUSADER (see PRINCE OF ORANGE)

CRUSSELLE 1957
A dramatic and popular cultivar introduced by American T. A. Crusselle in 1957, his name-sake camellia is a large, late-blooming flower of vivid red with darker shading. The loose peony form blooms have upright petals punctuated with groups of showy stamens. A dense bushy grower, it is suited to life as a container plant.

CRYSTAL LAKE (see COLONIAL LADY)

CZARINA
(see EMPEROR OF RUSSIA VARIEGATED)

DAIKAGURA (Great Sacred Dance) 1851
(syn: *IDATEN SHIBORI, KIYOSU*) Grown in Japan at least as far back as 1851 and probably well beyond, *DAIKAGURA* is considered one of the greatest camellias of all time. It is certainly one of the most variable. Medium to large in size, peony form in style, early blooming; it is usually described as bright pink splotched with white, but in the specimen I photographed in California, this colouring was reversed, to great effect.

DAIKAGURA PINK (see BENI DAIKAGURA)

DAIKAGURA RED (see BENI DAIKAGURA)

DAINTRIE SIEVERS 1964
Released in 1964 by Australian hybridist Keith Brushfield, *Daintrie Sievers* is a medium-sized bloom of loose peony form, opening late in the season. Its colouring is clear pink with orchid tonings.

DAINTY MAIDEN 1952
Not illustrated in this book, *Dainty Maiden* is a popular pink medium-sized cultivar of semi-double to peony form. It blooms mid season, has waved inner petals, and was first flowered in Sydney by the late Professor Eben Gowrie Waterhouse. He described it as a seedling from the Japanese variety *SUI BIJIN* or *Exquisite Beauty*. It is greatly suited to espalier training because of a spreading growth and somewhat weeping habit.

DAUTEL'S SUPREME 1961
Again a most variable camellia, the glowing *Dautel's Supreme* was introduced with understandable pride in 1961. It is a large to very large sport of *Mathotiana* (which see). Purplish-crimson in colour, with reflexed outer petals, it is centred with a variable pompon of stamens and petaloids, some marked in white. *Dautel's Supreme* blooms mid season.

DIDDY'S PINK ORGANDIE

DIXIE KNIGHT

DONA HERZILIA DE FREITAS MAGALHAES

DONCKELARII

DR BURNSIDE

DR JOHN D. BELL

DR KING

Japonicas

DAWN (see AKEBONO)

DEBUTANTE c. 1900
(syn: *Sara C. Hastie*) A popular American camellia of full peony form, *Debutante* was released in the early 1900s by Magnolia Gardens of South Carolina, and became an all-time favourite. A medium-sized bloom of clear light pink, it blooms early to mid season on a bush with light green foliage. Young plants frequently lose leaves, but this condition corrects itself with maturity.

DEMI TASSE 1962
A small-sized triumph for the McCaskill Gardens of California, *Demi Tasse* is a dainty semi-double bloom that resembles nothing so much as a perfect peach blossom. The golden centre generally includes a few petaloids.

DIANA (see IMURA)

DIDDY'S PINK ORGANDIE 1953
Delicately feminine both in flower style and coloration, this exquisite camellia has become a great favourite since its 1953 introduction. Medium-sized, more rose form than formal double, it blooms mid season on a bush of slightly pendulous growth. The imbricated petals shade from dawn-pink through blush to pure white at the petal edge. Over all, there is a fine pink veining.

DIDO 1861
Another Macarthur hybrid from Camden Park, *Dido* bloomed in 1850 and was first sold in 1861. It is a white semi-double bloom of medium size. Still grown, it is scarcely spectacular enough for modern popularity.

DIONYSIA PONIATOWSKI 1865
A perfect white camellia occasionally flecked with pink, *Dionysia Poniatowski* was named for a scion of Poland's royal house. Medium in size, formal double in style, it dates from 1865, a creation of Italian grower Boutourlin.

DIXIE KNIGHT 1955
A particularly fine informal double cultivar, *Dixie Knight* produces large, showy flowers of brilliant deep red — so deep, the buds are almost black. A long flowering period from mid season and vigorous, upright growth make it a popular choice for container work. It was released in 1955, and has several variegated forms. (See also photo p. 66)

DON PEDRO V, REI DE PORTUGAL 1872
The charming formal double *Don Pedro V* can be traced back as far as 1872 in Portugal, where it was tremendously popular. It has rounded petals of waxy texture, perfectly overlapped. The colouring is white, streaked with pale rose-pink, and the blooms open mid season. *Don Pedro V* is often found in old European gardens.

DR TINSLEY

DONA HERZILIA DE FREITAS MAGALHAES 1952

Nobody forgets the camellia with the longest name, even if it is unpronounceable to most of us! *Dona Herzilia* (if we may be familiar) is a Portuguese cultivar released by grower da Silva in 1952, and quite outstanding for the distinctively purple blooms it produces when grown in heavy clay or shale soils. Elsewhere it is a not particularly distinguished bloom of anemone form and dull red colour. Medium in size, and blooming mid season, *Dona Herzilia de Freitas Magalhaes* is named for a descendant of the explorer Magellan.

DONCKELARII 1834

Imported from China to Belgium in 1834 at the height of an earlier European camellia mania, this highly variable bloom has given rise to many other named strains and sports. But the original cultivar, still grown today, is a large semi-double flower of pure red, marbled in white. The blooms appear mid season on a slow-growing, bushy plant. (See also plate p. 38)

DONNA KAYE (see ARRABELLA)

DORIS MADALIA (see BEAUTY OF HOLLAND)

DOROTHY PARKER (see EMMETT PFINGSTL)

DR ALLEN AMES (see IMURA)

DR BURNSIDE 1962

There would appear to be a disproportionately large number of Western camellia cultivars named after family doctors — more than seventy are recorded! Of these, *Dr Burnside* at least is named by the doctor himself, a handsome, medium to large flower of blood red. It is a mid season bloom of semi-double to peony form.

DR JOHN D. BELL 1950

(syn: *Beau Harp Variegated*) Raised in Florida, the cultivar *Dr John D. Bell* is a variegated form of the red camellia *Beau Harp*, released in the same year. It is a medium to large camellia of peony form, blotched in white and with a magnificent stamen display among the inner petals. *Dr John D. Bell* flowers early to mid season.

DR KING 1945

An Australian medico joins the club in this 1945 presentation of Australia's Camellia Grove Nursery. *Dr King* is no longer propagated by them, but is certainly worth seeking out. It is a large semi-double bloom of light cherry-red, the petals dramatically ruffled around a gorgeous display of long stamens. It flowers mid to late season, and individual blooms tend to hang downwards.

DR SHEPHERD (see GRAND SULTAN)

DR TINSLEY 1949

More like a wild rose than a camellia, this

DRAMA GIRL

EASTER MORN

ECCLEFIELD

EDELWEISS

Japonicas

medium-sized charmer rings many changes on a theme of pale pink. The buds are brilliant pink in colour, and open to semi-double blooms of soft pink with deeper shaded edges and occasional petaloids. It is recommended for the cooler climate, where it flowers profusely in mid season.

DRAMA GIRL 1950
Howard Asper's *Drama Girl* never ceases to amaze with its reticulata-size flowers of deep salmon-rose, often streaked with paler pink. They are classed as very large and semi-double, and frequently produce a centre packed with petaloids. These enormous blooms need some protection and last a long time in mid season. They are so heavy that regular pruning of the long drooping lateral branches is needed to force a stronger, more compact growth. *Drama Girl* first bloomed at Escondido, California in 1950.

DUC D'ORLEANS
(see MARGUERITE GOUILLON)

DUC DE BRETAGNE 1848
A noble camellia with a noble name, from the days when France led the world in hybridising. *Duc de Bretagne* is an 1848 offering by nurseryman Drouard. A medium-sized rose form double of cherry-red, its centre often pales to a lighter shade.

DUC DE DEVONSHIRE (see C. M. HOVEY)

DUCHESS OF YORK (see LADY LOCH)

DUCHESSE DE CASES
(see DUCHESSE DE CAZE)

DUCHESSE DE CAZE 1908
(syn: *Duchesse de Cases, Hime, Juanita, Mrs Conrad Wall Jr, Opelousas Peony*) A 1908 French cultivar from the Guichard Nursery of Nantes, *Duchesse de Caze* has been known by many other names in many places. It is a medium-sized camellia of full peony form and great popularity. Basically flesh-pink, it is edged white, veined deeper pink. Blooms mid season.

DUKE OF YORK (see OTAHUHU BEAUTY)

DUNCAN BELL (see MENA LADNIER)

DURFEE ROAD (see CALIFORNIA)

EASTER MORN 1965
A very large semi-double camellia of palest peach-pink, *Easter Morn* may vary all the way to full peony form, when the flower's heart mingles beautifully waved inner petals among the golden stamens. Discovered as a chance seedling, it blooms mid to late season on a bush with exceptionally strong growth and large foliage.

ECCLEFIELD 1959
A strikingly handsome loose informal double cul-

tivar, *Ecclefield* develops large, waved white petals that form a high ruffle around a centre of stamens and scattered petaloids. The size is very large, the flowering period mid season and the bush itself has splendid foliage. *Ecclefield* was introduced by California hybridist Toichi Domoto.

ED ANDERSON (see TOMORROW)

EDELWEISS 1956
An exquisite white cultivar from San José, California, *Edelweiss* seems most variable in form; anything from loose informal double to a perfect anemone shape. Petals are irregular, fluted and notched, with a mass of curled petaloids. It blooms early to mid season, and was released in 1956. One wonders if it is not another sport of the *Elegans* group.

EDITH LINTON 1941
A decorative mutation from another Australian-raised sporting camellia, *Jean Lyne*, the popular *Edith Linton* was released by hybridist G. C. Linton in 1941 and named for his wife. It is a delightful semi-double flower of deep salmon shading to silvery rose-pink, and has occasional petaloids among the gold-tipped stamens. *Edith Linton* is medium-sized and blooms profusely throughout the season. It has one major fault — the flowers drop all too soon.

EDWARD BILLING (see LADY LOCH)

EGRET (see SHIRATAMA)

EIGHTEEN SCHOLARS 1955
A favourite camellia throughout China, the remarkable *Eighteen Scholars* does not seem to have been grown in the West before 1955, when it was imported from Taiwan by hybridist Ralph Peer. A medium-sized formal double bloom, it is noted for sporting up to 18 different varieties of white, pink and red on a single bush.

ELEANOR MARTIN SUPREME 1964
Another winner from Californian Caesar Breschini, *Eleanor Martin Supreme* was released in 1964. It is medium to large, semi-double, with wide cupped petals, and is coloured a wonderful cerise-red, moiréd with white. A mid to late season bloomer.

ELEANOR McCOWN 1942
A vibrant 1942 release by Shepp's Shade Gardens of Pasadena, *Eleanor McCown* is a medium-sized camellia of semi-double to anemone form. Opening mid season, the cupped blooms are white, lightly streaked with scarlet and pink.

ELEANOR OF FAIROAKS 1906
(syn: *Vedrine Variegated*) A sport of *Vedrine*, one of the most popular camellias in the early twentieth century, *Eleanor of Fairoaks* is, like its parent, a medium to large camellia of anemone

EDITH LINTON

ELEANOR MARTIN SUPREME

to loose peony form, flowering early to mid season. The blooms are brilliant ruby-red, lightly marbled in white toward the petal tips.

ELEGANS 1831
(syn: *Chandleri Elegans Pink, Chandleri Rubra, Elegans* [*Chandler*], *Red Elegans, Rosea Chandleri*) A famous camellia from English nurseryman Chandler, *Elegans* was released in 1831, and in the intervening years has sported a whole range of descendants in many parts of the world. Still elegant, this original flower is a large to very large cultivar of anemone form and slow, spreading growth. Its colour is a deep rose-pink with central petaloids occasionally spotted white. It blooms early to mid season. (See also photo p. 67)

ELEGANS CHAMPAGNE 1975
Latest and perhaps the most beautiful descendant of Chandler's original *Elegans* cultivar, *Elegans Champagne* was released only in 1975 by the Nuccio Nursery of Altadena, California. It is a plant of spreading bushy growth and deeply serrated foliage, producing typical *Elegans* anemone form flowers. These are waxy white with fimbriated outer petals and a centre of cream petaloids. Large blooms early to mid season.

ELEGANS (CHANDLER) (see ELEGANS)

ELEGANS (CHANDLER) VARIEGATED (see FRANCINE)

ELEGANS SPLENDOR 1969
(syn: *C. M. Wilson Splendor*) A direct sport of *C. M. Wilson* and thus ultimately of the original *Elegans, Elegans Splendor* was a 1969 introduction. The flowers are similiar in style to those of *Elegans Supreme* (which see) but tinted iridescent blush-pink edged with white. The petal edges are deeply serrated, the petaloid centre is large and fully double, and the flowers open mid season. Foliage too is elegantly serrated.

ELEGANS SUPREME 1960
A favourite sport of the original *Elegans* (1831), this deep rose-pink flower was developed in 1960. The large, deeply serrated guard petals have a delightful iridescence, and surround a double centre of matching petaloids, some serrated, some almost white. The blooms are large in size, peak around mid season and may fail to open properly if the weather is too mild. *Elegans Supreme* is a plant of compact growth and heavy, waved foliage. (Photo p. 54)

ELEGANS VARIEGATED (see FRANCINE)

ELEGANTISSIMA (see NAGASAKI)

ELENA NOBILE 1881
(syn: *Napa Red*) A memorable camellia from nineteenth century Italy, *Elena Nobile* has enjoyed continuous popularity since its release

ELEANOR McCOWN

ELEANOR OF FAIROAKS

ELEGANS

ELEGANS CHAMPAGNE

exactly a century ago by Cesare Franchetti of Firenze. It is a late-blooming camellia of medium size, with flame-red, rose form double blooms borne in profusion. Growth is slow.

ELISABETH 1845
(syn: *Elizabeth, Helene Longhi, Montironi, Teutonia White, Trois Maries, Victoria and Albert*) A charming old-world camellia originally from Italy, but first described and published by Verschaffelt in Belgium in 1851. It is a formal double of medium size, white with pink radial stripes. A late bloomer.

ELIZABETH (see ELISABETH)

ELIZABETH BAY 1962
Elizabeth Bay is an Australian cultivar registered in 1962, and not to be confused with the similarly named American variety, *Elizabeth le Bey* of 1948. *Elizabeth Bay* is a medium-sized peony form camellia, blooming mid season. It is soft rose-pink, occasionally mottled with a lighter tone. It is named for a suburb of Sydney with many older colonial houses.

ELIZABETH DOWD SILVER 1973
Progeny of the freely sporting American cultivar *Elizabeth Dowd* (a 1960 registration), *Elizabeth Dowd Silver* is a splendid large flower of rose form double style. The fully open bloom is soft blush-pink, shading to white at the frilled petal margins. It is marked with random flecks of deep pink, and shows occasional long petaloids among the widely flaring stamens. A mid season bloomer. (Photo p. 61)

ELIZABETH GRANDY
(see MARGARET HIGDON)

ELIZABETH JOHNSTON (see LADY LOCH)

ELIZABETH LE BEY 1948
A large camellia of deep rose-pink centred with erect petaloids, *Elizabeth le Bey* was introduced in Florida in 1948. The flower is loose to full peony form in style, and blooms right through the season.

ELLEN SAMPSON 1938
A fine container plant, *Ellen Sampson* was produced in 1938 by a New Zealand grower, and is popular throughout the southern hemisphere. The large semi-double blooms are carmine-pink, with two rows of large, waved petals surrounding a centre of gold-tipped stamens and small petaloids. *Ellen Sampson* blooms mid to late season. (Photos pp. 60, 67)

ELSIE RUTH MARSHALL 1965
Light pink with a mauve cast, this fascinating large bloom was introduced in 1965. Rose form double to loose peony form, its stamens are almost completely hidden beneath a centre of swirling upright petals. It is inclined to bloom late in the season.

ELEGANS SPLENDOR

ELENA NOBILE

EMILY BROWN (see HISHI KARAITO)

EMMETT PFINGSTL 1950
(syn: *Dorothy Parker, Joseph Pfingstl Variegated*) A dark red and white variegated form of the earlier cultivar *Joseph Pfingstl*, this great camellia has a medium to large flower. It varies widely in style from irregular semi-double to loose peony form with deeply waved inner petals. *Emmett Pfingstl* blooms early to mid season, and was introduced from Alabama in 1950.

EMPEROR FREDERICK WILLIAM
(see GIGANTEA)

EMPEROR OF RUSSIA 1856
Popular since 1856 when it flowered for the Belgian grower Van de Geert, the stunning *Emperor of Russia* is arrayed with blooms of Imperial scarlet. These are medium to large in size, peony form, and bloom mid season. The glowing red blooms are set off to perfection by a powdering of gold stamens and a background of strong, dark green foliage.

EMPEROR OF RUSSIA VARIEGATED
(syn: *Aspasia* [US], *Czarina, Great Eastern* [NZ]) A variegated form of the preceding cultivar, *Emperor of Russia Variegated* is deep red, marbled white. Because of an earlier confusion in nomenclature, this tremendous flower has attracted the several other names listed above. None of them is valid.

EMPEROR WILHELM (see GIGANTEA)

EMPRESS (see AKASHIGATA)

EMPRESS VARIEGATED (see ŌNIJI)

ERICA McMINN 1965
Named in 1965 for the wife of Australian hybridist Neville McMinn, the charming *Erica McMinn* is a small, formal double bloom of palest blush-pink, fading to silver-white. A dainty compact plant, it blooms mid season and is useful for tub work.

ERIN FARMER 1962   FRAGRANT
A wondrously beautiful and popular camellia registered in 1962, *Erin Farmer* bursts out in mid season with large semi-double to peony form flowers. These are white, flushed with orchid-pink among the deeply fluted petals. The gold-stamened flowers are of heavy texture, and make a wonderful display among the dark foliage.

EUGÉNIE DE MASSÉNA 1877
First described in the catalogue of English nurseryman Rollis in 1877, *Eugénie de Masséna* is a sport of the Portuguese *Don Pedro V*. Unique in appearance, *Eugénie de Masséna* is a sparsely-petalled formal double bloom of light pink, the petals radially veined with deeper pink and bordered in white. The flowers are small to medium in size, blooming mid season.

EULALIA SALLY (see LADY DE SAUMAREZ)

EXTRAVAGANZA 1960
Extravaganza indeed! This aptly named spectacular camellia is very large, anemone form and blooms mid season. It has rounded outer petals and a high domed centre of smaller petal growth. Both are vividly rayed and marked in light cherry-red against a white background.

EZO BROCADE (see EZO NISHIKI)

EZO NISHIKI (Ezo Brocade) 1859
(syn: *Brocade of Ezo Province, GONDŌ SHIBORI*) Traced back in Japan to at least 1859, the old variety *EZO NISHIKI* has several synonyms, among them *GONDŌ SHIBORI*, which was the label on the plant I photographed in Kyūshū. It is a large semi-double camellia of pink-flushed white, with profuse spatterings of red variegation. Blooming mid season, the plant has a strong, compact growth and was first received in the United States in 1930. (See also *Tricolor*).

F. M. UYEMATSU
(see ADOLPHE AUDUSSON VARIEGATED)

FAITH VARIEGATED 1956
The delicate colouring of Mississippi cultivar *Faith Variegated* is best appreciated in a semi-shaded position. It is a large, semi-double bloom of rose-pink, tending to anemone form, and flowering mid to late season. Both petals and petaloids are variegated white. A vigorous grower and a fine garden specimen.

FANCY 1945
A magnificent turkey-red bloom varying from peony form to formal double, *Fancy* was a 1945 release from the Armstrong Nurseries of California. The notched outer petals tend to fade lighter on mature blooms.

FANNY BOLIS (see LATIFOLIA VARIEGATA)

FANNY DAVENPORT (see GIGANTEA)

FASHIONATA 1964
A large semi-double camellia of most unusual colouring, *Fashionata* has been described as 'apricot-pink with an appealing silver sheen'. It has become one of the most popular introductions of recent years. The superb blooms are variable in form, often with the stamens obscured by a central arrangement of matching petaloids marked in white. A mid season bloomer.

FEATHERED ROBE (see HAGOROMO)

FEATHERS OF WILD GOOSE
(see TOKI NO HAGASANE)

FIMBRIATA 1816
(syn: *Alba Fimbriata, Fimbriata Alba*) This delicately fringed camellia sported in the early

ELIZABETH LE BEY

EMMETT PFINGSTL

EMPEROR OF RUSSIA

ERIN FARMER   EUGÉNIE DE MASSÉNA

EXTRAVAGANZA

EZO NISHIKI   江戸錦

Japonicas

nineteenth century on a bush of the older Chinese cultivar *Alba Plena*, and may well have been known to Chinese growers centuries earlier. It was first described, however, in 1816 by nurseryman Chandler of Vauxhall. Early blooming, medium-sized and formal double in style, it is a most decorative tub plant.

FIMBRIATA ALBA (see FIMBRIATA)

FINLANDIA VARIEGATED 1910
(syn: *Aurora Borealis, Margaret Jack, Speckles*) The great white cultivar *Finlandia* was imported from Japan to America in 1910, and immediately celebrated its arrival by sporting the brilliant variety we have illustrated. *Finlandia Variegated* is a medium-sized semi-double bloom with superbly fluted petals and a marvellous wide centre of stamens. It is lightly streaked with crimson at the petal edges, and blooms early to mid season.

FIREBRAND 1840s
An oldie but a goodie, as the disc jockeys say – glowing *Firebrand* was launched in the 1840s from South Carolina. It is a medium-sized semi-double bloom for mid to late season, and coloured the vivid scarlet you would expect from its name. There is also a variegated form.

FIREGOLD (see GRAND SULTAN)

FIREY KING (see C. M. HOVEY)

FIRST DAY OF 8TH MONTH
(see BENI HASSAKU)

FISHTAIL (see KINGYO TSUBAKI)

FLAME (Aust) (see MOSHIO)

FLAME (USA) 1917
Most vividly coloured of all camellias, the popular cultivar *Flame* was produced by California hybridist Domoto in 1917. It is a medium to large semi-double flower of flame-red, with a profuse mid season blooming habit. Not to be confused with the smaller *MOSHIO*, which is often called *Flame* in Australia.

FLAME VARIEGATED 1919
A variegated sport of the previous variety, *Flame Variegated* is an equally popular garden subject, due to its profuse, mid season flowering habit.

FLEUR DE PÊCHE (see PEACH BLOSSOM)

FLORE CELESTE (see ASPASIA)

FLOWER CREST (see HANA TACHIBANA)

FLOWER OF CRÊPE PAPER
(see HANA FŪKI)

FLOWER OF HONOUR (see HANA FŪKI)

FAITH VARIEGATED

FLOWER OF NOBLE FAMILY
(see HANA FŪKI)

FLOWERWOOD 1951
(syn: *Mathotiana Fimbriata*) A mildly fimbriated sport of the old *Mathotiana* cultivar (1840s) *Flowerwood* was released in 1951. It is a large to very large camellia of rose form double style; the deep rose petals are irregularly flushed with soft white patches.

FRA ARNALDO DA BRESCIA 1850
Typical of the rather ornamental camellias produced in Italy in the 1850s, *Fra Arnaldo da Brescia* has a distinguished pedigree. A formal double bloom of medium size, its rose-pink petals are softly striped with white. Blooming mid season, it was raised by Count Bernardo Lechi, and named for a prominent churchman of his home city, Brescia.

FRAGRANT STAR 1956   FRAGRANT
A delightful white camellia of more than interesting form and fragrance, *Fragrant Star* has been grown in California for more than 25 years. It is a large semi-double with elongated upright central petals, and blooms mid season.

FRAGRANT STRIPED (see COLONIAL LADY)

FRANCES BUTLER 1958
First exhibited by Californian Reg Ragland in 1958, the charming *Frances Butler* is now widely grown in Australia. It is a simple, medium-sized camellia of tulip form, the centre of each petal marked with a red line. The overall colouring is a deep coral-rose, and it blooms mid season.

FRANCINE c. 1860
(syn: *Chandleri Elegans Pink Variegated, Elegans [Chandler] Variegated, Elegans Variegated, Pride of the Emperor's Garden*) *Francine* is often used incorrectly as a synonym for *Elegans (Chandler)*, but is in fact the priority name for its variegated sport. Like the original, it is a large to very large anemone form bloom, but in this case, both petals and petaloids are blotched white. Blooms early to mid season. (Photo p. 54)

FRANCOIS WIOT 1868
(syn: *Lady of the Lake* [NZ]) Most exotic in appearance, *Francois Wiot* was first described in 1868 in Belgium, but is undoubtedly a Japanese import. The large, anemone form flowers are displayed like crimson jewels against gold-variegated foliage. A real eye-catcher.

FRAU MINNA SEIDEL (see USU OTOME)

FRIZZLE WHITE 1935
(syn: *Susan Carter*) White flowers are always popular, and this large semi-double camellia with crinkled texture is no exception. Upright central petals protect a high cylinder of gold-tipped white stamens, and the blooms peak mid season.

FASHIONATA

FIMBRIATA

FINLANDIA VARIEGATED

FIREBRAND

FLAME (US)

Japonicas

FUJI YAMA (see NOBILISSIMA)

FUYAJŌ 1935
(syn: *Nightless Quarter, Purpurea*) Darkest of dark purple-reds, the small single camellia *FUYAJŌ* is quite unforgettable as its bell-shaped blooms peep out from among long, elegant foliage. It is a Japanese registration of 1935, though probably much older. *FUYAJŌ* blooms mid season and may be a hybrid of *C. wabisuke.*

G. C. LINTON 1941
A seedling acquired by G. C. Linton from the Alexander Hunter estate, *G. C. Linton* is a medium-sized semi-double camellia flowering in mid season. The bloom is bright red with irregular petals.

GAIETY (see GIGANTEA)

GATHERING STORM (see OKI NO NAMI)

GAUNTLETTII (see SODE KAKUSHI)

GEISHA GIRL 1959
A charmingly variegated cultivar in the Japanese taste, *Geisha Girl* was actually originated in California in 1959. It is a large camellia, semi-double and open in style, blush-pink with fine red-pink stripes and dashes, particularly towards the petal edges. Flowers appear mid season.

GENERAL DWIGHT EISENHOWER 1946
FRAGRANT
General Dwight Eisenhower, named for the great wartime military leader and later President of the United States, is a medium-sized beauty of full peony form. The glowing red flowers appear mid season on a bush of strong, compact growth. Interestingly enough, the cultivar is mildly fragrant.

GENERAL LAMORCIÈRE
(see MARGUERITE GOUILLON)

GENERAL LECLERC 1950
Deep red camellias seem prone to be named for military leaders on either side of the Atlantic. France's contribution is the magnificent *General Leclerc*, released by the Guichard Soeurs Nursery of Nantes in 1950. It is a large semi-double to loose peony form bloom with irregular petals, and is at its best mid season.

GENEVIEVE DE BARBIER (see COLLETTII)

GEORGIA ROUSE 1964
A 1964 introduction from Mississippi, this magnificent camellia was named for the wife of its originator, Dr A. H. Rouse. The full peony form blooms of vivid medium pink and large size achieve almost a ball shape, with their waved upstanding petals. *Georgia Rouse* blooms early to mid season on a plant of vigorous, spreading habit. Blooms are exceptionally long-lasting.

FLAME VARIEGATED

FLOWERWOOD

FRANCES BUTLER

FRIZZLE WHITE

FUYAJO　　　　不夜城

GIGANTEA *1840s*

(syn: *Emperor Frederick William, Emperor Wilhelm, Fanny Davenport, Gaiety, Jolly Roger, Kelvingtoniana, Magnolia King, Mary Bell Glennan, Monstruoso Rubra*) How can any one camellia variety acquire so many names? Beauty and popularity are two requirements to be sure, but political patronage, mixing and loss of records and many other factors can be blamed as well. The European cultivar *Gigantea* was imported to the United States by the Magnolia Nurseries in the 1840s and given their name, *Magnolia King*. The Belgian grower Louis van Houtte released it in 1856 as *Kelvingtoniana*, the Germans named it for their Emperor later in the century. To the Italians it was always *Monstruoso Rubra*. It is a large to very large semi-double flower of true anemone form, raspberry-red, marbled with white. The blooms appear mid season on a bush with open weeping habit. The leaves too are large and decorative.

GIRARD DEBAILLON (see COLLETTII)

GLEN 40 *1942*

(syn: *Coquetti*) A popular 1942 introduction from the Azalea Glen Nursery in Alabama, *Glen 40* has won world popularity with its profuse blooming habits. It is a medium to large camellia of bright showy red, with mid to late season flowers variable, but generally rose form in style. (See also photo p. 42)

GLEN 40 VARIEGATED

(syn: *Thunderbolt*) A sport of the previously described cultivar, *Glen 40 Variegated* is a medium to large rose form double bloom of bright red, variegated white.

GLORIOSA (see REGINA DEI GIGANTI)

GODDESS (see BENTEN)

GOLDEN FLEECE *1970*

One of the finest cultivars from David Feathers, camellian extraordinaire of Lafayette, California, *Golden Fleece* is well described by its name. But for the record, it is a large, white, loose peony form flower with ruffled petals and glorious, widely flared stamens. Grown since 1970, it is a must for the lover of white blooms.

GOLDFISH CAMELLIA
(see KINGYO TSUBAKI)

GONDŌ SHIBORI (see EZO NISHIKI)

GOSHO GURUMA *1812*

(syn: *Rhodellia King, Royal Carriage*) A Japanese cultivar with a written history back to 1812, *GOSHO GURUMA* was made available to American collectors in 1935 through California grower Toichi Domoto. It is a stunning peony form camellia of brilliant deep red and medium size. Petals and petaloids are moiréd in white.

GEISHA GIRL

GENERAL DWIGHT EISENHOWER

GENERAL LeCLERC

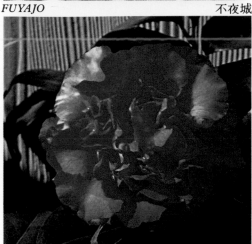

GEORGIA ROUSE

GIGANTEA

Japonicas

GLEN 40

GLEN 40 VARIEGATED

GOLDEN FLEECE

GOVERNOR EARL WARREN

GRAND FINALE

GOVERNOR EARL WARREN 1949

A medium to large rose-pink camellia, *Governor Earl Warren* was registered in 1949, and named for the Governor of California at the time. It is rose form double to loose peony form, and blooms mid season.

GOVERNOR MOUTON c. 1900

(syn: *Angelica, Aunt Jetty*) Introduced in the early 1900s by an unknown grower, *Governor Mouton* is a medium-sized camellia of semi-double to loose peony form and vigorous growth habits. Colouring is Oriental red, often splotched with white, and the blooms are at their best mid season.

GRACE ALBRITTON 1970

Popular with the boutonnière fans, *Grace Albritton* could win prizes whatever her size. The small, formal double blooms are perfectly imbricated, and are normally palest pink, shading deeper at petal edges. A mid season bloomer.

GRACE BURKHARD (see C. M. WILSON)

GRAN SULTANO (see GRAND SULTAN)

GRAND FINALE 1957

If *Grand Finale* were the only camellia originated by Harvey Short (and it is not) it could still claim to be the climax of a glorious career. It is very large, semi-double, and white with broad irregular petals. These have edge flutings and surround an enormous centre of crimped golden stamens. Blooms mid season.

GRAND PRIX 1968

A very large semi-double camellia of open recurved style, *Grand Prix* is a born prize winner with its irregular petal shapes and brilliant red colour. A 1968 introduction by Nuccio's Nurseries, it blooms mid season.

GRAND SLAM 1962   FRAGRANT

Nuccio Nurseries of California really did win the hand with this gorgeous bloom of deep glowing red and variable form. The rich colour is constant, but the large to very large flowers may be semi-double with a boss of gold stamens, or anemone form with a centre of swirling, deep red petaloids. Whatever their style, the flowers take every eye as they open mid season against a background of deep green foliage.

GRAND SLAM VARIEGATED

A fully variegated form of the preceding cultivar, its dark red petals are blotched with white.

GRAND SULTAN 1844

(syn: *Dr Shepherd, Firegold, Gran Sultano, Morague, Pasha of Persia, Shah of Persia, Te Deum*) If a multiplicity of names truly indicated a camellia's popularity, this magnificent flower of deep velvety red should top any list. Originated in Italy under the name *Gran Sultano* in 1844, it was first published in 1849 by the

Belgian Verschaffelt as *Grand Sultan*, which becomes the priority name. America introduced it as *Te Deum* in 1890, and the other names have been collected since then. It is typically a large formal double, but in warmer weather presents a centre mass of mixed petaloids and stamens. Growth is slow and open, and blooming period is mid to late season.

GRANDIFLORA ALBA (see SODE KAKUSHI)

GRANDIFLORA ROSEA 1890
(syn: *Louise Maclay*)   A grand old camellia from the naughty nineties, *Grandiflora Rosea* was raised by the Teagardens Nursery of South Carolina. It is a mid to late flowering semi-double camellia of deep pink, large size and with crinkled petals. Growth is generally slow.

GREAT EASTERN 1873
For more than a century (it was introduced by Australian nurseryman J. Harris in 1873) this splendid all-round camellia has shared names with that other glory of the Victorian age, the giant steamship *Great Eastern*, which opened the era of modern communications by laying the Atlantic Cable in 1865. This is a grand plant of iron constitution, heat and cold resistant, but with the forgivable habit of producing too many flower buds. After an early disbudding however, the remaining blooms are large and semi-double, with a noticeable 'hose-in-hose' form. *Great Eastern* flowers are a deep rose-red, varying toward purple in heavy soils. They have an inner arrangement of paler petaloids with occasional white markings. This remarkable flower blooms mid to late season. (See also photo p. 43)

GREAT EASTERN (NZ)
(see EMPEROR OF RUSSIA VARIEGATED)

GREAT SACRED DANCE (see DAIKAGURA)

GREAT SACRED DANCE RED
(see BENI DAIKAGURA)

GUEST OF HONOR 1955
Guest of Honor was produced by California's Harvey Short in 1955, and is a very large, loose peony form camellia of rosy salmon-pink. It blooms profusely mid season on a bush of dense growth habit. It has a less popular variegated form.

GUILFOLIUS HALLEANA (see HELENOR)

GUILFOYLE'S HELLENOR (see HELENOR)

GUILIO NUCCIO 1956
There are many *aficionados* of the camellia who believe *Guilio Nuccio* to be the finest japonica cultivar raised yet. Its flowers are as large as any reticulata — often 15 cm (6 in) across, and of a rich coral-rose shade, almost red. The petals are irregular and waved, surrounding a mixture of tall petaloids and golden stamens. The flowers

GRAND SLAM

GRAND SULTAN

GREAT EASTERN

GUEST OF HONOUR

Japonicas

GUILIO NUCCIO

GUILIO NUCCIO VARIEGATED

have a superb velvety texture, and the lush green foliage is of a weeping habit, often with divided 'fishtail' leaves inherited from its ancestor *KINGYO TSUBAKI* (which see). *Guilio Nuccio* was named for the patriarch of the Nuccio Nurseries in California, where it was bred before 1956.

GUILIO NUCCIO VARIEGATED
One of many sports and descendants of the brilliant *Guilio Nuccio* (which see) *Guilio Nuccio Variegated* is similar in every respect but colour to its predecessor. It is tinted a more intense red, with startling patches of pure white.

GULFPORT PURPLE 1950
The colour of this medium-sized anemone form camellia is difficult to describe. I would not say it was purple, but there do seem to be markings of at least magenta on its crimson petals. Early to bloom, *Gulfport Purple* was raised in Gulfport, Mississippi and released in 1950.

HAGOROMO (Feathered Robe) 1695
(syn: *CHŌ NO HAGASANE, Magnoliiflora*) Though *Magnoliiflora* has long been accepted as the European name of this lovely blush-pink camellia, there can be no doubt that the Japanese name *HAGOROMO* has priority, for the flower is recorded by this name as far back as 1695. *HAGOROMO* means 'feathered robe', and in Japanese folklore is the traditional raiment of an angel. *HAGOROMO* is a medium-sized semi-double bloom of 'hose-in-hose' form. It opens mid season on a compact bush with decorative, pale green leaves that taper to sharp, downward pointing tips. It was imported to Italy in 1886. (See also photo p. 58)

HAKU TSURU (White Crane) 1934
(syn: *White Stork*)   A Japanese cultivar of 1934 from the Chugai Nursery, *HAKU TSURU* is a medium-sized pure white camellia. Blooms vary from single to semi-double with large crinkled petals. It blooms mid season.

HAKUHAN KUJAKU
(White Spotted Peacock) 1956
(syn: *KUJAKU TSUBAKI, Peacock Camellia*)
A delightful Japanese novelty, the cultivar *HAKUHAN KUJAKU* can only be traced for certain back to 1956, but seems to be much older. It is a slender plant of much-branched weeping habit, and long willow-like foliage. The blooms, which appear mid season, are medium in size, and have a long lily-like shape, never opening fully. They hang from the branch tips like red and white shuttlecocks, or as the imaginative Japanese have decided, peacocks' tails.

HALL TOWNES (see REGINA DEI GIGANTI)

HANA FŪKI (Flower of Honour) 1930
(syn: *Chalice, Flower of Crêpe Paper, Flower of Noble Family, Mrs Howard Asper*)   An unusual

GULFPORT PURPLE

soft pink bloom of cup-like shape, *HANA FŪKI* is sometimes known as *Flower of Crêpe Paper* because of the almost artificial texture of the petals. Imported from Japan to California in 1930, it has achieved world popularity as a result of its great beauty and unique form. *HANA FŪKI* is a large semi-double flower, blooming mid season. It has several synonyms in the United States, but its Japanese name has priority, meaning a flower with unimpeachable ancestry, or from a noble family. *HANA FŪKI* shows round decorative buds, and sharply serrated foliage.

HANA FŪKI VARIEGATED
Similar to the preceding variety, but with the pink petals delicately blotched white. It reportedly enjoys a warm climate.

HANA TACHIBANA (Flower Crest) 1877
(syn: *KAKITSU, Wild Orange Blossom*) One of a number of Japanese cultivars imported by California's Star Nursery in 1930, HANA TACHIBANA is a wonderful large-sized deep pink camellia of full peony form. Outer petals are frequently marbled white, and flag-like petaloids break the circle of widely flared gold stamens. A medium to late bloomer.

HAPPINESS (see SODE KAKUSHI)

HARMONIOUS (see BENI BOTAN)

HARMONY (see TRIUMPHANS)

HARRIET BEECHER SHEATHER 1872
(syn: *Mrs H. B. Sheather*) One of the more successful camellia introductions in the colony of New South Wales, *Harriet Beecher Sheather* is nurseryman Silas Sheather's memorial to his wife, and is still grown over a century later. A charming, medium-sized formal double of rosy salmon, it seems almost hexagonal as the overlapping petals become more and more slender towards the centre of the flower. This charming survivor blooms mid season, and has given rise to a variegated sport.

HARRIET I. LAUB (see SHIRAGIKU)

HARU NO UTENA (see LADY VANSITTART)

HASSAKU (see BENI HASSAKU)

HATSUARASHI (see SHIRATAMA)

HAWAII 1961
Rather resembling the *Elegans* series to which it is related, *Hawaii* is a direct sport of *C. M. Wilson*, and was released in 1961. It is a medium to large pale pink camellia, with lighter fringed edges to the petals. The flowers open mid season and hold extremely well. (Photo p. 54)

HAZEL E. HERRIN 1949
An unusual, medium to large bloom of flat, open appearance, *Hazel E. Herrin* was registered in Florida in 1949. The semi-double flowers have broad, notched outer petals with large fluted petaloids — the whole a restful shade of old rose. They open mid season.

HELEN BOWER 1964
Helen Bower has been identified as a chimera, or sport created when one variety is grafted on another. In this case it is a new camellia that appeared when *Dr Knapp* was grafted on *Mathotiana Variegated*. It is a large rose form to formal double of rose-red. The petals are etched in purple-red and have occasional white markings. It appeared in Mobile, Alabama in 1964.

HELENE LONGHI (see ELISABETH)

HELENOR 1866
(syn: *Guilfolius Halleana, Guilfoyle's Hellenor*) Described at its 1866 introduction as 'a superior seedling raised by Michael Guilfoyle' (a nurseryman in New South Wales) *Helenor* has proved worthy of the praise, surviving for a further 115 years and finding her way into collections all over the world. A medium-sized camellia of peony form, it is tinted pale pink, flecked and striped with a darker tone, or (as the original description had it) 'carnation striped'. *Helenor* blooms mid season and has attracted a number of curious synonyms, largely because of the Victorian misspelling of the name. (See also photo p. 48)

HENRY PRICE 1965
An exquisite, large formal double bloom, bred by Australian E. G. Waterhouse, *Henry Price* has perfectly imbricated petals of a deep glowing pink, flushing almost to crimson at the centre. It blooms mid season.

HER MAJESTY QUEEN ELIZABETH II 1955
Although one might expect a certain patriotic enthusiasm from Commonwealth growers, this fine camellia does not seem to be widely listed. It is a medium to large salmon-rose bloom of loose peony form with ruffled petals and occasional light markings on the petaloids. Blooming mid season, it was released by Longview Nurseries of Alabama in 1955 shortly after the Queen's Coronation.

HERME (see HIKARU GENJI)

HERME PINK (see BENI BOTAN)

HERME RED (see BENI BOTAN)

HIIRAGIBA TSUBAKI (see HOLLY LEAF)

HIKARU GENJI (Brilliant Genji) 1859
FRAGRANT
(syn: *Herme, Jordan's Pride, Souvenir d'Henri Guichard*) It is impossible to please everyone, but I am prepared to incur the wrath of French,

HAGOROMO　　　　羽衣

HAKUHAN KUJAKU　　　　白斑孔雀

HANA FŪKI　　　　花富貴

HARRIET BEECHER SHEATHER

HAZEL E. HERRIN

HELENOR

HENRY PRICE

HISHI KARAITO

菱唐糸

Japonicas

German and American enthusiasts by insisting that this camellia is properly named *HIKARU GENJI*, and that it was so validly named and published in 1859. The French called it *Souvenir d'Henri Guichard* early this century, the Germans held out for *Herme* about the same time, the Americans pleaded ignorance and decided on *Jordan's Pride*. But *HIKARU GENJI* it was, is, and will remain. It is named for the romantic hero of the early Japanese novel *Tale of Genji*, a prince renowned for his elegance, and the name fits the flower to a 'T'. *GENJI* is a medium-sized informal double camellia of dark salmon-pink, bordered in white, streaked with scarlet. A centre of petaloids mixed with gold stamens completes the picture. It is also fragrant. Blooms mid season. (Photo p. 56)

HIKARU GENJI AKA (see BENI BOTAN)

HIKARU GENJI YOKUMOKU
(see BEAUTY OF HOLLAND)

HIME (see DUCHESSE DE CAZE)

HISHI KARAITO (Thread Stamens) 1875
(syn: *Emily Brown, Lacy Pink, Pink Lace, Thread of Diamond*) Most consistently popular of the small-class japonicas, *HISHI KARAITO* dates back well over a century in Japanese camellia literature, though it seems first to have been distributed by Kobe's Chugai Nursery in 1934. It is a delicate pink semi-double bloom with a centre of white petaloids. Growth is compact, and the flowers peak mid to late season.

HOLLAND RED (see ORANDA KŌ)

HOLLY LEAF 1954
A charming 1954 novelty from David Feathers of California, *Holly Leaf* blooms early in the season, but is probably grown more for its striking foliage than the medium-sized cardinal-red flowers. The latter are single with fine, twisted petals that have incurving edges and slight serration. The dense foliage resembles that of English holly, and the camellia is probably a hybrid of the Japanese *HIIRAGIBA TSUBAKI*, which has a similar appearance, though with small mid season flowers.

HOLLYHOCK (see KUMASAKA)

HON AMI (see KAMO HON AMI)

HONEYCOMB (see ANEMONIFLORA)

IDATEN SHIBORI (see DAIKAGURA)

IL CIGNO (see SHIRAGIKU)

IMBRICATA RUBRA PLENA
(see PRINCE EUGENE NAPOLEON)

IMPERATOR 1908
(syn: *Big Daddy*) A French camellia of 1908,

IMURA イ ム ラ

Imperator is a large bloom of full peony form, coloured deep red. A product of the Guichard Nursery of Nantes, it flowers mid season.

IMURA 1939
(syn: *Diana, Dr Allen Ames*) A pre-World War II masterpiece from Alabama's Overlook Nurseries, *IMURA* is a vision of sheer loveliness. Medium to large in size, the semi-double blooms are formal 'hose in-hose' style around a column of long golden stamens, and hang delicately from branch tips in mid to late season. The overall weeping, willowy form of the bush makes it perfect for hanging basket culture.

IN THE PINK 1971
A formal double cultivar of warm rose-pink with cyclamen veining, *In the Pink* was marketed by Kramer Bros of California in 1971. It is medium in size, vigorous, and blooms mid to late season. The waved petals frequently bear lighter or darker markings, always of pink.

INCARNATA (see LADY HUME'S BLUSH)

INDIA KRUGER (see LADY DE SAUMAREZ)

INDIAN CHIEF 1958
If you've an imagination, the ruffled, high-standing petals of this showy variety may remind you of an Indian chief's war bonnet. If not, then it is still a wonderful, large peony form camellia of vibrant red-pink. *Indian Chief* blooms early to mid season on a plant notable for its strength and vitality. It was originated in Georgia, and has a variegated sport.

IWANE (Solid Rock) 1877
(syn: *IWANE SHIBORI*) Listed in Japanese catalogues as far back as 1877, the delightful cultivar *IWANE* was rediscovered in a Victorian garden, for which it had been purchased years before under the label *Mars*. There is a suggestion of *Mars Variegated* at first sight, but only a suggestion. *IWANE* (known as *IWANE SHIBORI* in Japan) is a medium-sized semi-double camellia with 12 large, deeply veined petals and often one or two petaloids. The colour is rose-red and white, with the red markings often in moiré fashion. The plant is a slow grower, and blooms in mid season.

IWANE SHIBORI (see IWANE)

JANET WATERHOUSE 1952
An elegant white Australian cultivar raised from a seedling by E. G. Waterhouse, who named it for his wife. When young, the large flower has the appearance of a formal double, as the outer petals open to reveal a central cone. This later bursts apart to show golden stamens. In spite of the bloom's delicacy, *Janet Waterhouse* is a sturdy plant, with magnificent dark foliage.

JEAN CLERE 1969
Most recently reported sport of that inconstant

lady *Aspasia* is *Jean Clere*, registered in New Zealand, and named for the wife of its propagator, Richard Clere. The ravishing bloom is exactly the reverse of *Margaret Davis* — the petals are coral-pink or red, but with a narrow white picoteed border. It is a camellia as charming as its namesake whom I met while researching this book. (Photo p. 55)

JEAN LYNE 1941
An Australian seedling of unknown parentage, *Jean Lyne* was raised by Alexander Hunter of New South Wales, and named by another camellia enthusiast G. C. Linton in 1941. It is a medium-sized white bloom of variable form, generally semi-double, sometimes peony form. The petals are striped and flecked with soft carmine, sometimes flushed with pink. Of good bushy growth, it flowers mid season. (See also photo p. 49)

JEANNE KERR (see KUMASAKA)

JEFFREY HOOD 1969
A large to very large camellia, richly coloured deep pink, *Jeffrey Hood* was a 1969 registration from Arkansas, and is now widely grown. Flowering early to mid season, its blooms vary from semi-double with irregular petals to anemone form.

JENNY LIND 1854
Jenny Lind was described thus by its propagators, the English nursery firm of Henderson and Son: 'No other variety is more perfectly imbricated or has more numerous, better arranged or more ample petals ... blossoms of the purest white on which appear a few delicate and elegant bright red stripes'. Well, that was in 1854. Nowadays the once-famous cultivar seems to have faded like the memory of the Swedish nightingale herself. 'Medium size, formal double; white with a few faint pink streaks' is all they say. But it is still a nice camellia, blooming mid season.

JESSIE BURGESS 1960
A fine rose-coloured semi-double cultivar with a silvery-blue cast, *Jessie Burgess* has been rather outclassed since her launching in 1960. Still an elegant early bloomer though, with long twisted petals.

JESSIE GALE 1958
A medium-sized single camellia of light glossy red, *Jessie Gale* blooms mid season and is popular in the United States. It was distributed by the McCaskill Nursery in 1958.

JESSIE KATZ 1948
A large semi-double cultivar with crêped and wavy petals, *Jessie Katz* was released by the Magnolia Gardens, South Carolina in 1948. Attractive and hibiscus-like in form, the blooms are tinted watermelon-pink with an occasional blush of white. They are at their peak early in the season.

IN THE PINK

IWANE 岩根絞

JANET WATERHOUSE

JEAN CLERE

JEAN LYNE

JEFFREY HOOD

JESSIE KATZ

JULIA FRANCE

KATHERINE NUCCIO

KICK OFF

KIFUKURIN BENTEN   黄覆輪弁天

Japonicas

JIKKŌ (see CARDINAL'S CAP)

JINGLE BELLS 1959
A red sport of Nuccio's small camellia *Tinker Bell* (which see).

JOLLY ROGER (see GIGANTEA)

JORDAN'S PRIDE (see HIKARU GENJI)

JOSEPH PFINGSTL VARIEGATED (see EMMETT PFINGSTL)

JOSHUA E. YOUTZ 1915
(syn: *White Daikagura*)   This large white peony form camellia reached the USA from Japan in 1915. It is slow in growth and early blooming, the flowers sometimes tending to formal double style.

JUANITA (see DUCHESSE DE CAZE)

JULIA DRAYTON (see MATHOTIANA [US])

JULIA FRANCE 1958
Admired for its simplicity in Japan, *Julia France* is a superb semi-double camellia with fluted petals 'hose-in-hose' style. Large in size, it blooms in mid season. The colouring is an exquisite silver-pink. It was introduced in South Carolina in 1958.

KAGOSHIMA (see MATSU KASA)

KAISER WILHELM (see GIGANTEA)

KAKITSU (see HANA TACHIBANA)

KALLISTA
(syn: *Mrs H. Boyce Rosea*)   This is the deep pink to crimson sport of *Paolina Maggi*, large, formal double and blooming late in the season. It is a largely superseded cultivar named for the Victorian mountain district in which it was first noticed.

KAMO HON AMI 1935
(syn: *HON AMI, SŌTAN*)   Believed by many to be the most perfect white camellia ever grown, the chaste beauty of *KAMO HON AMI* is evocative of the tea flower, *C. sinensis*. How appropriate then, that it has been named for the most famous Japanese tea-master of all time. A large, single bloom of slightly cupped shape, it opens early to mid season, catching the light with its huge centre of gold to red tipped stamens. *KAMO HON AMI* has dark, lustrous foliage and is a joy to look at any time of year. It was introduced by the Chugai Nursery of Kobe in 1935, but may be the same as *Amabilis*, a cultivar described half a century earlier. (Photo p. 60)

KATHERINE NUCCIO 1950
A true labour of love from California's Nuccio Nurseries, the lovely *Katherine Nuccio* is an

KIN SEKAI   金世界

almost perfect formal double of brilliant rose-red. Medium in size, with slightly cupped petals, it blooms mid season, and was introduced in 1950.

KELVINGTONIANA (see GIGANTEA)

KICK OFF 1962
As camellias share the same season with football, it is perhaps appropriate to say that the 1962 season began with a sensational *Kick Off*! Large to very large, this rugged peony form flower is unexpectedly pale pink and frilly, with fine radial markings of deeper pink. It does in fact bloom early in the season, continuing to the cheers of the camellia crowd for several months. An introduction of the Nuccio Nursery.

KIFUKURIN BENTEN c. 1877
I do not believe this lovely camellia has been listed or illustrated in the West before, although it has a long Japanese history going back over a century. The single flower is a vivid cerise-pink; the dark foliage lightly marbled in paler green, irregularly edged and veined in creamy-yellow. It blooms mid season and is one of many popular Japanese cultivars with variegated foliage.

KIN SEKAI (nineteenth century)
A charming camellia in the variegated foliage style much appreciated in Japan, *KIN SEKAI* bears irregularly shaped single blossoms with only five petals of glowing carmine. These make a stunning contrast to the dark leaves which are curiously variegated along the centre line in green and olive. The effect is rather like an unfolded ink blot test. *KIN SEKAI* blooms early in the season.

KINGYO TSUBAKI (Goldfish Camellia) 1879
FRAGRANT
(syn: *Fishtail Camellia, KINGYOBA TSU-BAKI, Quercifolia*) Although its single flowers are sweetly scented, and tinted a delicious strawberry ice-cream shade, this curious variety of *Camellia japonica* is prized more for its unique foliage. Every dark, shining leaf is divided and twisted at the tip, like the tail of a fancy goldfish. And that is what the Japanese call it — *KINGYO TSUBAKI*, the *Goldfish Camellia*. Elsewhere it has been known as *Quercifolia (Oak Leaf)* or merely *Fishtail*, but the Japanese name is surely more appropriate. The plant is vigorous, blooming early to mid season, and a parent of many cultivars including *Guilio Nuccio* (which see).

KINGYOBA TSUBAKI (see KINGYO TSUBAKI)

KISHŪ TSUKASA
(Lord of Kii Province) 1937
(syn: *Admiral Nimitz, Captain John Sutter, SHUCHŪKA*) This favourite Japanese camellia, despite its long history, can only be dated with certainty back to 1937, when it was

KINGYO TSUBAKI   魚椿

KISHŪ TSUKASA   紀州司

KOKURYŪ　黒龍　KRAMER'S SUPREME

KUMASAKA　熊坂

KURO TSUBAKI　黒椿　KYŌ KANOKO VARIEGATED　京鹿子絞

Japonicas

listed by the Chugai Nursery of Kobe. It is a medium-sized formal double flower of rose-pink and white, blooming mid to late season.

KITTY 1955
A small japonica from Alabama's Azalea Glen Nursery, *Kitty* seems much like a paler version of *Grace Albritton* (which see).

KIYOSU (see DAIKAGURA)

KŌ BOTAN (see BENI BOTAN)

KOKURYŪ (Black Dragon) 1877
                                    FRAGRANT
(syn: *Carol Compton*) The favourite Japanese cultivar, *KOKURYŪ* can be dated back to 1877 with certainty, though it was not exported from Japan until 1930. It is a medium-sized bloom of dark glowing red, generally semi-double in style, but varying to loose peony form with irregular petals. The plant is a favourite bonsai subject, and blooms mid to late season.

KONA 1969
An unusual greenish-white sport of *Hawaii* (which see) *Kona* is a medium to large camellia of fimbriated style, like its parent and the related *Maui*. It blooms mid season, and was introduced only in 1969.

KOREAN CAMELLIA (see CHŌSEN TSUBAKI)

KRAMER'S SUPREME 1957　FRAGRANT
A wonderful turkey-red camellia from the Kramer Bros Nursery of California which may well deserve the 'supreme' epithet. It is a large to very large bloom of full peony form, blooming mid season, and of particular interest to hybridisers as it is quite fragrant. It was released in 1957. (See also photos pp. 41, 66)

KUJAKU TSUBAKI (see HAKUHAN KUJAKU)

KUMASAKA 1695
(syn: *Hollyhock, Jeanne Kerr, KUMASAKA BENI, Lady Marion, Maiden, Sherbrooke*) One of the oldest camellias in continuous culture, *KUMASAKA* (an old Japanese given name) is clearly recorded in Japan back to 1695, and was exported to the West in 1896 by Tokyo Nurseries. Since then it has attracted the many synonyms listed above. A medium-sized bloom of deep rose-pink, *KUMASAKA* varies from rose form double to peony form, with petals of varying size and shape. It blooms mid to late season.

KUMASAKA BENI (see KUMASAKA)

KURO TSUBAKI (Black Camellia) 1877
(syn: *The Black Camellia*) If this dramatic camellia is not truly black, then it is as dark as a red can get without blacking out altogether. Both buds and faded blooms are the colour of

LA PACE RUBRA   *LADY DE SAUMAREZ*

that old English favourite, a black pudding. It is a small semi-double camellia of cupped shape, and with red stamens. Blooming continuously from mid to late season, *KURO TSUBAKI* can be traced back to 1877, but was distributed generally in 1896. It is the parent of some interesting new hybrids.

KYŌ KANOKO VARIEGATED 1930
(syn: *Bandana of Kyōtō, KYŌKŌ*) The interesting Japanese variety KYO KANOKO was imported by California's Star Nursery in 1930 and has since produced several sports including *KYŌ KANOKO VARIEGATED.* This is a medium-sized camellia varying from semi-double to peony form, and blooming mid season. Its colour is basically white, slashed and spotted with several shades of carmine. The Japanese name means a dappled cloth or spotted scarf from Kyoto, but the allusion is obscure outside Japan.

KYŌKŌ (see KYŌ KANOKO VARIEGATED)

LA GRACIOLA (see ODORATISSIMA)

LA PACE RUBRA 1860
(syn: *Red Pressii*) Sport of the 1860 Italian cultivar *La Pace* (a seedling camellia of pinkish-white with carmine stripes) *La Pace Rubra* is a most elegant formal double of dark rose-pink. Medium in size, it blooms mid to late season and its outer petals have a tendency to reflex.

LACY PINK (see HISHI KARAITO)

LADINER'S RED
(see PRINCE EUGENE NAPOLEON)

LADY AUDREY BULLER (see NAGASAKI)

LADY CLARE (see AKASHIGATA)

LADY CLARE VARIEGATED (see ŌNIJI)

LADY DE SAUMAREZ 1920
(syn: *Eulalia Sally, India Kruger, Pride of Portland, Pride of Rosebud Farm, Tricolor Folki*) A sport of Siebold's original *Tricolor* (1832), *Lady de Saumarez* was released in 1920 by the Caledonia Nursery on the Isle of Guernsey. A medium-sized semi-double bloom, it is generally pale light red, blotched with white. It blooms mid season, and as you can see from the list of synonyms above, the same sport appeared in a number of different places. *Lady de Saumarez*, however, was the first listed and described, and thus has priority of name.

LADY HUME'S BLUSH 1806
(syn: *Buff, Incarnata*) One of the earliest and most popular of camellia cultivars, *Lady Hume's Blush* arrived in England from China in 1806. It is a small formal double bloom, white flashed with pink, and blooms quite early.

LADY KAY

LADY MACKINNON

LADY VANSITTART 春の台

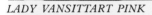

LADY VANSITTART PINK

LALLA ROOKH

LATIFOLIA VARIEGATA

Japonicas

LADY KAY 1949
A rather lovely sport of *Ville de Nantes, Lady Kay* was registered in California in 1949. Similar in form and habit to its parent (medium to large, loose to full peony form, with fimbriated petals) *Lady Kay* is a bright deep red, irregularly blotched with white. It blooms mid season.

LADY LOCH 1898
(syn: *Duchess of York, Edward Billing, Elizabeth Johnston, Pink Lady*) That remarkably unstable Australian cultivar *Aspasia* has sported many descendants at many times in many places; but none more often than the pale rose-pink variation edged in white. This has been grown and loved under the five different names listed above, but now the experts agree it was first validly christened in Australia in 1898 as *Lady Loch*, after the wife of the then Governor of Victoria. *Lady Loch* is a large informal double camellia, opening mid season. The inner petals are entwined with gold stamens. (Photo p. 55)

LADY MACKINNON 1891
An attractive sport of the earlier cultivar *Tricolor, Lady Mackinnon* was imported directly from Japan to England in 1891. It is a medium-sized semi-double bloom of slightly cupped form, coloured a rich crimson and mottled white. It blooms mid season, and is vigorous.

LADY MARION (see KUMASAKA)

LADY OF THE LAKE (NZ)
(see FRANCOIS WIOT)

LADY PARKER PEONY (see TRIUMPHANS)

LADY VANSITTART 1877
(syn: *HARU NO UTENA, Lady Vansittart Variegated*) Imported from Japan in 1877, this extremely variable camellia was named *Lady Vansittart* by Guernsey's Caledonia Nurseries — though it can be traced back at least ten years earlier under the Japanese name *HARU NO UTENA*. It is a medium-sized semi-double camellia with broad wavy petals, and in its most usual colour form is white flushed with rose-pink. *Lady Vansittart* has coarse rather holly-like foliage, and blooms mid to late season.

LADY VANSITTART PINK 1887
The self-coloured deep pink form of the previous entry was named *Lady Vansittart Pink* by the importers, Caledonia Nurseries in 1887, but is often sold as *Lady Vansittart Red.*

LADY VANSITTART RED
(see LADY VANSITTART PINK)

LADY VANSITTART SHELL
(see YOURS TRULY)

LADY VANSITTART VARIEGATED
(see LADY VANSITTART)

LEVIATHAN

LALLA ROOKH 1854

(syn: *Lallarook, Laurel Leaf, L'avenire, L'avvenire*) Named for the exotic heroine of Thomas Moore's poem 'Lalla Rookh', which was popular in the nineteenth century, this charming flower was released by the Guichard Nursery of France in 1893. But they had it from Italy, where the grower Corsi of Firenze described it in 1854 as *L'avvenire (The Future)*. It is a medium to large formal double bloom with generally incurved petal edges, coloured soft pink with white marbling caused by virus variegation. *Lalla Rookh* blooms mid to late season on a shrub with laurel-like foliage. It has been decided that the self-coloured pink variation grown in Europe should validly be named *L'avvenire*, the variegated 'Lalla Rookh'.

LALLAROOK (see LALLA ROOKH)

LATIFOLIA 1884

A once-popular Belgian cultivar of 1884, *Latifolia* is a medium-sized semi-double bloom of soft rose-red, blooming mid season. It is most often seen in its variegated form (which see).

LATIFOLIA VARIEGATA

(syn: *Fanny Bolis*) The variegated form of Belgian *Latifolia, Latifolia Variegata* is still seen in specialist collections, for its semi-double blooms are among the handsomest of camellias. A soft rose-red in colour, they are tidily marbled in white.

LAURA DASHER (see ROSEA SUPERBA)

LAURA WALKER 1956

Too reminiscent of many earlier cultivars to be considered a true novelty, *Laura Walker* has nevertheless built a world following thanks to her firm, compact growth and reliable blooming habits. The large semi-double to anemone form blooms are bright rose-red, with occasional white markings on the central petaloids. The flowers open early to mid season.

LAURA WALKER VARIEGATED 1956

A fully variegated form of the previously described cultivar.

LAUREL LEAF (see LALLA ROOKH)

LAURIE BRAY 1955

An extremely variable seedling of the Australian cultivar *Edith Linton, Laurie Bray* came from grower G. C. Linton in 1955, and possesses the same valuable attributes as its parent — hardiness, profusion of bloom and complete reliability. It flowers early to mid season, the blooms ranging in form from almost single to a simple informal double with petaloids among the stamens. *Laurie Bray* is medium to large in size, the colour a delicious pale pink, intensifying as the flower ages.

L'AVENIRE (see LALLA ROOKH)

L'AVVENIRE (see LALLA ROOKH)

LEVIATHAN 1862

(syn: *Maranui, Maranui Pink*) This camellia is certainly large, but not the *Leviathan* its name suggests. An Australian hybrid, it bears deep red-rose blooms that are very like those of a peony, with their raised ruffled centres. *Leviathan* was introduced in 1862 by nurseryman Thomas Shepherd of New South Wales, and later given several invalid names in New Zealand. It is a feature of many older Australian gardens.

LEWIS RED PEONY (see VEDRINE)

LILIAN PITTS 1946

Propagated in 1946 by the late Professor Waterhouse of Gordon, New South Wales from seed collected at the Linton estate, *Lilian Pitts* is a charming, early-blooming cultivar. Medium-sized, it is semi-double with two-thirds of the petals being white with streaks of cerise, the others almost pure cerise. There are frequently petaloids among the stamens. (Photo p. 49)

LILY CAMELLIA (see YURI TSUBAKI)

LILY PONS 1955

A camellia that is really different in its appearance, *Lily Pons* was released in 1955 and named for the reigning diva of the Metropolitan Opera. It is a pure white bloom, single to semi-double in form, with long lily-like petals surrounding a delicate centre of gold-tipped greenish stamens. *Lily Pons* produces its best blooms mid season.

LITTLE BIT 1958

A small charmer of anemone to peony form, *Little Bit* is normally cherry-red with white and deep pink stripes — but occasionally a plain red bloom is to be had. It was registered in California by Dr John D. Lawson, and blooms mid season. Reminiscent of *Tinker Bell* (which see).

LITTLE HOLLAND (see ORANDA KŌ)

LONJAN (see NAGASAKI)

LORD OF KII PROVINCE (see KISHŪ TSUKASA)

LOTUS (see SODE KAKUSHI)

LOUISE CENTURIONI (see CANDIDISSIMA)

LOUISE MACLAY (see GRANDIFLORA ROSEA)

LOVEBOAT 1981

Due for release in 1981, *Loveboat* is a brilliant new creation of northern California hybridist David Feathers. It is a cross of *Dr Tinsley* and *Debutante* and can expect a wonderful future. *Loveboat* is a medium-sized peony form camellia of delicate 'sweet pea' coloration — pink shading to a white centre. The flowers peak mid season on a bushy compact plant.

LILY PONS

LOVEBOAT

LOVELIGHT

MADAME HAHN

MARGARET DAVIS

Japonicas

LOVELIGHT 1960
Guaranteed to make the eyes of any enthusiast shine, the superb semi-double white camellia named *Lovelight* was introduced in 1960 by California grower Harvey Short. It is large with broad, crêped petals opening to a cup shape, and ultimately reflexing as the bloom ages. The showy boss of gold-tipped ivory stamens occasionally shows petaloid development. In addition, *Lovelight* features strong growth and magnificent foliage. A must for any collector.

LUCILLE FERRELL (see C. M. WILSON)

MADAM BUTTERFLY (see CHŌ CHŌ SAN)

MADAME HAHN 1915
A charming medium-sized camellia imported from Japan in 1915, the original name of *Madame Hahn* has been lost, but under her Western alias, she has remained tremendously popular. Semi-double, brilliant pink with a distinctive mauve tinge to the swirling petaloids, she is the essence of femininity. Blooms mid season.

MADAME HAHN VARIEGATED
(see SIERRA SPRING)

MAGNOLIA KING (see GIGANTEA)

MAGNOLIIFLORA (see HAGOROMO)

MAGNOLIIFLORA (UK)
(see PEACH BLOSSOM)

MAGNOLIIFLORA ALBA (see MIYAKO DORI)

MAHOGANY GLOW 1953
Small to medium in size, the blooms of magnificent *Mahogany Glow* are much admired for their deep red colouring, a tinge of which can also be seen on the foliage at certain times of the year. The late-blooming flowers are semi-double with notched petals, reducing in size towards the centre. *Mahogany Glow* is a 1953 creation of California hybridist Harvey Short.

MAIDEN (see KUMASAKA)

MAJESTIC (see BENI BOTAN)

MARANUI (see LEVIATHAN)

MARANUI PINK (see LEVIATHAN)

MARC ELEVEN 1969
The large cherry-red blooms of *Marc Eleven* appear on an outstanding plant with rapid, spreading growth and have brought it a measure of popularity in America. The blooms are semi-double with waved, upright petals in reticulata style. It flowers mid to late season, and was originated in 1969.

MARGARET DAVIS 1961
Named by her late husband for my old friend

MARGARET HIGDON

MARIANA

and founding president of the Garden Clubs of Australia, *Margaret Davis* first appeared in 1961 as a sport of the Australian cultivar *Aspasia*, in her own garden. Since then, this charming ruffled flower, reminiscent of a Victorian posy, has swept the world, winning many awards in many lands. It is an informal double camellia, medium in size, creamy-white, with the crowded petals edged brilliant rose or vermilion. Flowers open early to mid season. (Photo p. 55)

MARGARET HIGDON c. 1900
(syn: *Elizabeth Grandy*) A full-blown camellia of earlier style, *Margaret Higdon* was grown by South Carolina's Magnolia Nurseries in the early 1900s. She is rose form semi-double in style, and rose-red in colouring, sometimes with paler petal margins. Blooming mid season since the turn of the century, she will doubtless continue well into the next.

MARGARET JACK
(see FINLANDIA VARIEGATED)

MARGARET LAWRENCE (see VEDRINE)

MARGARET SANDUSKY
(see ROSEA SUPERBA VARIEGATED)

MARGARETE HERTRICH 1944
A white formal double camellia of superb shape and substance, *Margarete Hertrich* was released in 1944 by the Huntington Gardens of San Marino, California. It is named for the wife of their famous camellia collection's founder, William Hertrich. Medium in size, the bloom has many small notched petals, perfectly imbricated. The delicate flowers are popular in corsage work.

MARGUERITA (see NAGASAKI)

MARGUERITE GOUILLON 1850
(syn: *Duc D'Orléans, General Lamorcière*) The names of this fine cultivar read like a history of France, and it was released in that country in 1850 by the grower Drouard. A full peony form camellia of medium size, the colouring is delicate pink, striped and flecked with a deeper shade. A plant of strong growth, it blooms mid season.

MARIA ANTONIETTA 1853
Named in memory of the tragic Queen of France, *Maria Antonietta* was created by Ridolfi of Firenze in 1843. It is a large Italian-style formal double — brilliant cherry-red, striped white.

MARIANA 1852
(syn: *Red Waratah*) A dark crimson camellia of anemone form and medium size, *Mariana* was first flowered from a seedling at Camden Park, New South Wales in 1852, but there is some dispute as to whether this is the same camellia grown today. Today's *Mariana* is a rich crimson medium-sized flower, also of anemone form, but

is more often known by its synonym of *Red Waratah*, after the floral symbol of New South Wales.

MARK ALAN VARIEGATED 1958
One of my favourite camellias, *Mark Alan Variegated* blooms for me months on end, and the individual flowers hang on for weeks with no sign of fading. They are unusual semi-double blooms with elongated lily-shaped petals, centred with a striking mass of petaloids. Colouring is wine-red, marbled in white.

MAROON AND GOLD 1961
Small to medium, but spectacular as any camellia twice its size, *Maroon and Gold* is a worthy 1961 release from Nuccio's Nursery of California. Deep maroon, with gold-tipped maroon stamens, it has very much the black toning of *KURO TSUBAKI*, which is doubtless in its parentage. *Maroon and Gold* blooms mid to late season.

MARS 1911
Introduced in England by nurseryman William Paul in 1911, the spectacular japonica cultivar *Mars* is believed to have been a Japanese import, but has not been clearly identified. It is a large crimson semi-double bloom of loose peony form, with occasional white variation on the inner petals.

MARS VARIEGATED c. 1911
A sport of the English variety *Mars*, and like it introduced by Englishman William Paul in the early twentiety century, *Mars Variegated* is a most popular camellia in Australia. Large, semi-double blooms of glowing crimson and white appear in mid season, their petals surrounding a cylinder of prominent stamens intermixed with sparse petaloids. *Mars Variegated* is also prone to occasional foliage variegation. It is a recommended container plant.

MARTHA TUCK 1959
A fine semi-double white camellia of medium to large size, *Martha Tuck* was registered in 1959. Both petals and filaments are white, the former fluted, the latter few in number and tipped with gold stamens. *Martha Tuck* is a useful white for early season bloom.

MARY BELL GLENNAN (see GIGANTEA)

MARY PAIGE 1964
Named for his charming wife by prominent California camellian Harold Paige, this medium to large formal double camellia is soft, light pink with deeper shadings. It is a strong grower, a medium to late bloomer, and was registered in 1964.

MATHOTIANA (US) 1840
(syn: *Julia Drayton, Mathotiana Rubra, Purple Dawn, Purple Emperor, Purple Prince, William S. Hastie*) The *Mathotiana* camellia grown today (when it is grown) is apparently not the original

MARK ALAN VARIEGATED

MAROON AND GOLD

MARS

MARS VARIEGATED

Japonicas

MATHOTIANA SUPREME

MATTERHORN

MENA LADNIER

MIDNIGHT

European variety of that name, but is descended from a plant that arrived in America in 1840 and was possibly wrongly labelled. It still has priority right to the name *Mathotiana (US)* over the many synonyms with which it has been saddled since. A large to very large rose form double, it blooms mid to late season and has a somewhat purplish cast to its crimson petals.

MATHOTIANA FIMBRIATA
(see FLOWERWOOD)

MATHOTIANA RUBRA
(see MATHOTIANA [US])

MATHOTIANA SUPREME 1951
(syn: *Mima Mae*) This very large semi-double sport of *Mathotiana* has loose irregular petals, sometimes streaked with white. It blooms mid to late season and has floppy cream stamens. It was released by the Flowerwood Nursery of Alabama in 1951.

MATSUKASA (Pine Cone) 1681
(syn: *KAGOSHIMA*) Imported by American Toichi Domoto in 1932, *MATSUKASA* can be traced back in Japan to 1681. It is a medium-sized semi-double cultivar with a high centre, its wavy petals reflexed in pine cone style. Colouring is a rose-red, with slight white markings here and there. *MATSUKASA* blooms late.

MATTERHORN 1976
An exquisite formal double cultivar from hybridist David Feathers, *Matterhorn* is being propagated by the English Trehane Nursery, and should be a sensation when it is released. It is a white seedling of the Japanese *KINGYO TSUBAKI*, although the parentage is hard to spot. The medium-sized blooms appear mid season on a bushy compact plant.

MAUI 1975
A white anemone form sport of *Kona*, *Maui* was first listed in 1975 by the Nuccio Nurseries. It is a large camellia with rippled guard petals, and flowers mid season.

MAVERICK (see TOMORROW VARIEGATED)

MEHL'S RED (see VEDRINE)

MELINDA HACKETT 1966
A large medium-pink camellia of tight anemone form, *Melinda Hackett* was developed in South Carolina. It blooms early to mid season.

MENA LADNIER 1941
(syn: *Duncan Bell*) No longer new, the marvellous *Mena Ladnier* must have been a sensation when first shown in 1941 by its namesake grower. It is a large anemone form cultivar of deep pink, flushed blood-red, and with occasional white striations. *Mena Ladnier* blooms mid season but has been surpassed in style by several cultivars in the *Elegans* series.

MIDNIGHT 1963
Semi-double to anemone form, the dark red blooms of *Midnight* have superbly ruffled petals and a mass of tiny petaloids that almost completely obscure the stamens. It is a medium-sized flower, opening mid season on a densely foliaged bush. A 1963 introduction by Nuccio's of Altadena.

MIDNIGHT SERENADE 1973
For those who prefer a single flower (and a million Japanese camellia fanciers can't all be wrong) the 1973 introduction *Midnight Serenade* must be a milestone. It is a medium to large flower of brilliant darkest red, with irregular twisted petals and a compact display of gold-tipped stamens. California's Nuccio Nurseries propagated it and it blooms mid to late season.

MIKE WITMAN 1968
This beautiful frilled japonica hybrid blooms mid season, and is a full peony form double with loose, irregular petals. These are often notched and fimbriated and display more than a hint of long gold stamens. *Mike Witman* was registered in 1968.

MIKENJAKU (see NAGASAKI)

MILKY WAY (see AMA NO KAWA)

MIMA MAE (see MATHOTIANA SUPREME)

MISS ANAHEIM 1961
A soft pink semi-double cultivar of loose peony form, *Miss Anaheim* was introduced in 1961 by the McCaskill Gardens of Pasadena. Both petals and swirling petaloids have a slight mauve cast, and this lovely flower blooms mid season.

MISS CHARLESTON VARIEGATED 1961
A sport of the deep red 1961 cultivar *Miss Charleston*, this sensational bloom is large size, semi-double, with a high swirling centre. The petals are deep red blotched with white, the stamens pure gold. *Miss Charleston Variegated* blooms mid to late season.

MISS MUFFET 1962
A small japonica of anemone form, *Miss Muffet* was registered in 1962. Colouring is deep rose-red, blooming throughout the season.

MIYAKO DORI (Seagull) 1891
(syn: *Magnoliiflora Alba*) Most commonly known to Western gardeners as *Magnoliiflora Alba*, this elegant and popular camellia is surely better described by its evocative Japanese name *MIYAKO DORI*, meaning *Seagull*. It was so named because its blooming corresponded with the seagulls' annual migration. A large, pure white, semi-double bloom, with elongated gull-wing petals arranged 'hose-in-hose' form, *MIYAKO DORI* blooms mid to late season on a rather slow-growing bush. It was first recorded in Japan in 1891.

MIDNIGHT SERENADE

MME AMBROISE VERSCHAFFELT 1868
Named by Belgian hybridist Verschaffelt for his wife in 1868, this large formal to rose form double bloom has cupped petals and pink stripes against a white ground. It is fast-growing, and flowers mid season.

MONJISU (see MONJUSU)

MONJUSU (Crested Satin) c. 1868
(syn: *California Donckelarii Variegated*, *SHIBORI JESU*) The original Japanese name of this gaily variegated cherry-red cultivar is in dispute, for it seems to correspond with several old Japanese varieties. It was imported from Japan in 1895 under the name *MONJISU*, but is probably the older Japanese *MONJUSU* or *Crested Satin*, which is recorded back to 1868. The blooms are medium in size, rose form semi-double and appear in great profusion on a slow-growing bush.

MONSTRUOSO RUBRA (see GIGANTEA)

MONTIRONI (see ELISABETH)

MORAGUE (see GRAND SULTAN)

MOSHIO (Tide of Flowers) 1788
(syn: *Flame* [Aust], *Seaweed Salt*) The old Japanese camellia *MOSHIO* has been shown conclusively to be a sport of the even older variety *OKI NO NAMI* (which see) and is recorded back as far as 1788. A medium-sized semi-double of 'hose-in-hose' form, it blooms mid season on a dense upright bush. The colour, a pure intense red, has given it the popular name of *Flame* in Australia, but that name rightly belongs to a different camellia (see FLAME [US]). The Japanese name can be translated two ways — firstly the picturesque *Tide of Flowers*, but more literally *Seaweed Salt*. In the old days, Japanese salt was obtained by setting seaweed on fire — hence a bush in flame, a most apt description.

MRS ANNE MARIE HOVEY 1872
Apparently most variable in colour, this nineteenth century cultivar is for me a deep rose-pink, strongly blotched in white. It is a medium-sized camellia, classed as formally double, but the effect is spoiled by inward-turning edges of the massed centre petals. The plant blooms early to mid season.

MRS BERTHA A. HARMS 1949
FRAGRANT
One parent of several famous fragrant cultivars, *Mrs Bertha A. Harms* is in its own right a most attractive, large flower. Semi-double, with waxy pink-flushed petals of ivory-white, it blooms mid to late season. (Photo p. 193)

MRS CHARLES COBB c. 1900
Introduced in the early 1900s, *Mrs Charles Cobb* has retained popularity because of its remarkably free-flowering habit. It is particularly valuable in warmer climates where it begins blooming early in the season, continuing for several months. The plant is vigorous, spreading, and the large, loose semi-double to peony form blooms are a glowing dark red.

MRS CONRAD WALL JR
(see DUCHESSE DE CAZE)

MRS D. W. DAVIS 1954
Good looking at any time of year with its dense foliage cover, *Mrs D. W. Davis* achieves breathtaking loveliness in mid camellia season when its almost unbelievable blush-pink flowers unfurl from plump buds. These are frequently all of 17.5 cm (7 in) in diameter. Each bloom is semi-double with ten delicate pink shell-like petals in the form of a shallow dish. This is centred with a variable swirl of mixed petaloids and stamens. It was introduced in 1954, but its exact parentage is unknown.

MRS D. W. DAVIS DESCANSO 1970
Discovered in California's famous Descanso Gardens, this gorgeous camellia is a natural sport of the beautiful *Mrs D. W. Davis*. Identical both in growth habit and flower colour, it has in addition developed a full peony form in its bloom, and lightly fringed petals. It is not yet common, being introduced only in 1970.

MRS FRANCES SAUNDERS (see AMABILIS)

MRS H. B. SHEATHER
(see HARRIET BEECHER SHEATHER)

MRS H. BOYCE 1900
(syn: *Paolina Maggi Rosea*) A popular Australian cultivar, *Mrs H. Boyce* is a natural sport of the earlier variety *Paolina Maggi* which was introduced in Italy in 1855 and arrived in Australia within a few years. The pink sport was noticed in a Melbourne garden and propagated by Cremorne Nursery in 1900. Blooming late in the season, it is a formal double camellia, palest pink, the petal edges shading to white. The plant is bushy and suited to tub culture.

MRS H. BOYCE ROSEA (see KALLISTA)

MRS H. L. HINDBIGLER (see ŌNIJI)

MRS HOWARD ASPER (see HANA FŪKI)

MRS JIMMY DAVIS 1961
Introduced by American grower Wilson in 1961, the delightful *Mrs Jimmy Davis* bears large white blooms of anemone form. Both petals and petaloids are irregularly shaped and frequently notched, and are also enlivened by gay stripes and flecks of pink. The bush has an open upright habit, and flowers over a long period from quite early in the summer.

MRS SOL RUNYON (see ANEMONIFLORA)

MIKE WITMAN

MIYAKO DORI   都鳥

MONJUSU   紋繻

MOSHIO (FLAME [AUST]) 藻汐

MRS CHARLES COBB

MRS D. W. DAVIS

Japonicas

MRS SWAN 1945
Australian nurseryman Alexander Hunter gave this camellia to his daughter, after whom it was named in 1945. It has become popular with flower arrangers. A medium-sized bloom of rich salmon-pink, it has notched wavy petals and may vary from semi-double to loose peony form. The flowers open chiefly mid season, often with a display of petaloids among the flared golden stamens.

MRS T. R. McKENZIE (see VEDRINE)

MURASAKI TSUBAKI
(Purple Camellia) 1956
(syn: *SHIKON TSUBAKI*) One for the admirers of unusual camellia colouring, the remarkable *Purple Camellia* was registered by Eikichi Satomi of Tokyo. A medium-sized red bloom in formal double style, it has a distinct purple toning to the petal edges.

MYŌRENJI 1930
There is a series of charming medium-sized japonicas which have been given the name of the Buddhist Temple where they first grew — *MYŌRENJI*. Each is of cupped form, single, and with long petals surrounding a boss of prominent stamens. The growth is compact, the leaves glossy and prominently veined. *BENI MYŌRENJI* is scarlet; *SHIRO MYŌRENJI* white; and the illustrated *MYŌRENJI* an old-rose pink. The last-named was shipped to the United States in 1935 by the Chugai Nursery at Kobe.

NAGASAKI 1889
(syn: *Candida Elegantissima, Elegantissima, Lady Audrey Buller, LONJAN, Marguerita, MIKEN-JAKU, Nagasaki Special, Princess Nagasaki, S. Peter Nyce, TENNIN KWAN*) A Japanese variety, named for that unfortunate city which later became a target for the atomic bomb, *NAGASAKI* was first imported to England and introduced by G. Waller in 1889. It seems probable, however, that it is identical to the older cultivar *MIKENJAKU*, which is recorded back to 1859. *NAGASAKI* has from time to time achieved tremendous popularity under a wide range of popular, though invalid names. Its growth is slow, and the large semi-double blooms open in mid season. They are a deep red-pink, marbled in white. The outer petals are large, the inner petals smaller and lying flat.

NAGASAKI SPECIAL (see NAGASAKI)

NANCY BIRD c. 1940
Named for aviatrix Nancy Bird by veteran Australian nurseryman Walter Hazlewood, this splendid pink camellia is a sport of *Jean Lyne* (which see). The blooms are medium to large in size, semi-double and flushed a pale rose-pink except at petal edges, where there is a variable border of white. Occasional splashes of dramatic carmine-rose enliven an otherwise pastel flower

— symbolic perhaps of Nancy Bird's career. Occasional petaloids can be expected among the gold stamens of this lovely cultivar, which is profuse in its mid season blooming habit.

NAPA RED (see ELENA NOBILE)

NAPOLEON D'ITALIE 1849
A medium-sized formal double bloom of the type so popular in the mid nineteenth century, *Napoleon d'Italie* is typical in all respects but one — its coloration. The rose-red bloom is striped with a red so deep it might be black, and over all is a fine veining and mottling of this same dark shade. Not beautiful, but certainly memorable, *Napoleon d'Italie* blooms late in the season and was perfected in 1849 by Burnier and Grilli of Firenze.

NARARA 1960
Released by G. C. Linton of Somersby, New South Wales in 1960, *Narara* is a large white camellia of rose form double to peony form. Gold stamens, widely dispersed among fluted inner petals, give it a memorable appearance. *Narara* blooms late season.

NEIGE DORÉE (see SHIRAGIKU)

NELLIE BLY (see AKASHIGATA)

NEWINGTON 1960
Named for the famous New South Wales boys' academy in whose garden it first appeared, *Newington* is a large semi-double to anemone form flower of early blooming habit. Its colour is scarlet.

NIGHTLESS QUARTER (see FUYAJŌ)

NINA AVERY 1949
Released by Louisiana's Jungle Gardens in 1949, *Nina Avery* is a showy cultivar of medium size and semi-double to loose peony form. The outer petals have a 'sweet pea' coloration of white washed with rose-pink; the inner petals are wrinkled and punctuate a large boss of gold-tipped white stamens. Blooming period is mid season.

NISHIKI MINO (see EZO NISHIKI)

NOBILISSIMA 1834
(syn: *FUJI YAMA*) Long forgotten in most parts of the world, the Belgian variety *Nobilissima* was certainly among the noblest blooms of its day. Full peony form, medium in size and white with yellow shadings, it was of a type we would know and appreciate today. *Nobilissima* was introduced at Ghent in 1834. It blooms early to mid season.

NUCCIO'S GEM 1970
One of the most perfect of formal double camellias, *Nuccio's Gem* was introduced by the Nuccio Nursery of Altadena, California in 1970,

MRS SWAN

MYŌRENJI 妙蓮吉

and its popularity is showing no signs of abating. The plant has dense glossy foliage; the flower, medium to very large in size, is purest white and of a superb formal shape. It develops an interesting spiral pattern in the petals. *Nuccio's Gem* blooms profusely in mid season and has received world acclaim.

NUCCIO'S JEWEL 1977
Another brilliant introduction by California's Nuccio Nursery, this time in 1977, *Nuccio's Jewel* bears a medium-sized bloom of loose peony form. It is soft white, shaded and washed irregularly in orchid-pink towards the edges. Slow in growth, bushy in habit, it blooms from mid to late season. An ideal tub specimen.

NUCCIO'S PEARL 1977
A vintage year from the Nuccio Nursery for camellia lovers, 1977 also saw the introduction of *Nuccio's Pearl*, an elegant formal double bloom of medium size, flowering quite late in the season. They describe the colour as blush-white (an unbelievably pale pink) with both centre and outside petals pointed and toned a deeper orchid shade. The blooms are medium in size, developing on a bush that is compact in growth.

NUKI FUDE (Worn Paintbrush) 1868
A popular Japanese cultivar since 1868, *NUKI FUDE* was imported to the USA in 1930. It is a medium-sized single camellia, blooming mid season. It is either pink with radial crimson lines or vice versa, dependent on the individual plant. It also has finely frilled petal edges that have suggested the picturesque Japanese name.

ODORATISSIMA 1866   FRAGRANT
(syn: *La Graciola*) First listed by the Australian grower Guilfoyle in 1866, *Odoratissima* is a large rose-pink cultivar of semi-double to peony form. Charming enough, it has proved especially useful to hybridists, for it has a distinct perfume. Blooms mid to late season.

OKI NO NAMI 1695
(syn: *Gathering Storm, Waves in the Offing*) The late Professor E. G. Waterhouse traced this elegant Japanese cultivar back as far as 1695. It is a semi-double bloom approximately 7.5 cm (3 in) wide (medium size) and of most brilliant colouring. The ground tint is white with an overlaid reticulation of warm pink veins and lines, broken by irregular stripes and slashes of brilliant orange-red. It blooms mid to late season. A well-shaped bush in full flower is quite stunning.

OMEGA 1965
A large, loose semi-double camellia for mid season display, *Omega* was introduced in 1965. It is coloured blush-white, shading to coral at the petal edges.

ŌNIJI (Big Rainbow) 1932
(syn: *Empress Variegated, Lady Clare Variegated,*

NAGASAKI 長崎

NANCY BIRD

NUCCIO'S GEM

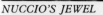

NUCCIO'S JEWEL

NUCCIO'S PEARL

OKI NO NAMI   沖の浪

ŌNIJI   大虹   OPTIMA ROSEA

Japonicas

Mrs H. L. Hindbigler, Rainbow, TAIYŌ NISHIKI) A variegated sport of the older Japanese cultivar AKASHIGATA, ŌNIJI is particularly valuable in cooler climates as it has an exceptional cold resistance. It is a large semi-double flower of deep pink, marbled white, and appears on a plant of vigorous spreading growth. Though undoubtedly a very old cultivar in Japan, it does not seem to have been recorded before 1932, and was sent to the United States in 1935 by the Chugai Nursery. It blooms early to mid season.

OPELOUSAS PEONY (see DUCHESSE DE CAZE)

OPTIMA ROSEA 1850
Still a glorious camellia when well grown, *Optima Rosea* has been around since 1850, when it was introduced in England. A large bloom varying from rose form to formal double, it has a colouring best established from our picture, but described as bright, deep pink streaked and bordered with crimson. The petals are distinctly cup-shaped. *Optima Rosea* blooms mid season.

ORANDA KŌ (Little Holland) 1733
(syn: *Holland Red*) If camellias could only speak, what a tale this bloom might have to tell! It can be traced with certainty in Japan's camellia literature back to 1733, but is almost certainly much older. The largest known specimen (recently identified by a Japanese expert) is in a private garden in Spain, just by the Portuguese border. This has a trunk more than 60 cm (24 in) in diameter and is believed to be at least several hundred years old. The question is how it got there, but the answer is lost in history, though it must have had something to do with the foreign trade concession at Deshima, an island off Nagasaki. There the Dutch had exclusive trade rights with Japan from 1640 to 1853 — but the Portuguese had the same privileges earlier, back to 1570. The Japanese name, interestingly enough, means *Little Holland*. Did the original plant grow in the Dutch concession at Deshima? Was it earlier taken to Spain by Portuguese traders, before 1570? *ORANDA KŌ* is a formal double bloom of deep pink, with a white central stripe on each petal. It blooms mid season. There is no report of it in any other European garden. (See also plate p. 34)

ORCHID PINK 1939   FRAGRANT
A camellia with a long history, *Orchid Pink* was discovered as a sport of the cultivar *Colonial Lady* in 1939. The *Colonial Lady* herself sported on *HIKARU GENJI*, which was brought from Japan in 1875. The blooms are medium-sized and semi-double, the colouring overall a pale pink with central petals bordered in a deeper shade and sometimes flecked with white. *Orchid Pink* blooms mid season.

OTAHUHU BEAUTY 1904
(syn: *Aspasia Rosea, Duke of York, Paeoniaeflora Rosea*) Here is yet another sport of the lovely

Aspasia — Otahuhu Beauty. Again, this is identical in form and growth to *Aspasia, Camden Park, Jean Clere, Lady Loch* and *Margaret Davis;* but this variation is self-coloured a deep rose-pink without any variegation. It was first named *Otahuhu Beauty* by its discoverer, New Zealand nurseryman Lippiat, in 1904.

OTOME SHIBORI (Striped Virgin) 1891
(syn: *Baronne de Bleichroeder, Bleichroeder, Otome Variegated*) Variegated sport of a popular Japanese variety which we can trace back to 1828, *OTOME SHIBORI* has had a controversial history of nomenclature. It was imported to the United States by California's Huntington Gardens in 1917 under its correct name, but was then incorrectly redistributed as *Baronne de Bleichroeder,* a Belgian cultivar similar in appearance. While it is still grown under the Belgian name, the Japanese has been proved to have priority. It is a medium-sized rose form double bloom of soft pink, finely striated with pale crimson. A charming cultivar, blooming mid season.

OTOME VARIEGATED (see OTOME SHIBORI)

PAEONIAEFLORA (see ASPASIA)

PAEONIAEFLORA ROSEA
(see OTAHUHU BEAUTY)

PALMERSTON (see CHŌ CHŌ SAN)

PAOLINA MAGGI 1855
In many old gardens, including my own, there is a white formal camellia that blooms so late in the season many buds are severely damaged by drying hot winds. But when an earlier flower does appear on some sheltered branch, it may open to a large, formal white blossom of great beauty. This is *Paolina Maggi,* an 1855 Italian cultivar of impeccable ancestry. The tree is rugged, with pale grey bark and large, light green leaves. The petals blush towards yellow at the centre, and *one* of them, somewhere in the flower, will always carry a tell-tale stripe of deep pink or red. (See also photo p. 52)

PAOLINA MAGGI ROSEA
(see MRS. H. BOYCE)

PARTY GIRL 1962   FRAGRANT
This large, semi-double pink bloom from Australia's H. K. Dettmann is distinctly perfumed, and will doubtless become popular with collectors of fragrant camellias. It is a late bloomer.

PASHA OF PERSIA (see GRAND SULTAN)

PAT NIXON 1969
A delightful sport of the earlier *Richard Nixon* (which see), this large anemone form bloom was propagated by Kramer's Nursery of California in 1969. Blush-pink, veined with deeper pink, it flowers right through the season, and was named for the wife of the former US President.

ORANDA KŌ   オランタ紅   OTAHUHU BEAUTY

OTOME SHIBORI   乙女絞

PAOLINA MAGGI   PETER PAN

PHILIPPA IFOULD

PINK DIDDY MEALING

PINK FROST

PINK GOLD

Japonicas

PAUL JONES SUPREME 1968

A large flat semi-double camellia of blush-white, striped carmine, the spectacular *Paul Jones Supreme* was registered in 1968 by E. G. Waterhouse. He named it for the Australian artist whose painting of *Camellia chrysantha* appears on page 10 of this book.

PAULETTE GODDARD 1945

A wonderful dark red camellia named for the durable Hollywood star, *Paulette Goddard* was perfected in 1945. Mid to late season in bloom, it is a medium-sized cultivar of most variable appearance, as befits the namesake of a famous actress. It can be semi-double, anemone form, or loose peony form. The growth is vigorous and there is a stunning variegated sport.

PAYNE'S RED (see VEDRINE)

PEACH BLOSSOM 1920

(syn: *Fleur de Pêche, Magnoliiflora* [UK]) The charming medium-sized japonica known as *Peach Blossom* was listed by England's Caledonia Nursery in 1920, but may well have been around for almost a century longer. It is semi-double, with delicate pink petals set well apart and flushed deeper at the flower's heart. Bloom on this compact bush peaks mid season.

PEACOCK CAMELLIA
(see HAKUHAN KUJAKU)

PEARL OF CHINA (see SEMI-DOUBLE BLUSH)

PEONY (see YUKI BOTAN)

PETER PAN 1950

Not, as one might expect, a small camellia, *Peter Pan* is a medium-sized bloom of variable form — semi-double, anemone or full peony. The colouring, too, shades from a creamy-pink through blush to cerise-pink at the petal edges, and central petaloids are a combination of all three. Flowering mid to late season, it was developed in 1950 in Virginia.

PHILIPPA IFOULD 1968

An Australian seedling propagated in 1968, *Philippa Ifould* is a charming formal double bloom in softest peach-pink. A florist's dream, the petals sparkle in the sun as tiny white variegations catch the light. *Philippa Ifould* is medium-sized, and blooms mid to late season. The delicate flowers need morning protection from winter sunlight.

PIE IX 1850

Not the same cultivar as *Pope Pius IX* (a synonym for *Prince Eugene Napoleon*), *Pie IX* is a splendid Italian camellia of earlier times, first listed by the Belgian grower Verschaffelt in 1850. A medium-sized formal double bloom, it has cherry-red outer petals, pink-striped white middle petals, and pink inner petals. Blooms mid season.

PINK JADE

PINK PAGODA

PINK PEARL

PINK POPPY

PIRATE'S GOLD

POMPONIA

PINE CONE (see MATSUKASA)

PINK BALL 1935
A medium-sized soft pink cultivar of full peony form, *Pink Ball* was imported to the US from Japan by Toichi Domoto in 1935. It is a delicate bloom, peaking at mid season.

PINK DIDDY MEALING 1950
A pink sport of the 1948 cultivar *Diddy Mealing*, this medium-sized bloom varies from rose form double to peony form. A delightful pale pink, it blooms mid season on a bush of slightly pendulous growth.

PINK FROST 1970
A sport of the cultivar *Pink Pagoda*, *Pink Frost* is a medium to large formal double camellia introduced in 1970. Its colour is silvery-pink with a faint white border to each petal.

PINK GOLD 1960
A large semi-double camellia with occasional petaloids, *Pink Gold* was announced in 1960. The petals shade from pale orchid-pink to a deeper tone at the margins; the widely flared yellow stamens are bright with golden anthers. Early to mid season flowering habit.

PINK HERME (see BENI BOTAN)

PINK JADE 1965
A charming development by California's Harold R. Paige, *Pink Jade* first bloomed in 1965, though it was not registered until 1980. A seedling from japonica *Mrs Bertha A. Harms*, it is a blush-pink semi-double bloom of 'hose-in-hose' form, flowering mid to late season. It has not yet been widely propagated, which seems a shame. The large, crisp, jade-like blooms are long-lasting and described by an American grower as resembling 'a larger and more beautiful *Magnoliiflora*' (see HAGOROMO).

PINK JORDAN'S PRIDE (see BENI BOTAN)

PINK KAGURA (see BENI DAIKAGURA)

PINK LACE (see HISHI KARAITO)

PINK LADY (see LADY LOCH)

PINK PAGODA 1963
A medium to large formal double camellia of interestingly waved form, *Pink Pagoda* was registered in 1963. It is rose-pink in colour, and blooms mid season.

PINK PARADE 1972
A 1972 release from California's Monrovia Nursery, *Pink Parade* is a startling raspberry-pink semi-double bloom of large size. Petals are fluted and upright, playing hide and seek with the gold-tipped stamens. A splendid choice for mid season.

PREMIER VARIEGATED

PRINCE EUGENE NAPOLEON

PRINCE FREDERICK WILLIAM

PROFESSOR CHARLES S. SARGENT

PROFESSOR GIOVANNI SANTORELLI

PUKEKURA

Japonicas

PINK PEARL 1895
(syn: *Badgen's Beauty, Burgdorf Beauty*) A sport of the older variety *Pink Perfection* (see USU OTOME), *Pink Pearl* came to Australia from Japan in 1895. Small in size, its pale pink outer petals shade to a high pointed ivory centre. It blooms right through the camellia season.

PINK PERFECTION (see USU OTOME)

PINK POPPY 1941
A small single camellia, occasionally varying to semi-double, *Pink Poppy* came from the Gerbing Camellia Nursery of Florida in 1941. The simple blooms (very much like those of a Shirley poppy) are soft pink, with an enormous rosette of gold stamens. It blooms mid season.

PINK SILK SATIN (see REGINA DEI GIGANTI)

PIRATE'S GOLD 1969
A large red semi-double camellia, occasionally varying to peony form, *Pirate's Gold* can easily be mistaken for a reticulata hybrid with its waved upstanding petals. But it is, in fact, pure japonica, registered in 1969. Flowers peak mid to late season on a rather spreading bush.

POLAR BEAR 1957
This large white seedling from *Great Eastern* was raised by Professor Waterhouse in Australia and released in 1957. It is a large chalky-white semi-double bloom of 'hose-in-hose' style. The rounded outer petals enclose an open centre of small petaloids mixed with short stamens. It is a plant of husky growth and dark handsome foliage, blooming mid season.

POMPONIA 1822
Imported from China to England, where it was renamed in 1822, *Pomponia* is typical of many other Chinese cultivars. It is a large full peony form flower, with high ruffled petals. These are white, occasionally marked in deep pink, and swirl among decorative golden stamens.

POPE JOHN XXIII 1967
A medium to large formal double, *Pope John XXIII* has heavy, white, velvet-textured petals. It blooms mid season and was registered in 1967 in California.

POPE PIUS IX
(see PRINCE EUGENE NAPOLEON)

POWELL'S PINK (see BENI BOTAN)

PREMIER VARIEGATED 1973
A variegated sport of the earlier American cultivar *Premier*, this is a spectacular though rather untidy camellia of large peony form. The colour is bright rose-red, blotched white, and it was registered in 1973. The petals are irregular in size and shape.

PRIDE OF DESCANSO (see YUKI BOTAN)

PRIDE OF HOUSTON (see ROSS)

PRIDE OF PORTLAND
(see LADY DE SAUMAREZ)

PRIDE OF ROSEBUD FARM
(see LADY DE SAUMAREZ)

PRIDE OF THE EMPEROR'S GARDEN
(see FRANCINE)

PRINCE ALBERT (see ALBERTII)

PRINCE EUGENE NAPOLEON 1859
(syn: *Imbricata, Ladiner's Red, Pope Pius IX, Rubra Plena*) One of the most widely grown of formal double camellias, the brilliant cherry-red *Prince Eugene Napoleon* was introduced by Belgian horticulturist de Costa in 1859, and named to celebrate the birth of the future Prince Imperial. It is a medium-sized bloom with small overlapping petals that become progressively smaller towards the centre, where they are sometimes streaked with a lighter shade. It blooms mid season and is known by many names, a proof of continued popularity.

PRINCE FREDERICK WILLIAM 1872
In spite of its name, this popular formal double camellia is Australian, raised by Silas Sheather at his Parramatta nursery. He named it for the Prussian prince who had married Queen Victoria's eldest daughter and namesake, and it was first listed in 1872. *Prince Frederick William* is overall rose-pink, and in their early stages the blooms have a rosebud form. Later, however, the overlapping petals reflex and the flower opens out to a flat, perfect formal shape. A mid season bloom.

PRINCE OF ORANGE 1950
(syn: *Crusader*) As the name might suggest, *Prince of Orange* is a large camellia of deep orange-red. It varies from loose peony form to anemone in style, and blooms mid season on a rather heavy-set bush.

PRINCESS BACIOCCHI 1930
A tricky problem — both in nomenclature and spelling. There are two camellias validly named *Princess Baciocchi* in one spelling or another. (1) The earlier (1850) is a medium-sized Italian variety — crimson, with white radial bars. It is spelled *Princesse* (French) or *Principessa* (Italian) *Bacchiocci* (two 'Cs' in each case). (2) The one grown today is *Princess* (without an 'E') *Baciocchi* (with one 'C' initially). It is a medium-sized deep carmine bloom of semi-double to peony form that came from the Armstrong Nurseries of California in 1930. Both are splendid camellias, but if you live in Europe you probably grow No. 1, in America No. 2. In Australia, you might grow either.

PRINCESS LAVENDER 1950
Though it is certainly one of those in between

112

QUERCIFOLIA

colours, I wouldn't describe this camellia as lavender. Lavender-pink only with a stretch of imagination, it is a decorative semi-double of large size with a spiral petal arrangement, and blooms mid season. It was registered by a Florida grower in 1950.

PRINCESS LUCILLE
(see BEAUTY OF HOLLAND)

PRINCESS NAGASAKI (see NAGASAKI)

PROFESSOR CHARLES S. SARGENT 1925
One of the more majestic of peony form cultivars, *Professor Charles S. Sargent* was a 1925 release from South Carolina's Magnolia Gardens. It is a glowing dark red with a balled centre somewhere between peony and anemone form. It blooms mid season on a strong-growing plant.

PROFESSOR GIOVANNI SANTORELLI 1860
An older bloom of full, lush appearance, *Professor Giovanni Santorelli* is a product of 1860, the height of Italy's camellia rage. It is a medium-sized rose form double bloom, coloured usually in overall deep pink with stripes and blotches of white and several intermediate shades. Il Professore blooms mid to late in the camellia season.

PUKEKURA 1952
This beautiful, though somewhat variable, creamy-white camellia takes its name from the New Zealand park in which it originated in 1952 — *Pukekura* — 'the chief's hill'. It is a large semi-double to peony form flower with rounded outer petals and an informal centre compounded of folded petals and golden anthers. It blooms mid season.

PURITY (see SHIRAGIKU)

PURPLE CAMELLIA (see MURASAKI TSUBAKI)

PURPLE DAWN (see MATHOTIANA [US])

PURPLE EMPEROR (see MATHOTIANA [US])

PURPLE PRINCE (see MATHOTIANA [US])

PURPLIANA (see COLLETTII)

PURPUREA (see FUYAJŌ)

QUAKER LADY 1959
A salmon-pink sport of the 1957 *Carter's Carnival*, *Quaker Lady* is a large, semi-double white bloom, striped pink and rose. Growth is slow but upright, and flowers appear mid to late season. *Quaker Lady* was a 1959 introduction by Carter's Camellia Gardens of California.

QUEEN JULIANA (see SOUTHERN CHARM)

QUEEN VICTORIA c. 1840

R. L. WHEELER

RED ENSIGN

Japonicas

RED GIANT

RED RED ROSE

RICHARD NIXON

ROMANY

Wherever there's a Prince Albert, there just has to be a camellia named for Queen Victoria, a camellia enthusiast herself. Here it is — a formal double of course, in the style favoured by the Victorians — this time crimson, spotted white, almost like an heraldic depiction of ermine. *Queen Victoria* was imported from Europe to America in the 1840s by South Carolina's Magnolia Gardens, and blooms mid to late season.

QUERCIFOLIA
(syn: *KINGYO TSUBAKI* [Aust]) The camellia called *Quercifolia* is often said to be synonymous with the Japanese *KINGYO TSUBAKI*, but they seem quite different to me, so I make no apologies for including both. *Quercifolia* in Australia blooms later (mid season). It is semi-double as opposed to the single form of *KINGYO TSUBAKI*, and the blooms are a much deeper shade of pink (though still not crimson, as *Quercifolia* is described in the Southern California Camellia Society's *Camellia Nomenclature*). The foliage on specimens I have seen also has a much less developed 'fishtail' effect than on the real *KINGYO TSUBAKI*.

R. L. WHEELER 1949
One of the most beautiful and popular cultivars of modern times, *R. L. Wheeler* is a product of Wheeler's Central Georgia Nurseries, USA. The enormous blooms of rich rose-pink are semi-double to anemone form with a frequent appearance of white-variegated petaloids among the gold stamens. *R. L. Wheeler* has bushy growth, large attractive foliage and a plant in full bloom has a quite arresting splendour. Try it in a container.

R. L. WHEELER VARIEGATED
A sport of the previous variety in which the petals are fully variegated in rose-pink and white. Otherwise, similar in all respects.

RADIANT GLOW (see BENI BOTAN)

RAINBOW (see ŌNIJI)

RAINSFORD CANTELOU
(see REGINA DEI GIGANTI)

REBEL YELL 1961
Though I may earn the undying enmity of camellia growers in the old Confederacy, I must say that *Rebel Yell* seems a singularly inappropriate name for such a beautiful, tranquil flower. And beautiful it is — a large, semi-double to peony form bloom with swirling petals. The ground colour is white, but spotted, striped and rippled in red. It was developed by Wheeler's Central Georgia Nurseries and released in 1961.

RED ELEGANS (see ELEGANS)

RED ENSIGN 1955
A 1955 release from Australian G. C. Linton, *Red Ensign* is surely a camellia to put out the flags for. Large, single to semi-double, it is coloured a vivid crimson with drooping pale creamy-yellow stamens. Inner petals have a crushed effect, and there are sometimes petaloids. Blooms mid season.

RED GIANT 1954
(syn: *Apache*) Growers can never get enough spectacular red camellia cultivars, so the strong-growing *Red Giant* achieved instant popularity when it was announced in 1954. Developed in Georgia, it is a large, loose peony form bloom with frequent petaloids. It is very like a reticulata, and blooms mid season.

RED HERME (see BENI BOTAN)

RED JORDAN'S PRIDE (see BENI BOTAN)

RED PRESSII (see LA PACE RUBRA)

RED, RED ROSE 1969
Something of an improvement on the old *Prince Eugene Napoleon* of a century earlier, *Red, Red Rose* has taken many prizes since its 1969 release. It is a brilliant rose-red formal double bloom with a high rose-like centre. Varying from medium to large in size, it blooms mid season, and is a product of the McCaskill Gardens, Pasadena.

RED WARATAH (see MARIANA)

RED WINE 1958
Christened as his namesake by Dr M. B. Wine of Georgia, 1958's *Red Wine* is a noteworthy addition to the ranks of deep red camellias. It is a medium-sized semi-double bloom with two rows of wide petals surrounding several folded petaloids that almost obscure the stamens. It blooms mid season.

REFINEMENT (see SHIRAGIKU)

REG RAGLAND 1954
Red, but variably marked in white, the popular *Reg Ragland* has been grown world-wide since its 1954 introduction in California. It is a large to very large semi-double bloom with a mass of yellow stamens guarded by small upright petals. Blooming may be any time in the season.

REGINA DEI GIGANTI 1855
(syn: *Gloriosa, Hall Townes, Pink Silk Satin, Rainsford Cantelou, Rosalie, W. H. Hastie*) A medium to large camellia of bright pink, *Regina Dei Giganti* (Queen of the Giants) is hardly what we would call a giant camellia today. It was introduced in 1855 by Charles Luzzati of Italy, and its range of synonyms is proof (if needed) that it has rarely been out of popularity since. A semi-double bloom with fluted petals, it flowers mid to late in the season.

RENJO NO TAMA (see SHIRAGIKU)

ROSA MUNDI

RESTIVE LION (see ARAJISHI)

RHODELLIA KING (see GOSHO GARUMA)

RICHARD NIXON 1954
The name of a controversial President can be remembered one way without controversy — *Richard Nixon*, the camellia. Whether or not he loved flowers I cannot say, but camellia fans certainly love the camellia named for him. It is a large anemone form bloom, with upright crinkled petals, registered in 1954. Blooming throughout the season, it is white, flushed and striped in several shades of pink and carmine.

RISING SUN ON RIVER YODO
(see YODO NO ASAHI)

ROBERT E. LEE c. 1900
Southern patriots are rightly fond of a magnificent dark red camellia produced in the early 1900s. Its name is *Robert E. Lee*, and you'll find it growing throughout the old Confederacy. A product of South Carolina's Magnolia Gardens, it is a medium-sized semi-double bloom, with loose irregular petals. The velvety red of these is veined even darker red, and the stamens are similarly toned. It blooms mid season.

ROBIN [Aust] 1952
As there are several camellias named *Robin*, arguments still rage as to which has priority of name. At this time, the honour would seem to belong to the lovely 1952 registration of Australia's Professor Waterhouse. It is a medium-sized bloom, single and cherry-red, flowering mid season.

ROI LEOPOLD (see ROMANY)

ROMA RISORTA 1866
A medium-sized camellia of rose form double style, *Roma Risorta* was first listed by Italian grower Delgrande in 1866. Its petals are streaked and blotched deep rose-pink against a paler pink background. Flowering is mid season.

ROMANY 1937
(syn: *Belgium Red, Roi Leopold*) Bright red with occasional splashes of white, the 1937 registration *Romany* may be identical to the older Italian cultivar *Roi Leopold*, listed by Franchetti in 1855. Medium in size, formal double, and blooming mid season, they share the same characteristics.

ROSA MUNDI 1832
Named for a rose that has been popular since medieval times, this medium-sized formal double camellia was developed by the English hybridist Press. It is pink, streaked with white and a deeper cerise shade.

ROSALIE (see REGINA DEI GIGANTI)

ROSE HILL RUBRA (see ST ANDRÉ)

ROSE OF CHINA (see SEMI-DOUBLE BLUSH)

ROSE OF DAWN (see HAGOROMO)

ROSEA CHANDLERI (see ELEGANS)

ROSEA SUPERBA 1890
(syn: *Ada Wilson, Laura Dasher*) A rose-pink sport of the older variety *Mathotiana* (1840s) *Rosea Superba* was introduced to America in the 1890s. The blooms, like those of *Mathotiana*, are large to very large, rose form double in style, and appear early to mid season

ROSEA SUPERBA VARIEGATED
(syn: *Margaret Sandusky*) A second generation sport, *Rosea Superba Variegated* has again the characteristics of *Mathotiana*, but the colouring is deep rose-pink, variegated in white.

ROSS 1955
(syn: *Pride of Houston*) Discovered in an Alabama cemetery in 1945, *Ross* is a fine semi-double camellia of medium size. The flowers open late, and are white-spotted against a background of salmon-pink.

ROSY DAWN (see BENI BOTAN)

ROYAL CARRIAGE (see GOSHO GURUMA)

RUBAIYAT 1969
With a bush of this variety beside you, the wilderness would indeed be 'paradise enow'! Introduced in 1969 by the Julington Nursery of Jacksonville, Florida, *Rubaiyat* is a large formal double camellia, with waxy rounded petals. These are a deep wine-red, with veining that is almost blue. Flower time is mid to late season.

RUBESCENS MAJOR 1895
An 1895 creation of French grower Guichard, *Rubescens Major* is a large formal double flower of rose-red, veined crimson. It blooms mid season.

RUBY GLOW (see VEDRINE)

S. PETER NYCE (see NAGASAKI)

SAKURABA TSUBAKI
(Cherry-Leaf Camellia) 1867
(syn: *Cherry Blossom*) Known and loved in Japan for over a century, the charming *SAKURABA TSUBAKI* or *Cherry-Leaf Camellia* is admired as much for its foliage as for its flowers. Blooms are pale pink, medium in size, with fringed petals and irregular marking of pale red and light green. The delicately fringed leaves resemble those of a flowering cherry. It blooms mid season and has been recorded in Japanese camellia literature as far back as 1867.

SARA C. HASTIE (see DEBUTANTE)

SAWADA'S DREAM 1958
Possibly the most perfect of all formal double camellias, *Sawada's Dream* shows strong, pointed

ROSEA SUPERBA

SAKURABA TSUBAKI　　桜葉椿

SAWADA'S DREAM

SENATOR DUNCAN U. FLETCHER

SEPPOZAN 雪宝山

SHIRAGIKU 白菊

SHIRO CHAN

SHOW TIME

Japonicas

petals arranged in a perfect spiral form. Purest white at the centre, these graduate almost invisibly to palest flesh-pink in the outer one-third of each flower. The blooms are medium to large in size, and seem at their best around mid season, though they commence opening earlier. *Sawada's Dream* was a 1958 triumph for the Overlook Nurseries of Crichton, Alabama.

SCATTERING CAMELLIA
(see CHIRI TSUBAKI)

SCENTED TREASURE 1950   FRAGRANT
Exploring an old garden in the winter of 1980, I was first attracted to this marvellous camellia through its perfume, of which I had been aware from a distance of many yards. It is a handsome peony form bloom of rose-red, and the perfume, too, I should describe as mighty like a rose. Medium in size, the blooms hang on pendant branchlets from a bush of compact growth. It was registered by Harvey Short of California, and the parentage is unlisted. (Photo p. 192)

SCENTSATION 1967   FRAGRANT
A lightly scented japonica from California's Nuccio Nurseries, *Scentsation* is a medium to large peony form bloom of silvery-pink, bloomin mid season. The plant is popular with growers breeding for fragrance. (Photo p. 190)

SCHEHERAZADE 1957
As gorgeously coloured as any episode from the *Thousand and One Nights*, this medium to large bloom is tinted a brilliant coral-rose, spangled overall with a golden haze. Semi-double to anemone form, it was raised by Californian McCaskill Gardens, and blooms mid season.

SEAGULL (see MIYAKO DORI)

SEAWEED SALT (see MOSHIO)

SEMI-DOUBLE BLUSH 1937
(syn: *Celtic Rosea, Pearl of China, Rose of China*) Not the most spectacular of camellias, *Semi-Double Blush* has enjoyed a certain popularity since its 1937 importation from Japan by Alabama's Kiyono Nurseries. It is a simple semi-double camellia of blush-pink, medium in size and almost 'hose-in-hose' form. A slow-grower, it blooms mid season.

SEMI-DOUBLE ROSEA
(see SERGEANT BARRIOS)

SENATOR DUNCAN U. FLETCHER 1943
A reliable garden camellia of semi-double to peony form, *Senator Duncan U. Fletcher* is somewhat variable in colour, from rose-red to a darker shade. The slow-growing plant blooms mid to late season, and the blooms are of medium size. It was originated in Florida in 1943.

SEPPOZAN 1964
A small semi-double camellia of brilliant rose-

SIERRA SPRING

SILVER CHALICE

red, *SEPPOZAN* was imported from Japan in 1964 by California's Nuccio Nurseries. It is profuse in its flower production, early to mid season in bloom, and has been classed as a member of the japonica sub-species *C. rusticana*. Growth is slow and bushy.

SERGEANT BARRIOS 1940
(syn: *Semi-Double Rosea*) A brilliant rose-red, with occasional petaloid markings in white, *Sergeant Barrios* was a most successful 1940 release by the Semmes Nursery of Alabama. The large blooms are semi-double with waved petals. Blooming period is mid season.

SHAH OF PERSIA (see GRAND SULTAN)

SHANGRI LA (see BENI DAIKAGURA)

SHEPHERD'S RED (see SPECIOSISSIMA)

SHERBROOKE (see KUMASAKA)

SHIBORI JESU (see MONJUSU)

SHIKON TSUBAKI (see MURASAKI TSUBAKI)

SHIN AKEBONO (see AKEBONO)

SHIRAGIKU (White Chrysanthemum) 1695
(syn: *Harriet I. Laub, Neige Doreé, Purity, Refinement, RENJO NO TAMA*) A very old formal double variety which can be traced back to 1695 in Japan under the name *SHIRAGIKU*, this has elegantly fluted white petals, cream at the base. As each bloom opens, one is irresistibly reminded of a gardenia — but alas, without the perfume. *SHIRAGIKU* is medium-sized, late-blooming and appears on a bush of strong, upright growth. Although its Japanese name has priority, I must say I find the French synonym more evocative — *Neige Doreé* means 'gilded snow'.

SHIRATAMA (White Bead) 1907
(syn: *Egret, HATSUARASHI*) A white camellia named *SHIRATAMA* was reported growing in Japan by Englebert Kaempfer in 1712. Unfortunately, he left no description, so we cannot tell if it was this same perfect white flower first described in 1907 by a Japanese grower. It is a medium-sized flower of pure white, rose form to formal double and blooms mid season.

SHIRO CHAN 1953
A snow-white sport of *C. M. Wilson*, and thus second generation sport of the old *Elegans*, *SHIRO CHAN* has the perfect anemone form of all its relations. It is a large to very large camellia, registered by Toichi Domoto of the USA in 1953. The white colouring is relieved by a basal flush of pink as the blooms open.

SHIRO MYŌRENJI (see MYŌRENJI)

SHOW TIME 1979
A 1979 release by Nuccio's Nurseries of

SILVER TRIUMPH

SILVER WAVES

SODE KAKUSHI

神隠

SPECIOSISSIMA

SPENCER'S PINK

SPRING SONNET

SPUTNIK

ST ANDRE

Japonicas

Altadena, California, *Show Time* is a very elegant, very large camellia of clear light pink. Semi-double, its petals and petaloids are fluted. Blooms open early to mid season on a strong upright plant. This is one show that can open in my garden anytime.

SHUCHŪKA (see KISHŪ TSUKASA)

SIERRA SPRING 1949
(syn: *Madame Hahn Variegated*)   A lightly variegated sport of the 1915 cultivar *Madame Hahn*, *Sierra Spring* was registered only in 1948 by C. Marshall of Sierra Madre, California. Soft bright pink, blushed with white, it is a medium-sized semi-double bloom like its parent, with a similar profuse flowering habit.

SILVER CHALICE 1963
A 1963 success for Nuccio's Nursery of California, the gorgeous *Silver Chalice* ranks in the forefront of white camellias. It is a large fully peony form flower for mid season display, with strong upright petals deeply swirled and fluted, revealing just a tantalising glimpse of gold. The flowers are a brilliant silver-white.

SILVER TRIUMPH 1973
Nuccio Nurseries' 1973 entry in the whiter-than-white camellia stakes, *Silver Triumph* blooms early to mid season. It is an outstanding semi-double camellia, large to very large in size, and with prominent gold stamens. The petals are notched and somewhat crumpled after opening.

SILVER WAVES 1969
An earlier white entry from California's Nuccio Nurseries, *Silver Waves* was released in 1969. Again, it is a large to very large camellia, semi-double, with white wavy petaloids among a flared centre of creamy stamens. For such a large flower, *Silver Waves* blooms profusely on a vigorous bushy plant.

SLEEVE HIDER (see SODE KAKUSHI)

SNOW CHAN 1957
(syn: *White Elegans*)   *Snow Chan* is yet another sport of the *Elegans* series in the third generation, as it sprang from a bush of the earlier *Shiro Chan*. This time it really is pure white, and the blooms large to very large. Nuccio registered it in 1957.

SNOW PEONY (see YUKI BOTAN)

SNOWMAN 1964
A large white semi-double camellia registered in 1964, *Snowman* has a rather unusual combination of notched, incurved outer petals and twisted inner petals. Tall spreading growth has made it a popular choice for tub planting. Bloom period is mid season.

SODE GAKUSHI (see SODE KAKUSHI)

SUNSET GLORY

SWAN LAKE

TABBS

TAFFETA TUTU

THE CZAR

SODE KAKUSHI 1879
(syn: *Gauntlettii, Grandiflora Alba, Happiness, Lotus, Sleeve Hider, SODE GAKUSHI, Yokohama*) This great white camellia of waterlily form was imported to the United States from Japan in 1909, and can be traced back to 1879. It is a very large pure white flower, peaking mid season, but often opens only to a cupped form.

SOLARIS (see C. M. HOVEY)

SOLID ROCK (see IWANE)

SŌTAN (see KAMO HON AMI)

SOUTHERN CHARM 1955
(syn: *Queen Juliana*) *Southern Charm* seems a rather saccharine name for the dramatic appearance of this wonderful white camellia, but alas, it has priority over the later attempt of *Queen Juliana*. It is a large semi-double bloom, peaking mid season, and was originated in Alabama.

SOUVENIR D'HENRI GUICHARD
(see HIKARU GENJI)

SPECIOSISSIMA 1862
(syn: *Shepherd's Red*) Developed by the well-known Shepherd's Nursery of Rooty Hill, New South Wales and first distributed in 1862, *Speciosissima* greatly resembles another fine Australian flower, the native waratah, *Telopea speciosissima*, and was doubtless named to take advantage of the resemblance. It is a large anemone form camellia of pure carmine-red, the flat outer petals arranged about a waratah-like central cushion of petaloids. It commences flowering early and continues for months. (See also photos pp. 47, 60)

SPECKLES (see FINLANDIA VARIEGATED)

SPENCER'S PINK 1940
With a dash of beginner's luck, an Australian housewife bought this seedling from a door-to-door salesman in the 1930s. When her property was sold to Sir Baldwin Spencer some years later, the camellia was described and given his name in 1940. It is a profuse and early bloomer of low spreading growth. The large single blooms have slightly waved petals and matching pink stamens. Its parentage is unknown.

SPRING SONNET 1952   FRAGRANT
A 1952 sport of *Colonial Lady* from Pasadena's McCaskill Nursery, *Spring Sonnet* presents an exquisite picture in pale pink with irregular mauve-pink petal edges. It is a medium-sized informal double bloom, descended from the brilliant *HIKARU GENJI*, and blooms mid season.

SPUTNIK 1959
It is often said that nothing is so stale as yester-

TIFFANY

TOKI NO HAGASANE 鴇の羽重

TOM CAT

TOM HERRIN

TOM KNUDSEN

Japonicas

day's news. The *Sputnik* after which this noble flower was named is today scarcely remembered outside Russia, but the flower itself may serve to remind us of the primitive vehicle that won the race into the cosmos. It is a medium-sized semi-double bloom of deep red, with upright petals slightly reminiscent of the satellite's antennae. Blooms mid to late season.

ST ANDRÉ 1931
(syn: *Rose Hill Rubra*) A dazzling scarlet camellia from between the wars, *St André* found its way from England to the United States in 1931, but was probably not new even then. It is a medium-sized mid season cultivar, varying from semi-double to anemone form, and in spite of its colour, stands up well to sunlight.

STRAWBERRY BLONDE 1949
A sport of a different colour from nineteenth century's *Aspasia*, *Strawberry Blonde* was released in California in 1949. It is a medium-sized informal double bloom, this time of light salmon-pink, daintily speckled with a deeper tone.

STRIPED VIRGIN (see OTOME SHIBORI)

SUNSET GLORY 1951
A ruffled anemone form camellia of vivid carmine-pink, *Sunset Glory* has notably long guard petals. It blooms right through the season on an open upright bush. Another success for Harvey Short of California, this time in 1951.

SUNSET OAKS 1965
A dazzling sport of the earlier *Finlandia*, *Sunset Oaks* was developed and released by Kramer Bros of California in 1965. It is a semi-double bloom of medium size, with swirling petals and occasional petaloids. The colour is just like a peach Melba — golden peach-coloured stamens, with petals like icecream, stained at the edges with vivid strawberry sauce. Its blooming peaks mid season.

SUSAN CARTER (see FRIZZLE WHITE)

SWAN LAKE 1971
Swan Lake has magnificent rose form double blooms whose ruffled petals recall the fluttering plumage of Tchaikovsky's tragic Swan Princess. Large in size, and blooming mid season, it was released in 1971 by California's Monrovia Nursery — but you'll find it everywhere that camellias and Tchaikovsky are known and loved. Unfortunately, there is already an earlier Australian camellia with the same name — a problem the Camellia Nomenclature Committees are still trying to sort out.

T. S. CLOWER JR 1950
A fine formal double camellia from Mississippi, *T. S. Clower Jr* nostalgically evokes the charm of that state's old camellia gardens. Medium in size, the white satin of its petals is broken at intervals with a tasteful narrow stripe of deep pink. Regis-

tered in 1950 by the Clower family of Gulfport, it blooms mid season on a bush of slender open growth.

TABBS 1856
Named for his pet tabby cat by the early Australian hybridist, Michael Guilfoyle, *Tabbs* is a sport of the earlier triumph *Helenor*. It has a medium-sized crimson bloom marbled and blotched with white in a truly tabby pattern. It is still seen in old Australian gardens.

TAFFETA TUTU 1959　　　FRAGRANT
Soft peach-pink blending to palest lemon-yellow at the centre, the petals of this large cultivar remind us of a ballerina's skirts. The blooms vary from semi-double to loose peony form, with inner petals and petaloids deeply frilled. As an added bonus, this mid season camellia is slightly fragrant. It was developed in Fresno, California and registered in 1959.

TAIYŌ NISHIKI (see ŌNIJI)

TE DEUM (see GRAND SULTAN)

TEMPLE INCENSE 1955　　　FRAGRANT
A delightfully fragrant camellia, *Temple Incense* is a chance seedling of the earlier cultivar *Arrabella*, which it closely resembles. Medium in size and semi-double, its salmon-pink blooms show petals that are deeply notched, fimbriated and occasionally striped in deeper pink. It blooms mid to late season and was raised by Californian hybridist David L. Feathers. (Photo p. 190)

TENNIN KWAN (see NAGASAKI)

TEUTONIA WHITE (see ELISABETH)

THE BLACK CAMELLIA (see KURO TSUBAKI)

THE CZAR 1913
The precise origin of this popular crimson camellia (one of the most widely grown in Australian gardens) is obscure, for research has failed to locate it in Japan, Europe or America. The original plant was purchased from the estate of a deceased gardener Neil Breslin, in Camberwell, Victoria, in 1913, but where he got it is a mystery. It may have been a chance seedling. The purchaser, R. W. Hodgson, a Victorian nurseryman, raised 800 plants from the original stock and they created a sensation when released in the 1920s. The original plant is now in Melbourne's Royal Botanic Gardens. *The Czar* is a very large semi-double bloom with heavily veined, reflexed petals. The flowers are sun-resistant, but when grown in shade or in heavy soil, frequently become toned with a rich imperial purple, particularly on the ruffled petal edges. *The Czar* blooms mid season.

THE CZAR VARIEGATED
A variegated form of the previously described

TOM THUMB

TOMORROW

TOMORROW CROWN JEWEL

TOMORROW, LEANNE'S

TOMORROW PARK HILL

TOUCHDOWN

Japonicas

cultivar, *The Czar Variegated* can be quite striking with its white-blotched petals.

THE RADIANT GENJI (see HIKARU GENJI)

THREAD OF DIAMOND (see HISHI KARAITO)

THREAD STAMENS (see HISHI KARAITO)

THUNDERBOLT (see GLEN 40 VARIEGATED)

TIDE OF FLOWERS (see MOSHIO)

TIFFANY 1962
A gorgeously ruffled loose peony form cultivar, *Tiffany* seems as rare and priceless as anything its namesake jeweller sells. Large to very large in size, its orchid-pink petals shade to deeper pink. Lavishly swirled and upright, they reveal just a tantalising glimpse of gold. *Tiffany* is a release from La Cañada, California in 1962.

TINKER BELL 1958
Very reminiscent of *Little Bit* (which see) Nuccio's small japonica *Tinker Bell* is also of anemone form, but with a fuller centre and more ruffled petals. Early to mid season in bloom, it is white, striped pink and deep rose-red.

TOKI NO HAGASANE (Feathers of Wild Goose) 1879
(syn: *Bessie Morse Bellingrath*, *Betty Hopfer*, UBANE) A charming old Japanese camellia dating back to 1879, TOKI NO HAGASANE has been plagued with synonyms. However, as it can be found listed in Japanese catalogues of 1934 and much earlier under that name (before it was exported to the West) the name must be considered valid. It means *Feathers of Wild Goose*, and is a medium-sized semi-double cultivar of white, delicately flushed with pink. The underpetals, too, are deeper pink and most obvious when in bud. Blooms late.

TOM CAT 1964
Rose-pink tom cats are as rare as pink panthers, but somehow the name doesn't seem too out of place in this memorable semi-double cultivar with irregularly fluted petals. *Tom Cat* is large in size, blooms mid to late season and was registered in 1964.

TOM HERRIN 1962
This very Japanese-style camellia was raised and named in Florida in 1962. It is large, semi-double and crêpy white, lavishly rayed in carmine. It sometimes sports solid red blooms, and flowers mid season.

TOM KNUDSEN 1965
Named in 1965 for a prominent California garden figure, *Tom Knudsen* is a splendid red camellia with darker veining. Medium to large in size, rose form double to fully peony in style, it blooms early to mid season.

TRICIA

TRICOLOR

TRIUMPHANS

TWILIGHT

VEDRINE

TOM THUMB 1957
Most original in colouring, the small cultivar *Tom Thumb* produces perfect formal double blooms in mid season. Every mid pink petal is variably bordered in soft white — a great success for its originator, A. Krueger of California.

TOMORROW 1953
(syn: *Ed Anderson*) Pride of the camellia country around Thomasville, Georgia, the very large glowing *Tomorrow* was first presented in 1953 by the Tick Tock Nurseries, and has become the sport parent of more than half a dozen gorgeous varieties. The original *Tomorrow* is a large to very large camellia, varying from irregular semi-double to full peony form. It is tinted a showy light strawberry-red over all, with occasional petaloids marbled in white. Blooms early to mid season.

TOMORROW CROWN JEWEL 1967
An early sport of *Tomorrow*, this splendid cultivar was launched in 1967. Called *Tomorrow Crown Jewel*, it is pure white with an occasional fleck of red on one or more petals. Its style and habit duplicate those of the original parent.

TOMORROW, LEANNE'S 1964
An early discovery in the complicated sporting life of *Tomorrow*, this showy variant appeared in Natchez, Mississippi in 1964. It is coloured a delicious coral-red with occasional white markings, but otherwise possesses all the attributes of the original parent.

TOMORROW PARK HILL 1964
It sometimes seems all growers of *Tomorrow* can get in on the sporting act. This time it was Hollywood grower Ralph Peer who hit the jackpot with a second generation sport of the great camellia favourite. His *Tomorrow Park Hill* of 1964 is a very large informal double, shading from bright pink outer petals to a softer shade towards the centre. The flower is spattered with faint white variegation which enhances its delicate charm. Do not be misled though, the growth is robust in every way.

TOMORROW SUPREME
(see TOMORROW VARIEGATED)

TOMORROW VARIEGATED 1957
(syn: *Maverick, Tomorrow Supreme*) The simplest sporting form of *Tomorrow*, this has the original strawberry-red colouring, but blotched white in a quite irregular pattern.

TOMORROW'S DAWN 1960
Mississippi again was the birthplace of an excellent sport of the original *Tomorrow*. Similar in form to its beautiful sisters, *Tomorrow's Dawn* graduates from white at the petal edges to deep soft pink at the centre of the flower. Odd white petaloids may appear, as may occasional streaks of red throughout the flower.

VILLE DE NANTES RED

Japonicas

VIOLET BOUQUET

VIRGINIA FRANCO ROSEA

TOMORROW'S TROPIC DAWN 1967
If by now you are thinking that *Tomorrow* can't make up its mind, you may be right. This second generation sport (and there is no sign of the camellia stabilising yet) is white with the occasional red ray, the whole flower fading to blush as it ages. It appeared in 1967 in Fresno, California.

TOUCHDOWN 1962
A deep rose-pink sport of the cultivar *Kick Off*, *Touchdown* was also released in 1962 by Nuccio of California. It is a large to very large camellia of loose peony form, blooming mid season. A truly outstanding cultivar.

TRICIA 1974
So pale a pink you'd almost think it was white, the lovely *Tricia* is a sport of cultivar *Pat Nixon*, and like that camellia, of *Richard Nixon*. A large anemone form flower with upright crinkled petals, it may bloom at any time in the season. Registered in 1974 by Kramer Bros of California.

TRICOLOR 1832
(syn: *Tricolor* [*Siebold*], *Wakanoura Variegated*) *Tricolor* is an old camellia with a new name problem. It was imported from Japan under the name *EZO NISHIKI* in 1832 by German nurseryman Franz von Siebold, who rechristened it *Tricolor* for the European market. It is a medium-sized semi-double flower of white, streaked with carmine-red, and blooms mid season. By the time it got to America, there were several other camellias known as *Tricolor* — hence the ugly decision to name it there as *Tricolor (Siebold)*. It has since been reimported by another American nursery as *EZO NISHIKI* again. I still think of it as *Tricolor*, and it is the parent of many different sports. I make no apologies for including entries under both headings — *EZO NISHIKI* and *Tricolor*; the two camellias seem quite different to me.

TRICOLOR FOLKI (see LADY DE SAUMAREZ)

TRICOLOR (SIEBOLD) (see TRICOLOR)

TRIUMPHANS 1834
(syn: *Allen's Pink, Harmony, Lady Parker Peony, Triumphant*) Its grandiose name is quite appropriate for the old European variety *Triumphans*, first recorded in Belgium in 1834. A splendid large peony form bloom of rose-pink, with occasional white markings, it swept the world and was known by many names at different times and in many lands. The flowers open mid season.

TRIUMPHANT (see TRIUMPHANS)

TROIS MARIES (see ELISABETH)

TWILIGHT 1964
A 1964 release from the Nuccio Nurseries of California, *Twilight* celebrated the end of a summer's day with a large formal double bloom of palest blush-pink. It flowers mid season on a plant with strong handsome growth.

UBANE (see TOKI NO HAGASANE)

USU OTOME 1875
(syn: *Frau Minna Seidel, Pink Perfection*) One of the most popular of camellias in Victorian times (under the synonyms *Frau Minna Seidel* and *Pink Perfection*) this cultivar has finally been reallotted its original Japanese name *USU OTOME*. It is a sport of the Japanese variety *OTOME* (1828) and was brought to the United States in 1875. A small formal double of palest shell-pink, it is ideal in size for personal adornment. It blooms throughout the season.

VALENTINE (see AKEBONO)

VARIEGATA 1792
This early variety is not sold today, and is probably only grown in very old gardens of China and perhaps certain English collections. It is amply recorded, however, in English journals at the time of its importation by Chandler in 1792. It is (or was) a medium-sized semi-double bloom of deep rose-pink, mottled in white. Flowering period is mid season.

VEDRINE c. 1900
(syn: *Bolen's Pride, Cleo Witte, Lewis Red Peony, Margaret Lawrence, Mehl's Red, Mrs T. R. McKenzie, Payne's Red, Ruby Glow*) An immensely popular camellia in the early 1900s, ruby-red *Vedrine* was first recorded in Louisiana at the turn of the century. It bears a strong resemblance to many other anemone form camellias of that time (*Anemoniflora* and *Speciosissima* being two examples). It is a medium to large bloom, flowering early to mid season. Its provenance is unknown.

VEDRINE VARIEGATED
(see ELEANOR OF FAIROAKS)

VENUS DE MEDICIS 1868
The almost legendary *Venus de Medicis* was believed to be an early Australian seedling, but is now known to be Italian, for it was imported to England from Italy in 1868. It is a large formal double bloom of vivid cherry-red. Growth is slow and rather pendulous.

VICTOR EMMANUEL (see BLOOD OF CHINA)

VICTORIA AND ALBERT (see ELISABETH)

VILLE DE NANTES 1910
A sport of Siebold's 1834 cultivar *Donckelarii*, *Ville de Nantes* is first recorded by the French grower Heurtin of Nantes in 1910. It is a medium to large semi-double camellia with upright petals that are spectacularly fringed. It is dark red, blotched white, and blooms mid to late season.

VILLE DE NANTES RED 1910
This is a solid red form of the previous variety,

VIRGINIA ROBINSON

and like it, has intriguingly fringed petals.

VIOLET BOUQUET 1969   FRAGRANT
This 1969 registration by Mrs W. H. Gates of Louisiana would seem to be a real colour break, though it is not the most beautiful of blooms. Certainly it matches its name *Violet Bouquet*, for it is a sort of ruffled anemone form bloom with a distinct violet tinge, varying to purple in some soils. It blooms early to mid season.

VIRGINAL 1945
A 1945 seedling from Australian hybridist G. C. Linton, *Virginal* is often described as greenish white, though I haven't observed the phenomenon personally. It is otherwise a medium-sized semi-double bloom, sometimes verging on anemone form. It blooms mid season.

VIRGINIA FRANCO 1856
Not very large by modern standards, the small blooms of *Virginia Franco* remind us of an earlier day, when camellias were commonly worn in the hair of ladies, and in the lapels of their escorts. Named by an Italian collector, Santorelli in 1856, this delicate charmer is formally double with the centre petals often lightly fringed or feathered. The colouring is creamy-white, blushed with rose and streaked with deeper rose. The blooms appear mid season. That they have retained popularity is a tribute to their charm.

VULCAN

VIRGINIA FRANCO ROSEA 1875
A sport of the preceding variety, *Virginia Franco Rosea* was first described in 1875 by Shepherd and Co., an early Australian nursery firm. It may have originated in Australia. Identical in form to the paler flower, this formal double sport is tinted a rich rose, fading to flesh tone at petal margins. The centre of the flower, too, is often lighter.

VIRGINIA ROBINSON 1957
A charming semi-double confection of pale orchid-pink, *Virginia Robinson* blooms profusely on a compact, strongly growing bush. The blooms appear mid to late season, and the plant is a 1957 registration of the Nuccio Nursery.

VITTORIO EMANUELE II 1867
A multi-coloured extravaganza from 1867, *Vittorio Emanuele II* is still popular with Italian collectors, though rarely grown elsewhere. It is a formal double bloom of medium size, sometimes with a centre of compact petaloids. The colouring is flesh-pink, flushed rose, and with occasional red stripes.

VULCAN 1958
Glowing like the forge of the ancient fire god for whom it was named, *Vulcan* is a large to very large camellia shading from deep fiery red at the outer petal edges to white heat at its heart. The blooms may be semi-double to peony form, often with irregular centre petals. It blooms early to mid season and was registered in 1958.

W. H. HASTIE (see REGINA DEI GIGANTI)

WHITE EMPRESS

WHITE NUN

WILDFIRE

YODO NO ASAHI　　　淀の朝日

YOURS TRULY

Japonicas

WAIWHETU BEAUTY 1951
A medium-sized semi-double camellia with loose waving petals, *Waiwhetu Beauty* is a New Zealand cultivar of 1957. Flowers open mid season in a delicious shade of light pink.

WAKANOURA VARIEGATED
(see TRICOLOR)

WALTER HAZLEWOOD 1973
Surely some sort of hybrid of the old *BOKUHAN (Tinsie)*, *Walter Hazlewood* looks more like a whole bouquet of camellias than a single bloom. It is medium in size and more of a deep liver colour than red, the petals swirling among white petaloids and gold stamens. It may bloom at any time throughout the season.

WARATAH (see ANEMONIFLORA)

WARATAH WHITE (see ANEMONIFLORA ALBA)

WAVES IN THE OFFING (see OKI NO NAMI)

WHITE ANEMONE (see ANEMONIFLORA ALBA)

WHITE BEAD (see SHIRATAMA)

WHITE CHRYSANTHEMUM
(see SHIRAGIKU)

WHITE CRANE (see HAKU TSURU)

WHITE DAIKAGURA
(see JOSHUA E. YOUTZ)

WHITE ELEGANS (see SNOW CHAN)

WHITE EMPRESS 1939
Certainly aristrocratic in her lineage, the noble *White Empress* is a dramatically large semi-double camellia with deeply fluted petals. The splendid white blooms open early to id season. *White Empress* dates back to 1939, an early creation of Albama's Overlook Nurseries.

WHITE JORDAN'S PRIDE
(see COLONIAL LADY)

WHITE NUN 1959
One of the very largest white camellias, semi-double *White Nun* blooms mid season. The blooms are classed as very large, and their broad crêpy petals surround a comparatively small boss of pale lemon stamens. It is a 1959 release of Pasadena's McCaskill Gardens.

WHITE POPPY (see AMABILIS)

WHITE SPOTTED PEACOCK
(see HAKUHAN KUJAKU)

WHITE STAR (see CANDIDISSIMA)

WHITE STORK (see HAKU TSURU)

WICKE 1950
The small semi-double blooms of American cultivar *Wicke* are so variable in colour that one sometimes finds white, red, pink and variegated blooms all on the one bush when they are at their mid season peak. *Wicke* was registered by H. H. Harms of Portland, Oregon.

WILD ORANGE BLOSSOM
(see HANA TACHIBANA)

WILDFIRE 1963
A 1963 release from the Nuccio Nurseries, *Wildfire* is a medium-sized semi-double cultivar of brilliant orange-red coloration, with an iridescent finish. The blooms have a 'hose-in-hose' effect, with central petals somewhat cupped around gold stamens, which often include an odd petaloid. The 1 cm (½ in) blooms catch every eye, whether flowering in containers or in the open garden.

WILLIAM S. HASTIE (see MATHOTIANA [US])

WILLIAM S. HASTIE (MISSISSIPPI)
(see C. M. HOVEY)

WINGS (see BENI BOTAN)

WORN PAINTBRUSH (see NUKI FUDE)

YEZO NISHIKI (see EZO NISHIKI)

YODO NO ASAHI (Rising Sun on River Yodo) 1877
Traced back in Japan to 1877, the splendid *YODO NO ASAHI* reached the United States in 1930, and Australia some time later. It is a splendid large bloom of vermilion-red, with widely flaring stamens. White markings are recorded, and the blooms may vary from single to peony form. The Japanese name alludes to the rising sun over a well-known Japanese river. A late bloomer.

YOKOHAMA (see SODE KAKUSHI)

YORK AND LANCASTER 1844
An 1844 novelty from a New York grower named Prince, the interesting rose form double *York and Lancaster* bears two sorts of flower — white-spotted rose, and rose-spotted white, rather like the Japanese *CHIRI TSUBAKI*. It is medium in size, and blooms mid to late season.

YOSHUMI 1964
A small bright red camellia of profuse blooming habit, *YOSHUMI* was imported in 1964 directly from Japan by the Nuccio Nurseries of California. It is believed to be a member of the *C. rusticana* subspecies of *C. japonica*. Blooms are semi-double, with pointed petals. *YOSHUMI* flowers mid to late season.

YOURS TRULY 1949
(syn: *Lady Vansittart Shell*) The Japanese

YOSHUMI よしうみ YURI TSUBAKI 百合椿

camellia *HARU NO UTENA* travelled halfway round the world to Guernsey in the English Channel Islands where, in 1887, it was rechristened *Lady Vansittart*. Later it was exported to the United States, where it sported frequently, finally producing in 1949 the beautiful cultivar now called *Yours Truly*. This is a medium-sized semi-double bloom of pale pink, streaked with carmine and bordered white. The shining holly-like leaves are particularly noticeable when it is grown as a container plant.

YUKI BOTAN (Snow Peony) 1877
(syn: *Peony, Pride of Descanso*) Dating from 1877 in Japan, the lovely *YUKI BOTAN* reached the West in 1895. It is a large white camellia of semi-double to loose peony form. Faint yellow shading is visible at the base of the irregular petals. Blooms mid season.

YURI TSUBAKI (Lily Camellia) 1829
A Japanese variety of considerable antiquity, *YURI TSUBAKI* can be found in illustrations back to about 1700 and is listed in an 1828 catalogue. The carmine-red 'hose-in-hose' blooms have long lily-shaped petals and never open fully. They are seen early to mid season.

ZAMBO 1874
An Australian cultivar of 1874, *Zambo* is more widely remembered than it deserves to be, I suspect because it is always the last-listed bloom in any catalogue. It is a medium-sized formal double, coloured mauve-pink with purple overtones, rather like a faded cabbage rose. A novelty, but little more.

ZAMBO

THE MINIATURE CAMELLIAS
A small reaction

Miniature camellias can hardly be considered a novelty, for flowers of the majority of wild species fit easily into the miniature classification of well under 6.5 centimetres (2½ inches). It is an undeniable fact, though, that even without the application of size-boosting gibberellic acid, show blooms of *Camellia japonica* have been growing larger and larger for several generations. For those who appreciate the manageable size of the early cultivars, the introduction of the reticulata hybrids must have been the last straw.

What gentleman could consider wearing a bloom of *Howard Asper* unless he were setting out to emulate the young man in Gilbert and Sullivan's *Patience* who 'strolled down Piccadilly with a sunflower, or a lily, in his medieval hand'? What lady could imagine twining such a bloom in her hair unless she was planning to win a prize for the most novel hat.

There have been miniature japonica cultivars for a long time. *BOKUHAN (Tinsie)* has been grown since 1719, and probably longer, while its negative reverse bloom *ASAHI YAMA* can be seen in Yoshiaki Andoh's accompanying picture of a delightful seventeenth century screen. They have, however, only come into their own in recent years, and I like to think this is a reaction to the over-large show blooms that seem to be taking over the camellia world. Note the dates in the comprehensive list of entries that follows.

Only five varieties date back before World War II; only 15 were grown prior to 1959. The vast majority (over 45) were introduced within the last 20 years.

Yes, the miniature (or, some would say, normal size) camellias are making a big comeback, with no sacrifice to enthusiasts in colour, shape or style. All the normal colour shades and variegations can be found among the tiny blooms we have listed; every camellia style from single to formal double is there. It needs only the lead of a few hardy souls who are not afraid to wear their favourite flower, and we may see a wholesale return to the customs of the early nineteenth century, when camellias were not hidden away in gardens, but flaunted before the whole world.

(All miniature camellias described in this chapter are cultivars of *C. japonica*. Other miniature blooms will be found in the chapters on camellia species, the sasanquas and the camellia hybrids.)

卜伴

Above: Popular miniature camellia BOKUHAN (also known as GAKKŌ and Tinsie) has been around since 1719 at least, but is probably much older.

Opposite: These two lost camellia cultivars are known only from this exquisitely painted seventeenth century screen by Ogata Korin. The red-centred variety, ASAHI YAMA is the exact negative reverse of popular miniature BOKUHAN. Photo courtesy Yoshiaki Andoh.

BOB'S TINSIE

BONBON BLUSH

CONFETTI BLUSH

FAWN

Miniatures

ANGEL'S BLUSH 1945
(syn: *Maria Martini, Melissa Martin*) A delightful semi-double miniature of rose-pink, blooming mid season. From Alabama.

BABY SARGENT 1949
Resembling the full-size japonica *Professor Sargent*, this novel miniature bears peony form blooms rarely above 6 cm (2½ in) diameter. They are dark ruby-red, and bloom mid season.

BABY SIS 1954
A sweet single miniature with the stamens converted to petaloids, *Baby Sis* is white, broken with an occasional pink stripe. It has a solid pink sport, *Baby Sis Pink*. Blooms mid season.

BILLY GATES 1976
One of the more recent miniature introductions, *Billy Gates* is a fiery red varying from anemone to peony form. A mid to late bloomer.

BIMBO 1961
A rose-pink miniature of semi-double form, *Bimbo* was introduced by A. M. Hartman of California. It blooms mid season.

BLACK DOMINO 1961
More like a small rose than a camellia, *Black Domino* is single, black-red with dark red stamens. A late bloomer from Harvey Short.

BOB'S TINSIE 1962
Almost pure scarlet, the miniature *Bob's Tinsie* retains just enough white to remind us of the old Japanese cultivar for which it was named. Anemone form, it blooms mid season.

BOKUHAN 1719
(syn: *GAKKŌ*, Tinsie) Sole modern survivor of ancient Japanese miniatures, *BOKUHAN* can be traced back to at least 1719. Since it was imported to the West it has been commonly known as *Tinsie*. The tiny anemone form flowers are deep ruby-red, the inner petaloids white, flushed with pink. Blooms mid season.

BONBON 1961
Bonbon is a miniature peony form camellia with the colouring of old-fashioned peppermint candy. It resembles a striped carnation and blooms mid season.

BONBON BLUSH 1971
Even the miniatures sport happily. *Bonbon Blush* is almost identical to the previous variety, but the red splashes occur on a background of deep pink. Petal edges are still white.

BONBON RED 1970
A pure deep red sport of *Bon Bon*, this dainty bloom obligingly appeared in Alabama in 1970. Like its sport parent, it blooms mid season.

BONSAI 1955
The perfect flower size for a bonsai camellia, *Bonsai* produces miniature anemone form blooms of rose-red, flowering mid to late season.

BOUTONNIÈRE 1840s
One of the oldest miniature camellias in cultivation, *Boutonnière* was developed in Europe. The rose form double blooms are dark red, with centre petals streaked white. Blooms mid to late season.

BRIGHT SPRITE 1952
A novel colour break in the miniature field, *Bright Sprite* is a loose semi-double bloom of bright orange-red, blooming early to mid season.

BROZZONI NOVA 1855
One of the few miniatures to survive from the great days of the Italian camellia craze, *Brozzoni Nova* was raised by Franchetti, and is a formal double bloom of light pink, paler towards the centre. It blooms mid season.

CHINESE LANTERNS 1972
A dainty rose form double miniature of palest blush-pink, *Chinese Lanterns* most resembles a rosy buttercup when fully open. It blooms mid season, and was released in Georgia.

CONFETTI 1971
One of the most popular miniature introductions of recent years, the delightful *Confetti* is white, spattered with red spots and may vary from anemone form to formal double. Blooms mid season.

CONFETTI BLUSH 1971
Seemingly closely related to *Bonbon Blush* (which see) *Confetti Blush* was registered in the same year. A miniature of anemone form, it is pink with white edgings and an occasional red stripe. It shows a great display of gold stamens among blush-tinted petaloids.

CONFETTI RED 1971
A solid red sport of *Confetti* (see above).

CROWNING GLORY 1977
An exquisite miniature of anemone form from Californian David Feathers, *Crowning Glory* is white, tipped lavender-pink. The blooms open all season on a bush of compact size.

DOLLY DYER 1973
To my knowledge the first miniature camellia registered in Australia, *Dolly Dyer* was named for a popular television personality. Rose form double in style, it opens early to mid season, and the blooms are plain scarlet.

DOMOTO'S PETITE 1965
Produced by California's Toichi Domoto in the mid 1960s, *Domoto's Petite* is a charming peony form miniature of palest mauve-pink. Blooms mid to late season.

ELLEN DANIEL 1971
A 1971 release from Alabama, *Ellen Daniel* is a

full peony form miniature of blush-pink, striped in deeper pink and red. The crowded petals are often reflexed and fluted. Blooms mid season.

FAIRY GARDEN 1962
A delightful single miniature opening only to a cone shape, *Fairy Garden* was a 1962 introduction of Californian Harvey Short. Mid season.

FAWN 1973
A perfect mid season charmer, McCaskill's 1973 cultivar *Fawn* is a miniature semi-double with irregular, pointed petals and occasional petaloids. Its colouring is cream, with outer petals shaded blush.

FIRCONE 1950
A sweet blood-red miniature from Oregon's Rhodellia Nursery, *Fircone* is semi-double, and blooms profusely in mid season.

FIRCONE VARIEGATED 1950
The variegated sport of the previously described variety — red with irregular white blotches.

FLOWER IN SNOW (see SECCHUKA)

FRANCES COUNCILL 1971
A perfect miniature bloom of formal double style, *Frances Councill* is snowy white, and blooms early to mid season.

GAKKŌ (see BOKUHAN)

GARDENIA c. 1900
A charming miniature camellia from Edwardian times, *Gardenia* is a pure white formal double, blooming late. It does look like a gardenia.

GINGER 1958
A creamy-white miniature of peony form, *Ginger* blooms late in the season. It has deeply fluted petals that almost obscure the pale yellow stamens.

HOPKIN'S PINK 1959
What *Carter's Sunburst* is to full-size camellias, *Hopkin's Pink* may be to the miniatures. The original peony form miniature has upstanding fluted inner petals, and is tinted pale blush, with a red marking somewhere on the flower. It blooms mid to late season.

HOPKIN'S PINK DAWN 1969
See above. Soft pink, shading to white at edges.

HOPKIN'S RED 1969
Pure red sport of *Hopkin's Pink*.

HOPKIN'S ROSE PINK 1966
The deeper rose-pink sport of *Hopkin's Pink*.

IMP 1973
A formal double miniature, blooming mid season, *Imp* is tinted a deep, dark pink.

JANE EAGLESON 1973

A superb formal double miniature of deepest red. Blooms early to mid season.

JOSH SPROTT 1977
An exquisite miniature of formal double style, *Josh Sprott* is coloured vivid pink, more the colour you would expect in a *X Williamsii* hybrid. A recent release of Louisiana's Tammia Nursery, it blooms mid season.

LITTLE AGGIE 1976
From California hybridist Milo Rowell, a contribution to the miniature fans. *Little Aggie* is single, with petaloded stamens, the whole a most unusual light purplish-pink. A mid to late season bloomer.

LITTLE DAVID 1958
A miniature formal double bloom of rose-red, hail-spotted with white. Mid season bloomer.

LITTLE POPPY 1973
Rather like the larger *HISHI KARAITO* (which see) *Little Poppy* is a miniature anemone form camellia of soft pink, centred with cream petaloids. A mid season bloomer.

LITTLE RED RIDING HOOD 1965
Varying from peony form to formal double, *Little Red Riding Hood* is a showy miniature of deep crimson. Blooms mid to late season.

LITTLE SLAM 1969
Like a perfect miniature of the large variety *Grand Slam*, *Little Slam* is a 1969 registration from California's Nuccio Nurseries. Peony form, early to bloom, it is coloured a rich red.

LITTLE 'UN 1959
A slow-growing plant of compact size, *Little 'Un* is a perfect choice for the bonsai fans, with miniature semi-double blooms of rose-pink. A late bloomer.

MAN SIZE 1961
Just right for a formal boutonnière, the miniature anemone form blooms of *Man Size* are almost whiter than white. Blooming mid season, it is probably the same as the Japanese *SHIRO KARAKO*, which is recognised back to 1859.

MARIA MARTINI (see ANGEL'S BLUSH)

MELISSA 1961
A dainty semi-double miniature of blush-pink. Very feminine and blooming mid season.

MELISSA MARTIN (see ANGEL'S BLUSH)

MEMENTO 1959
Coral-rose is the colouring of this miniature anemone form bloom from California's Harvey Short. It opens mid season.

MEN'S MINI 1971
I presume the extraordinary name of this minia-

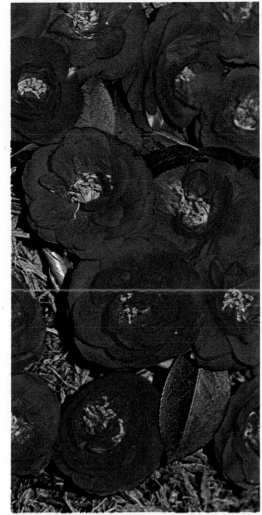

FIRCONE

HOPKIN'S PINK

LITTLE SLAM

Miniatures

MAN SIZE

TINSIE BLUSH

TINSIE SEEDLING

ture camellia means that it is suitable for a boutonnière — but it could have been more carefully expressed. The semi-double blooms are deep red with a silvery sheen, and open mid to late season.

MIDGET WHEELER 1974
A pretty colour effect on this dainty miniature camellia. Formal double in style, it is flesh-pink, spattered irregularly with deep rose. A mid to late season bloomer.

MINUTE 1962
A perfect formal double camellia of miniature size, *Minute* is tinted light pink, and blooms mid season. From the Wheelers of Georgia.

MOMOIRO BOKUHAN (see TINSIE BLUSH)

PEARL'S PET 1959
A dainty rose-red miniature of pure anemone form, *Pearl's Pet* blooms on a fast-growing bush of normal size. Early to mid season.

PEE WEE 1959
A miniature red camellia of typical anemone form, *Pee Wee* blooms mid to late season.

PINK SMOKE 1965
A loose anemone form miniature from David Feathers of Lafayette, California, *Pink Smoke* is an unusual lavender-pink. Blooms mid season.

RED BUTTON 1960
Almost indistinguishable from *Bob's Tinsie*, the tiny *Red Button* was registered two years earlier. It is a deep red miniature bloom of normal anemone form, and flowers mid season.

ROSY POSY 1959
A tiny semi-double camellia shaped something like a fircone, McCaskill's quaintly named *Rosy Posy* is bright pink. It blooms mid season.

RUNT 1962
An interesting miniature of full peony form, *Runt* was released in 1962 by Wheeler's Central Georgia Nurseries. It is light pink, deeply ruffled, and blooms mid season.

SECCHUKA (Flower in Snow) 1935
One of the few recent Japanese contributions to the miniature field, SECCHUKA was released by the Chugai nursery of Kobe. It is single, pure white streaked with red. Early blooming.

SHIRO KARAKO (see MAN SIZE)

SNOW BABY 1965
Pure white and perfectly anemone form, this charming miniature is a release of McCaskills Nursery, California. It blooms mid season.

SUGAR BABE 1959
A dark pink miniature in formal double style, *Sugar Babe* shows a tendency to petal edging in

a lighter tone. It blooms mid season.

TAMMIA 1971
An unusual miniature deserving greater attention, *Tammia* is formal double with inward-curving pointed petals. These are white, centred and edged pink. It blooms mid to late season.

TINSIE (see BOKUHAN)

TINSIE BLUSH 1976
(syn: *MOMOIRO BOKUHAN*) This recent American sport of *Tinsie* is anemone form and pale pink all over. It is probably the same as an earlier Japanese sport recorded under the name *MOMOIRO BOKUHAN (Peach-Coloured Bokuhan)*.

TINSIE SEEDLING 1970s
Discovered in Australia, the dramatic *Tinsie Seedling* is fully double. The deep crimson blooms appear to be several different flowers, each with its own cluster of gold stamens and white petaloids, the whole enclosed in a single row of guard petals. Mid season bloomer.

TINY TOT 1961
A miniature formal double bloom from Harvey Short of California, *Tiny Tot* is white with an occasional pink flash. Blooms mid to late season.

TOOTSIE 1967
A miniature formal double bloom of chalk white, with its petals arranged in the form of a five-pointed star. *Tootsie* blooms mid to late season.

TRUDY 1952
A very different miniature camellia, *Trudy* is a five-petalled single bloom of red, with matching red stamens. It blooms mid season.

WART 1962
This unfortunately named miniature is in fact a charming semi-double bloom of deep pink, with a paler centre and reverse. A slow grower, it blooms late in the season.

WHITE BUTTONS 1960
A perfectly miniature formal double bloom of stark white makes *White Buttons* the perfect choice for a boutonnière. Mid season bloomer.

WIDDLE WUN 1975
Widdle Wun (Ugh!) is a rose-pink bloom of anemone form, blooming mid season.

ZING 1973
Trust McCaskills to bring nomenclature back in line! *Zing* is the perfect epithet for this formal double miniature of bright rose-red. It blooms mid season, and is a real charmer.

THE HIGO CAMELLIAS
Kumamoto's Glory

It is a curious paradox that the more strongly ancient Japanese culture became appreciated in Western countries, the less highly it was regarded in its home islands.

Modern visitors to Tokyo (in particular) have lamented the lack of interest by younger Japanese in their traditional forms of art, music, cuisine and costume; they are appalled by the proliferation of Western-style high-rise buildings that have blotted out so many gardens, so many vistas. If it were not for the exotic ideographs in dazzling neon, the visitor might well believe he had accidentally stumbled into central New York, or Sydney's Kings Cross, or Dusseldorf, so omnipresent are the logotypes of American Express, Kentucky Fried and other multinational corporations.

As with culture in general, so with camellias in particular. While European fortunes were changing hands over the importation of new camellia varieties, so the Japanese lost interest in their priceless heritage of the camellia and its associated culture.

This marvellous Higo camellia depicted on an old Japanese silk fabric is not dissimilar to many of the modern Higo cultivars.

As cities expanded under the influence of Westernisation, priceless camellia trees were ripped out or planted over with concrete. As a consequence, of more than 700 camellia varieties depicted in the seventeenth century manuscript *Chinka Zufu*, perhaps no more than 20 can still be recognised among those cultivated today. At Japanese camellia shows, it is often the newer American cultivars, imported at great expense, that take the prizes.

The native wild forms can still be found on hillsides throughout the southern islands, and perhaps that was the trouble — familiarity breeding contempt. But elegant cultivated flowers, often the result of once-in-a-lifetime sporting or careful hybridisation, were formerly to be found in old gardens everywhere.

Fortunately, all traces of the old camellia culture were not lost. In the southern island of Kyūshū, in Kumamoto province, a group of flower-lovers banded together in the early nineteenth century to form the Hana

Detail of a shop curtain from Kumamoto City, capital of the Higo province of Kumamoto.

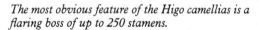

The most obvious feature of the Higo camellias is a flaring boss of up to 250 stamens.

Ren, an association devoted to the collection, preservation and improvement of certain local flower varieties. Among these were the now world-famous Higo camellias — Higo being the old-time name of the district in which these unique flowers were first selected and developed during the samurai culture. So seriously did the members of the Hana Ren take their self-appointed task that they succeeded in passing laws to register the varieties and forbid their export from the old Higo area.

The Higo camellia that they developed so well does not closely resemble any naturally occurring species; in fact, as modern plant scientists have discovered, the Higo style camellias are hybrids of selected varieties of *Camellia japonica* crossed with the lesser-known *Camellia rusticana* from the mountains of Honshū, and probably with other, rarer species as well. If anything, they are more closely related to the rusticanas, but are obviously the result of several centuries of selection and improvement.

They are a *style* of flower, rather than a species, their two most obvious features being their profusion of stamens, and the fact that they are all flat and single (or very nearly so). With rare exceptions the petals number between five and nine, and may be uneven in length. They are noticeably thick and leathery and often have an iridescent colouring overlapping their basic tint. The number of stamens vary from 100 to as many as 250 in an individual flower. These may be white, gold, or even pink or red to match the flower's overall colouring. These stamens may be arranged in a dense, columnar form; like half of a dandelion flower; or ideally, in *Ume jin* form. That is, like the flower of the plum blossom, *Prunus mume*, where the stamens are flattened out into a wide ring or crown, leaving a single pistil or female organ projecting in solitary splendour in the centre of the blossom. The colourings vary widely, but are all pure and brilliant — scarlet, crimson, white or pink, or the Higo's particular glory, the *Nishiki* or brocaded patterns, in which swirls, rays or flecks of a contrasting colour overlay the base tint.

Since the Higo camellias have such a varied parentage, it is not surprising to find that they sport freely, solid-colour blooms frequently appearing on plants of the brocaded forms.

Several of these beautiful flowers are even perfumed, a rarity among camellias in general; and their leaves vary widely according to variety. Some leaves are particularly thick and strong, a feature greatly valued by the Japanese enthusiasts who appreciate the camellia plant in all seasons.

Western collectors generally prefer to grow their Higo hybrids in the open garden, but in Japan, they are more often seen as bonsai plants, the chosen variety being grafted onto an ancient camellia branch or root and trained to display the bloom against a background of powerful form and windswept branches.

Now that the camellia hobby has come full circle in Japan, as witnessed by a proliferation of books and exhibitions, the carefully preserved Higo cultivars have come to be regarded almost with the awe accorded national treasures, and hobbyists are busy exploring old cemeteries and ruined gardens in many other parts of the country formerly known for their camellia culture. Through these efforts, it is not too much to hope that many other fine cultivars from Japan's past may be rediscovered and reintroduced to a waiting world of camellia lovers.

A wonderful old bonsai plant of Higo cultivar YAMATO NISHIKI *at a Japanese exhibition.*

Higos

ASAHI NO MINATO 旭の湊

DEWATAIRIN

AKATSUKI NO KAORI   FRAGRANT
(syn: *Dawn Fragrance, Scent of Sunset*) Uncommonly for a camellia, this aptly named single pink bloom has a faint but distinct fragrance. Larger than average, it has ten petals, but only 80 white stamens. Each bloom has the typical Higo style, and the leaves are average in size.

ALPINE SNOW (see MINE NO YUKI)

ANGEL'S WING (see HAGOROMO)

ASAGAO
(syn: *Morning Glory*) Softly pink, this charming Higo camellia would resemble the morning glory flower for which it was named if it were not for a stunning burst of 140 golden stamens. One of the most widely grown of camellias in its native province, it is often trained as a bonsai because of its medium bushy growth. Among the largest of Higo flowers, *ASAGAO* averages 12 cm (4¾ in) in diameter, and has six or seven petals. The blooms open early to mid season.

ASAHI NO MINATO
(syn: *Port of the Rising Sun*) Basically crimson, with an overlay of pink iridescence (like the calm waters of a harbour at dawn's first light) this showy camellia is typical of the Higo form, with seven or eight irregularly shaped petals and 130 yellow stamens. The flowers average 10 cm (4 in) in diameter and open early to mid season. Growth is fast.

ASAHI ZURU
(syn: *Crane Dance at Dawn*) A swirl of white breaks the crimson surface of this medium-sized Higo beauty, suggesting the flash of white cranes dancing in the red-hued waters of an estuary dawn. The 130 stamens are also white, surrounded by seven to nine petals. Foliage size and growth are average.

BAR NONE (see DEWATAIRIN)

BIG CUP (see DEWATAIRIN)

BLESSED PEACE (see DEWATAIRIN)

BROCADE OF ANCIENT CHINA
(see SHOKKŌ NISHIKI)

BROCADE OF OLD JAPAN
(see YAMATO NISHIKI)

BROCADE OF OLD KYOTO
(see KYŌ NISHIKI)

CAPITAL CITY SPRING
(see MIYAKO NO HARU)

CHERRY BLOSSOM PALACE
(see GŌSHO ZAKURA)

CHERRY VIEWING (see SAKURA GARI)

CHŌJU RAKU
(syn: *Happy Ever After*) A recent introduction in Japan, this deeper pink sport of *OSARAKU* (which see) bears large blooms with seven to eight fluted petals and 150 widely flared white stamens. The flowers open early to mid season, and the slow compact growth makes it a useful bonsai subject.

CRANE DANCE AT DAWN (see ASAHI ZURU)

CROWN PRINCE (see SHIN TSUKASA)

CRYSTAL PURE (see SUISHŌ HAKU)

DAIHASSU (see DEWATAIRIN)

DAITAIRIN (see DEWATAIRIN)

DAWN FRAGRANCE
(see AKATSUKI NO KAORI)

DEWATAIRIN
(syn: *Bar None, Big Cup, Blessed Peace, DAIHASSU, DAITAIRIN, Golden Temple, HATSU ZAKURA, OSAKAZUKI, TAI HAI, TAIHEI RAKU*) One of the earliest blooming Higos, often appearing at the same time as the sasanquas, this gorgeous hybrid is first described in the *Kadan Chinkin Shō* of 1695, and has become popular world-wide. Large, rose-pink and single, it is really quite variable. Commonly with reflexed petals, centred with a mass of pink petaloids and golden stamens, at times it produces stamens alone. The plant's growth is vigorous.

FACE OF THE SUN (see HI NO MARU)

FEATHERED ROBE (see HAGOROMO)

FUJI
(syn: *Mount Fuji*) A particularly striking plant with large shining leaves, *FUJI* is the most popular of white Higos for bonsai training. The irregularly shaped flowers open early with a flush of palest pink, fading to white as they expand to full size over several days. Each blossom is six-petalled with 160 light gold stamens. It is appropriately named for Japan's most popular mountain peak.

GENTLE BREEZE (see SOYO KAZE)

GLORY OF SHOWA (see SHŌWA NO HIKARI)

GOLDEN TEMPLE (see DEWATAIRIN)

GORGEOUS FIREBIRD (see REIHO)

GŌSHO ZAKURA
(syn: *Cherry Blossom Palace, Pink Palace*) Palest pink buds open slowly to display a rich confection of colour in this stunning Higo flower — 120 yellow stamens perfectly set off against six

FŪJI   不二

GŌSHŌ ZAKURA 御所桜

reflexed cherry-pink petals. These flowers are borne profusely all over a plant of vigorous habit, appearing from early in the season for several months. They are quite fertile and frequently set seed.

GREAT MOUNT ASŌ (see Ō ASŌ)

HAGOROMO
(syn: *Angel's Wing, Feathered Robe*) One of the most spectacular of Higo camellias, *HAGOROMO* sets over 200 red stamens in a cup of five to eight petals of glowing, fiery red. The leaves are large and glossy, the individual blossoms 10 cm (4 in) or more in diameter.

HAKU TSURU
(syn: *White Crane*) Largest of all the white Higos, the elegant *HAKU TSURU* may reach 11 cm (4½ in) in diameter and is completely white in its nine petals and 120 stamens. The flower holds particularly well, a characteristic that perhaps accounts for its being named after the crane, Japanese symbol of longevity. *HAKU TSURU* bears occasional seed.

HAKUTAKA
(syn: *SHIRA TAKA, White Hawk*) Set a golden eye in the centre of a disc of purest white, and to the poetic Japanese mind you have suggested the purity and the power of a white hawk! 10 cm (4 in) in diameter, each bloom has six petals, 140 stamens and is surrounded by particularly large, dark leaves.

HAPPY EVER AFTER (see CHŌJU RAKU)

HATSU ZAKURA (see DEWATAIRIN)

HI NO HAKAMA
(syn: *Scarlet Skirts*) A vivid flash of crimson-scarlet, a soft froth of white stamens and the viewer is instantly reminded of a dancer's skirts as this stunning flower opens. Only medium-sized when fully developed, it has up to eight irregularly rippled and waved petals, and 120 stamens.

HI NO MARU
(syn: *Face of the Sun, Japanese Flag*) Commonly known as *Japanese Flag*, the original name of this spectacular Higo has many possible translations — *Sunshine, Rising Sun, Face of the Sun* among them — all suggesting the majestic beauty of the sun's disc at dawn. The six wavy petals are blood-red in colour and seem to be reflected in a glow of 120 stamens which are soft pink.

HOST OF HEAVEN (see JITSU GETSU SEI)

ICHU
(syn: *Royal Decoration*) The Japanese *aficionado* who named this elegant bloom was reminded of the spectacular badges of rank worn by medieval courtiers. And indeed the bloom is

HI NO HAKAMA 緋の袴

JITSU GETSU SEI 日月星

KŌBAI   紅梅

KYŌ NISHIKI   京錦

Higos

spectacular: 10 cm (4 in) across, deepest red, and with a cockade of 120 pale-topped white stamens. There are always six or seven petals and the plant often sets fruit.

IMA KUMAGAI
(syn: *IMA KUMAGAYA, Modern Kumagai*) An improved version of the older Higo variety *KUMAGAI* (which see), *IMA KUMAGAI* is a vigorous plant with large foliage. The medium crimson blossoms have six or seven petals and a profuse 180 stamens. They average 10 cm (4 in) in diameter.

IMA KUMAGAYA (see IMA KUMAGAI)

JAPANESE FLAG (see HI NO MARU)

JITSU GETSU SEI
(syn: *Host of Heaven, Sun, Moon and Stars*) In full bloom, the flowers of this vigorous Higo suggest the firmament in spectacular display. The medium-sized dull crimson blossoms are streaked with soft white patches of varying size, no two petals alike. The petal count varies from five to eight, the stamens (a mixture of pink and white) number 150 in each bloom.

KIYŌ
(syn: *Shining Sun*) A delicious warm pink in colour, the blooms of *KIYŌ* have six petals, 100 golden yellow stamens, and average 9 cm (3½ in) across. Not the best of the pinks, but very lovely.

KŌBAI
(syn: *Red Apricot Blossom*) The large blossoms of this outstanding Higo bear more than a super-ficial resemblance to the red apricot blossom or *Ume*, regarded as a symbol of spring throughout Japan. Light crimson in colour, with five to six petals enclosing a spectacular display of 100 flar-ing white stamens, each bloom may be 11 cm (4½ in) wide. The foliage is also large.

KUMAGAI
Named for the hero of a popular drama in the *Kabuki* theatre, *KUMAGAI* bears perhaps the largest warm crimson flowers of any Higo, each a gigantic 13 cm (5¼ in) in diameter. Five to seven petals and up to 150 white stamens produce a display that is indeed theatrical. Individual leaves are large in proportion.

KYŌ NISHIKI
(syn: *Brocade of Old Kyoto*) Soft pink of various shades streaked with white suggests the delicate workmanship of fine brocade from Japan's most cultivated capital. Each bloom is 10 cm (4 in) across with five to six petals and a splash of golden stamens, from 130 to 150 in number. The flowers appear mid season.

LIFESPAN (see TENJU)

LORD OF THE CHERRIES (see SAKURA TSUKASA)

MIYAKO NO HARU 都之春

REIHŌ 黎峰

SAKURA TSUKASA 桜司

SHIN TSUKASA 新司

MANZAI RAKU

(syn: *Ten Thousand Years of Happiness*) Ten thousand years of happiness, a popular theme in Japanese court music, makes an appropriate name for the cheerful beauty of this fine modern Higo. Large-leafed, fast in growth, and individual blooms are 12 cm (4¾ in) in diameter and coloured a delicious deep rose-pink with white swirls. Five or six petals and 110 white stamens complete the flower form.

MINE NO YUKI

(syn. *Alpine Snow*) Snow on a mountain peak in the light of setting sun suggests the name of this attractive Higo. It has rose-pink petals with occasional blotches of deep crimson and a spray of 120 flaring pink stamens. *MINE NO YUKI*'s blooms are 10 cm (4 in) in diameter, mid season, and are often followed by fruit.

MIYAKO NO HARU

(syn: *Capital City Spring*) The gaiety of spring gardens in Japan's old capital of Kyōtō is conjured up by the pink and gold blooms of this splendid Higo. Less elaborate than other varieties with its six petals and only 70 stamens, *MIYAKO NO HARU* has small foliage and blooms mid season. It is popular as a pot and garden subject.

MIYAKO OSARAKU

(syn: *Wishing for the Stars*) Relatively small in size, the simple rose-pink blooms of this popular variety contrast well with 70 light gold stamens. Individual flowers are often as small as 6 cm (2½ in) but appear profusely.

MODERN KUMAGAI (see IMA KUMAGAI)

MORNING GLORY (see ASAGAO)

MOUNT FUJI (see FUJI)

NIOI FUBUKI   FRAGRANT

(syn: *Scented Storm*) Widely grown in California, this beautiful Higo seems not to be listed under that name in Japan. A plant of vigorous growth, it flowers mid to late season. The individual blooms have white, wavy petals, striped in rose-pink, and the high crown of stamens often includes a few petaloids. The flowers are pleasantly fragrant. (Photo p. 194)

Ō ASŌ 1958

(syn: *Great Mount Aso*) The sunset-tinted peak of Kumamoto's mighty Mt Aso suggested the name of this very large Higo. Late blooming, the flowers are 12 cm (4¾ in) wide, flushed crimson on a pale pink ground. Eight rippled petals and 120 widely flared pink stamens help identify it.

Ō ZORA

(syn: *Vault of Heaven*) Smallest of the Higos, the delectable *Ō ZORA* rarely exceeds 6 cm (2½ in) in diameter, but has remained a favourite because of its charming combination of pale pink

petals and white stamens. The petals are six in number, the stamen count 120.

OSAKAZUKI (see DEWATAIRIN)

OSARAKU

(syn: *Perhaps!, Pleasure of Longevity*) Perhaps the most dignified of flowers? The suggestion was implicit in the original name of this beautiful Higo, one of the largest in cultivation. It is medium in size, tinted a clear soft pink, with 120 pale gold stamens. The count of the irregularly fluted and rippled petals varies between six and seven.

PERHAPS! (see OSARAKU)

PHOSPHORESCENT FIRE (see SHIRA NUHI)

PINK PALACE (see GŌSHŌ ZAKURA)

PLEASURE OF LONGEVITY (see OSARAKU)

PORT OF THE RISING SUN
(see ASAHI NO MINATO)

RED APRICOT BLOSSOM (see KŌBAI)

REIHO

(syn: *Gorgeous Firebird*) A recent development, this enormous pure white Higo is a sport from *Ō ASŌ*, which has already been described. Like the flower from which it sprang, the blooms may be 12 cm (4¾ in) across.

ROYAL DECORATION (see ICHU)

SAKURA GARI

(syn: *Cherry Viewing*) Gayest time of the year in Japan's calendar, the season of cherry-blossom viewing is suggested by this brilliant Higo. Six or seven petals of vivid cherry-blossom pink fade to white as they meet 140 golden stamens and summon up spring festivals in the mind's eye. The plant has particularly large leaves, and flowers are a full 10 cm (4 in) in diameter.

SAKURA TSUKASA

(syn: *Lord of the Cherries*) A warm cherry-pink deepening a shade or two towards the rippled petal edges, sets apart the spectacular *SAKURA TSUKASA*, 'Lord of the Cherries'. Six petals, and 100 gold-tipped white stamens complete the picture.

SCARLET SKIRTS (see HI NO HAKAMA)

SCENT OF SUNSET (see AKATSUKI NO KAORI)

SCENTED STORM (see NIOI FUBUKI)

SCREEN OF APRICOT BLOSSOM
(see UME GAKI)

SHIN ONOME

(syn: *Sunrise Sky*) The vivid effect of a dawn

SHIRA NUHI 不知火

SHOKKŌ NISHIKI 蜀紅錦

SHŌWA NO HIKARI 昭和の光

TAKASAGO 高砂

Higos

sky is counterfeited in this deep rose-pink flower streaked with scarlet. 10 cm (4 in) in diameter, its spectacular display includes 200 flared pink stamens.

SHIN TSUKASA
(syn: *Crown Prince*) Vibrant crimson-pink is the best description of this dramatic 11 cm (4½ in) bloom, in which the petal colour is completed by a mass of 140 pale red stamens, tipped with gold. The flower petals are deeply reflexed, and the plant is a popular bonsai subject.

SHINING SUN (see KIYŌ)

SHIRA NUHI
(syn: *Phosphorescent Fire*) The colour of this popular Higo variety is hard to describe. Overall a vivid scarlet, it has a curious overlay of frosty pink iridescence, reminding Kumamoto camellia lovers of the phosphorescent lights seen off the seacoast on summer nights. Occasionally, this phosphorescence develops into paler streaks in the flower. Medium in size, it has six or seven petals and 130 flared stamens, sometimes including petaloids.

SHIRA TAKA (see HAKUTAKA)

SHIRA YUKI
(syn: *Snow White*) Second in popularity to the variety *FUJI*, this early-blooming Higo is frosty white with eight rippled petals and 100 dark-tipped white stamens. It is used in the garden and as a bonsai.

SHOKKŌ NISHIKI
(syn: *Brocade of Ancient China*) A rare semi-double type among the Higos, *SHOKKŌ NISHIKI* has a unique colouring. The basic faded crimson of the petals is broken by waves of white in a distinctly moiré effect, reminiscent of the patterns in a rich silk brocade. The medium-sized blooms may have 14 petals and from 100 to 150 white stamens. They appear mid season.

SHŌWA NO HIKARI
(syn: *Glory of Showa*) A truly spectacular modern Higo, *Glory of Showa* has a basically elliptical shape, each rich strawberry-pink bloom lavishly streaked with glowing crimson. There are six petals (occasionally cream-edged) and 200 white stamens which may include petaloids.

SNOW WHITE (see SHIRA YUKI)

SOYO KAZE
(syn: *Gentle Breeze*) A medium-sized Higo of delicate colouring, this quaint flower has been named for the gentle breezes of the Kumamoto coast. Seven or eight light pink petals and a burst of 150 white stamens add up to a perfectly charming flower.

TENJU 丹質

SUISHŌ HAKU
(syn: *Crystal Pure*) Clearest white both in petals and stamens, the delicate *SUISHŌ HAKU* is a welcome addition to the range of white Higo camellias.

SUN, MOON AND STARS
(see JITSU GETSU SEI)

SUNRISE SKY (see SHIN ONOME)

TAI HAI (see DEWATAIRIN)

TAIHEI RAKU (see DEWATAIRIN)

TAKASAGO
Reflexed petals of soft mauve-pink are the most outstanding feature of the Higo cultivar *TAKASAGO*. Stamens are gold and project in a mass, rather than flaring widely. It is an early bloomer with medium to large flowers.

TEN THOUSAND YEARS OF HAPPINESS
(see MANZAI RAKU)

TENJU
(syn: *Lifespan*) A unique shade of raspberry-pink sets apart *TENJU*, although it also has other outstanding features such as reflexed petals and more than 100 widely-flaring pale pink stamens and petaloids. Flowers mid season.

UME GAKI
(syn: *Screen of Apricot Blossom*) The soft crimson colouring of a popular variety of Japanese apricot blossom has inspired the name of this colourful Higo in which a starburst of 150 pale red stamens are surrounded by seven deeper petals. Flowers may be 12 cm (4¾ in) wide, foliage is also large.

VAULT OF HEAVEN (see Ō ZORA)

WHITE CRANE (see HAKU TSURU)

WHITE HAWK (see HAKUTAKA)

WISHING FOR THE STARS
(see MIYAKO OSARAKU)

YAMATO NISHIKI
(syn: *Brocade of Old Japan*) The rich brocades of Japan's past are suggested by this radiant bloom, perhaps the largest of the patterned Higos. 11 cm (4½ in) white flowers are irregularly shaped, streaked in pink and red, and feature a widely flared centre of 200 or more gold-tipped white stamens. It is a parent of *KUNI NO HIKARI* and *SHOWA NO HIKARI*.

YAMATO NISHIKI 日本錦

THE RETICULATA CAMELLIAS

Including hybrids with reticulata parentage

An introduction by Thomas J. Savige

'Spring arrives early in the first month of the year in Yunnan,
The camellia trees are in full bloom,
Their beauty surpasses that of the apricot and peach flowers
and decorates the gardens and makes them like red-cloud islands.'
                                    YANG SHEN, Ming Dynasty.

The province of Yunnan lies across the Tropic of Cancer in western China, at altitudes mostly over 1,000 metres (3,300 feet).

Known variously as the Land of Eternal Spring, and Kingdom of the Flowers, it is renowned for the wealth of its plant life. Here are found, in their natural habitat, a wide range of *Magnolias, Rhododendrons, Peonies, Chrysanthemums, Primula, Liliums, Prunus, Clematis* and many other plants long familiar in Western gardens. There are also over 40 species of the genus *Camellia*, many unknown as living plants beyond China.

Scattered throughout the remaining natural forests from Kunming to the mountainous Santai Shan, and across to Tali and Likiang, where the great mountain ridges of Nu Shan and Yun Ling Shan separate the headwaters of the Salween, Mekong and Yangtze Rivers, *Camellia reticulata* can be found in all its glory, at altitudes of up to 3,500 metres (10,500 feet). It exists in the wild in scattered stands, and as isolated specimens, some of them hundreds of years old and up to 20 metres (65 feet) in height.

Because of the unusual beauty of its blooms, selected plants of *Camellia reticulata* have been grown in China for many hundreds of years. Originally treasured by Buddhist monks in their monastery gardens, they also became popular among the people, and the wealthy used them as gifts of great prestige for weddings, birthdays, and particularly the New Year, which is their flowering time in Yunnan.

The earliest record of these camellias in China is the *Cha Hua Pu*, a listing of 72 varieties by Chao Pi, a Chinese naturalist of the early eleventh century. They were particularly popular during the Ming period, when they had already been cultivated for over 500 years. It was recorded in the *Ching Tai Tu Ch'ing*: 'There is a camellia from Chou Nan, at the entrance to the temple of the Heavenly King. It blooms in the winter months and its flowers are three colours: pink, vermilion and pure white interspersed. As the blooms wither they do not fall to the ground. The people believe it to be a deity and dare not pluck it.'

In the *Yunnan T'ung Tse* it is stated: 'The camellias of Yunnan are the rarest flowers in the world'. The *Yu Chuan T'eng Mei* of the Ming Dynasty tells that these camellias had ten distinguishing characteristics and that 100 poems had been written about them.

The Chinese names for this species of camellia are: *NAN SHAN CHA* or *Southern Mountain Camellia*, and *SHAN CHA HWA* or *Mountain Camellia of China*. It is the floral emblem of Yunnan.

Over the centuries, the plants having the most beautiful flowers were selected and propagated, often becoming family treasures, and were given poetic names such as *Nine Hearts and Eighteen Petals, Precious Pearl,*

Mr Savige is, at the time of writing, President of the International Camellia Society. He lives in Wirlinga, NSW.

Opposite: The beautiful reticulata known as SONGZILIN (Pine Cone) *was brought from China by plant collector Robert Fortune in 1847, and is commonly sold under his name. New Zealand hybridist Colonel Tom Durrant photographed this magnificent specimen in his garden at Tirau.*

Below: Probably the earliest picture of a reticulata painted outside China, this painting from the Chinka Zufu *illustrates a variety known to the Japanese as* NANKIN, *suggesting that it did come from southern China.*

Purple Gown and *Butterfly Wings*. Sometimes descriptive names were applied, such as *Peony Flower, Pinecone Scales* and *Chrysanthemum Petals*; even humorous ones such as *Ape's Lips, Empty Mouth* and *The Drunken Lady Yang*.

Special flower variations were sometimes given names of their own. In the case of *ZIPAO* or *Purple Gown*, there are *White-striped Purple Gown, Gold-striped Purple Gown, Vermilion Purple Gown, Nine Hearts Purple Gown* and *Cornelian Purple Gown*. In such cases it is still not established whether these were stable sports or casual variations.

As China fell into dissolution following the Opium Wars and the breakdown of the last ruling dynasty, many monastery and private gardens were reduced to ruin. Later, continuous fighting between warlords, the Kuomintang, Japanese and Communist armies left little time for attention to horticultural matters. During these years, many of the old forms of *Camellia reticulata* lost their identity and it was not until the period known to the Chinese as 'Liberation', when the Communist regime gained full control and was able to introduce stability once more, that an interest in horticulture generally, and *C. reticulata* in particular, began to regenerate.

The ancient Black Dragon Temple at Kunming, in Yunnan province, is noted for its reticulata trees. Here is BAOZHUCHA *or* Red Jewelry, *not yet known in the West. Photo Tom Savige.*

The first evidence of this was a booklet written by Fang Shu-mei, a native of P'an Lung Shan, called *A Short History of the Chan Nan Camellias*. The booklet comprises a collection of poems written about the reticulata throughout history, and gives evidence of the seventy-two varieties. From this book, it can be seen that a great proportion of the ancient names are still retained today.

Further setbacks, however, occurred with the outbreak of the Cultural Revolution, when universities, technical and research institutes and botanic gardens were closed or had their activities severely curtailed. Many temples and monasteries were abandoned due to bans on religion; so that it was not until about 1976, with the end of the Cultural Revolution, that botany and horticulture again began to flourish.

After Fang Shu-mei's publication, other Chinese horticulturists began to take an interest in collecting and identifying the old cultivars of *C. reticulata*. A Mr Y. T. Liu, manager of the Enterprise Bureau of Yunnan, built up a collection of plants in a garden near Kunming, and this became the basis of the large 'Reticulata Forest' near the Kunming Botanical Institute.

Shortly after this, Dr Te-tsun Yü became Director of this Institute on his return from the United Kingdom, where he had spent some time at the Edinburgh Botanic Gardens and Wisley. Whilst in England, he submitted a paper on the camellias of Yunnan at the Royal Horticultural Society's Magnolia and Camellia Conference, which was published in their 1950 report. In this, he identified and described eighteen different cultivars.

However, there had previously been published in the 1938 *Journal of the R.H.S.* an article by the Chinese botanist Dr Hsu-hsen Hu entitled 'Recent Progress of Botanical Exploration in China' in which he said 'Yunnan is famous for the numerous varieties of beautiful camellias. Over seventy varieties, all of great beauty, are cultivated in Yunnanfu. It is a matter not ascertained, but probably true, that there may be more than one species which contributes to the wealth of cultivated camellias in Yunnan.'

The significance of this was not followed up until 1947, as will be seen later.

It now becomes necessary to turn back in time to the export of the first *Camellia reticulata* from China.

The first record of such a camellia growing outside China is in the Japanese *Kadan Chinkin Shō*, published in 1695. The camellia was named *TŌ TSUBAKI (Chinese Camellia)* and is believed to be *Captain Rawes*, as there is no record of a fertile *C. reticulata* in Japan, and the illustration is of a semi-double flower. It was imported in the Enpō era 1673–1680.

The 'wild form' of Camellia reticulata *was collected in the south of China by Englishman George Forrest in the 1920s.*

In 1820, Captain Rawes, an East Indiaman skipper, brought to England on a voyage from China a semi-double form of *C. reticulata*. He gave this plant to a relative of horticultural bent, Thomas Carey Palmer. In 1826 it flowered for the first time in Palmer's glasshouse at Bromley, Kent. In 1824, a second plant was imported by John Dampier Parks, who had been in China collecting for the London Horticultural Society. It was from a flower of this plant that botanist John Lindley described and named the species. It is strange in retrospect that the type specimen of a species should be a most anomalous garden form, so that the wild form, when eventually found, was designated *forma simplex*.

The second cultivar eventually became known as *Captain Rawes*, and proved to be a highly sterile triploid. Recent research has established the possibility that the first specimen of *C. reticulata* (that introduced by Captain Rawes) may be a different cultivar from the Parks introduction and fertile, and may still exist in some old European collections. These early plants almost certainly came from the Canton flower markets as this area was, and still is, one of the great trading ports of China, and also closest to Yunnan.

About 1846, the plant collector Robert Fortune returned from China with a collection of plants which included a deep pink reticulata of formal double shape. Because of its difference from the type, it was originally called *C. reticulata Var. Flore-Pleno*, but was later renamed *Robert Fortune* in honour of its 'discoverer'.

In the 1920s another plant collector, George Forrest, collected botanical specimens and seed in the Chinese provinces of Yunnan and Sichuan. Amongst the plants grown from this seed by J. C. Williams of Cornwall, were some recognised as the wild forms of *C. reticulata*, and these were figured and described in *Curtis's Botanical Magazine* t.9397, 1935.

In 1944, Dr Walter Lammerts, while at the University of California, alerted by reading Dr Hu's article in the 1938 *R.H.S. Journal*, wrote to him. Dr Hu referred him to Professor Yü at Kunming, to whom he wrote in 1948. In the meantime, Lammerts had joined the research staff at Rancho del Descanso Nursery (now Descanso Gardens) at La Cañada, California.

At last, in early 1948, he received a reply from the Kunming botanist, Professor T. Tsai, to the effect that about twenty different cultivars of reticulata were available. Twenty plants were imported into America,

Captain Rawes *was the first reticulata seen in the West. It flowered in 1826, five years after its importation. Here is a contemporary impression of it from an old French print.*

Camellia reticulata

DAGUIYE 大桂叶

MAYE DIECHI 麻叶蝶翅

Top: DAGUIYE (Large Osmanthus Leaf) *was imported by Colonel Durrant of New Zealand in 1964.*

Above: MAYE DIECHI (Reticulate-leaf Butterfly) *was a 1949 reticulata import. In the West, it was named for its originator* Professor Tsai, *of the Kunming Botanical Institute.*

Below: Buddha *is a Chinese reticulata hybrid, but without a Chinese name. It first flowered in the United States.*

of which fifteen survived. Early in 1949 Walter Hazlewood, a well-known Australian nurseryman, imported six plants but because they were heavily virus-infested, he had them destroyed. In this same year, Ralph Peer of Los Angeles also imported twenty plants by air express, of which only three survived. However, two of the survivors were of varieties lost by Dr Lammerts. Descanso imported further scions and another batch of plants, finally resulting in fourteen different new cultivars being available in the West.

These original fourteen cultivars were:

1. *SONGZILIN* or *Pine Cone*. Since distributed as *Pagoda*, identical with *Robert Fortune*.
2. *JUBAN* or *Chrysanthemum Petals*. This was distributed under an earlier transliteration as *TSUEBAN*.
3. *ZIPAO* or *Purple Gown*, as it is known in the West.
4. *DAYINHONG* or *Great Spinel Pink*. Released under the synonym *Shot Silk*.
5. *LIUYE YINHONG* or *Willow-Leaf Spinel Pink*. Released in America as *Willow Wand*.
6. *XIAOGUIYE* or *Small Osmanthus Leaf*. Sold in the West as *Osmanthus Leaf*, although most plants distributed under this name have turned out to be *Willow Wand*.
7. *DATAOHONG* or *Large Peach Red* was renamed *Crimson Robe* for Western consumption.
8. *MUDAN CHA* or *Tree Peony Camellia*. This retained its Chinese name under the earlier transliteration, *MOUTANCHA*.
9. *HOUYE DIECHI* or *Thick-Leaf Butterfly Wings* was abbreviated to *Butterfly Wings*.
10. *MAYE DIECHI* or *Reticulate-Leaf Butterfly*, also called *DIECHI MUDAN* or *Butterfly Peony*. As this was a seedling raised by Professor Tsai, it was given his name in the West.
11. *DALI CHA* or *Dali Camellia*. As Dali or Tali is a place name, it is known as *Tali Queen*.
12. *DAMANAO* or *Large Cornelian* became known simply as *Cornelian*. It is one of the rare variegated forms of the Yunnan reticulatas.
13. *BUDDHA*. This new seedling from Kunming had never received a Chinese name, and was given the name *BUDDHA* in the United States.
14. *CONFUCIUS*. This also was an unnamed seedling from Kunming.

For a considerable time after these importations, it was thought that twenty different cultivars were included, until it was established that some were duplicates, incorrectly identified. For example, the large red and white variegated cultivar *Cornelian (DAMANAO)* was also erroneously distributed as *Lion Head (SHIZITOU)* and *Chang's Temple (ZHANGJIA CHA)*. The true cultivars of these names were later introduced by Colonel Tom Durrant of New Zealand.

Ralph Peer in 1952 imported another sixty-five plants which were distributed to the Royal Horticultural Society in England, Huntington Gardens of California and the Melbourne Botanic Gardens. In 1957 he also sent a set of plants to Colonel Durrant, awakening his interest in their tangled nomenclature. In 1964, in an endeavour to clear this up, Colonel Durrant personally imported twenty-eight plants in fourteen varieties from Kunming. From these he was able to dispel the nomenclature confusion and establish a further five cultivars.

The five new forms established by Colonel Durrant were:

15. *DAGUIYE* or *Large Osmanthus Leaf*.
16. *ZAOTAOHONG* or *Early Peach Red*, mostly known as *Early Crimson*.
17. *ZHANGJIA CHA* or *Chang's Family Camellia*. In the previous importation, *DAMANAO* had been incorrectly distributed as this camellia under the name *Chang's Temple*, and this now became the synonym of the true variety.
18. *SHIZITOU* or *Lion Head*. From the previous importation, *DAMANAO* was also incorrectly distributed as this cultivar, of

which it is a variegated form. The self-coloured cultivar now retains the synonym *Lion Head*.

19. *ZAO MUDAN* or *Early Peony*.

Then, in 1970, the late Dr Kinhachi Ikeda of Japan made contact with Professor T.T. Yü, now of the Beijing University, and with Dr Wu Chen-Yu, the present Director of Kunming Botanical Institute. By correspondence and the importation of plants from China, he established fifty-four varietal names of Kunming reticulátas. Later he brought out from China another twelve cultivars.

These 12 reticulatas are not in general distribution, but they are:

20. *MEIHONG GUIYE* or *Carmine Osmanthus Leaf*.
21. *XIGUIYE* or *Willow-Leaf Large Osmanthus*.
22. *PINBAN DALI CHA* or *Flat-Petal Tali Camellia*.
23. *SONGZIKE* or *Pine Cone Shell*.
24. *HENTIANGAO* or *Envious of Heaven's Height*, also called *The Dwarf* and *Dwarf Rose*.
25. *MANAO JUBAN* or *Cornelian Chrysanthemum Petal*.
26. *KUNMING CHUN* or *Kunming Spring*.
27. *FENHONG DIECHI* or *Pink Butterfly Wings*.
28. *PINHONG* or *Supreme Red*, also called *YIPINHONG* or *First Class Red*.
29. *YINFEN MUDAN* or *Pink Peony*.
30. *HONGWAN CHA* or *Crimson Bowl Camellia*.
31. *YINGCHUN HONG* or *Welcome Spring Red*.

Finally, in 1979 and 1980, parties of Japanese, American and Australian horticulturists were able to visit Kunming and see these magnificent plants in their country of origin. It was learned there had been considerable activity by the staff of Kunming Botanical Institute in bringing together as many cultivars of *C. reticulata* as could be located, as well as some selected clones from the wild, until in all, 105 cultivars were identified. Much of the identification work was done by Xia Li-Fang, the wife of the Vice-Director, Dr Chang Ao-lo.

The Institute is about to publish an illustrated book on these 105 reticulatas which, it is hoped, will be the definitive work on the reticulatas of Yunnan. Most of the balance of the 105 cultivars are becoming available to the Western world as, in 1979, shipments of scions and plants of sixty-four cultivars were received by Dr Bartholomew, Curator of the Botanic Gardens of the University of California, including a further twenty clones not previously imported. However, in all these camellias, the cultivar *Captain Rawes* has never been relocated in China, and has recently been returned to its country of origin!

The new reticulatas published to date from the group imported by Dr Bartholomew are:

32. *DALI DIECHI* or *Tali Butterfly Wings*.
33. *JINGAN CHA* or *Tsingan Camellia*.
34. *JINPAOHONG* or *Brocade-Gown Red*.
35. *JINRUI FURONG* or *Golden Stamen Hibiscus*.
36. *LUANYE YINHONG* or *Ovate-Leaf Spinel Pink*.
37. *MAYE TAOHONG* or *Reticulate-Leaf Crimson*.
38. *SAI TAOHONG* or *Superior Crimson*.
39. *YUDAIHONG* or *Red with a Jade Belt*.
40. *ZUIJIAOHONG* or *Intoxicatingly Charming Red*.
41. *DANDAHONG* or *Pale Red*.
42. *JINXIN BAOZHU* or *Golden Heart Jewelry*.
43. *XIAOYE MUDAN* or *Small Leaf Peony*.
44. *SAI MUDAN* or *Superior Peony*.

This makes a total of forty-four different cultivars out of the 105 listed by the Kunming Botanical Institute.

One of the best-known camellias in Kunming is the beautiful *BAOZHU CHA* or *Red Jewelry*, formerly known as *Noble Pearl*. The true cultivar has not yet bloomed outside China, though it is now in propagation. Another famous camellia is *TONGZIMIAN* or *Baby Face*, an almost white reticulata which is also not yet available in the West.

The impact of the reticulata cultivars, particularly in America, Australia and New Zealand, has been considerable. Immediate attempts at

The upright petals and bold stamens of Francie L. *are typical of many modern reticulata hybrids.*

Rob Roy *is an interesting hybrid, crossing* reticulata DAYINHONG (Shot Silk) *with the earlier Williamsii hybrid,* X J. C. Williams.

Fluted Orchid *was one of the first American hybrids of* C. reticulata, *crossing* DATAOHONG (Crimson Robe) *with* C. Saluenensis. *This delicate bloom was originated in 1960.*

The dazzling reticulata hybrid Brilliant Butterfly *was originated in New Zealand. Its flat, open flowers are the result of crossing the wild reticulata with* HOUYE DIECHI.

hybridisation were made, starting with Dr Lammerts using pollen from some of the blooms which were open on receipt of the first shipment. In 1943, 1949 and 1950 he made a large number of crosses onto plants of *C. japonica*. Only a limited number of seeds matured, and a percentage of these lacked viability. The developing seedlings seemed to show little evidence of hybridity and appeared very similar to their seed parent *C. japonica*. The programme was dropped and no further work was done until David Feathers of Lafayette, California began to make the same crosses.

He was able to demonstrate that the first generation cross onto *C. japonica* is very similar to the seed parent. Hybridisers in America, New Zealand and Australia were soon active and crosses were made between *C. reticulata* and a number of other camellia species and hybrids, such as *C. saluenensis, C. X Williamsii, C. sasanqua, C. pitardii, C. granthamiana* and *C. fraterna*, so that a flood of magnificent new hybrids has become available around the world. In general, the most spectacular results have been from the cross *C. reticulata X C. japonica*. This obvious cross would never have been possible in Yunnan, as *C. japonica* is not a native of China and only a very few double varieties such as *Alba Plena* are grown there, and these of doubtful fertility.

There has been considerable discussion among taxonomists on the origin of the Yunnan reticulatas. Using scientific methods of investigation, botanists have developed the theory that these camellias are the result of ancient hybridisation, or the infusion of more than one species into a base taxon.

Taxonomical investigations confirm what is quite obvious to the naked eye, that there is considerable variation between the cultivars. Compare the enormous, drooping and often variegated foliage of *DAMANAO (Cornelian)* with the slender, more densely-grouped leaves of *LIUYE YINHONG (Willow Wand)*.

Undoubtedly the possibility exists that these large, elaborately flowered, selected forms are caused by some hybridity as, in the forests, the wild form reticulata grows in association with other species, in particular *C. pitardii var. Yunnanica, C. saluenensis* and *C. semiserrata*, with all of which it is compatible.

The Yunnan reticulatas and their hybrids display blooms of a splendour and size rarely seen in any other flower. Their colouring is rich and often iridescent, and with a flowering period considerably longer than that of most other species, at least on mature plants. Individual blooms may expand for several days after opening, and last for weeks.

Reticulatas in general require more care in planting and placement than other camellia species. They prefer a lighter, better drained soil. In areas of deep, well-drained soils such as the pumice of the North Island of New Zealand, where their root penetration is 3 metres (10 feet) or more, they develop into large, splendidly foliaged plants. However, in shallower soils and in containers, because of their reduced root systems and sparse foliage, their requirements of moisture and fertiliser are less. A single mulch of cow manure in spring can be sufficient.

Unlike the japonicas, they do not enjoy heavy shade, and should be placed where they are exposed to full sunlight for at least part of the day. This may cause young spring foliage to droop, but that is unimportant provided the plant is sheltered from strong wind. The leaves will quickly recover in the evening.

Reticulata foliage seems particularly attractive to caterpillars and should be sprayed as a protection when the young leaves are developing. This spring growth is sometimes accompanied by a heavy fall of older leaves, which again is quite natural, and no cause for alarm. Additional watering will make no difference whatever, and is inadvisable.

Reticulatas are above all specimen plants, and should be used as such; their strong, open growth and heavy, dull foliage make them less suitable than japonicas where a windbreak or dense foliage cover is needed. Allow for plenty of future space, both vertical and lateral, at planting time, and do not try to reduce their bulk by excess pruning. This, by the way, should only be done towards the end of the flowering season.

One final note on the Chinese names of the reticulatas, and their spelling in English: the cultivar names used above, and in the dictionary that follows, are transliterated directly from the Chinese, and follow the phonetic transcription of Chinese characters by the official *Hanyupinyin* system, mostly known simply as 'Pinyin'.

In pronouncing Pinyin, it must be remembered that while this is a phonetic rendering of the Chinese name in Roman letters, the letters do not always have the same value as in English. For instance:

X is pronounced as the 'sh' in she;
Q is pronounced as the 'ch' in cheer;
R is pronounced as the 's' in leisure;
Z is pronounced as the 'ds' in reads;
C is pronounced as the 'ts' in hats.

Because of the difficulty Westerners have in pronouncing the Chinese names at all, the use of English synonyms has become widespread in most cases; usually incorporating an allusion to the Chinese name. For example, the two characters for *Purple Gown, ZI PAO*, mean just that, while *JU BAN* translates directly as *Chrysanthemum Petals.*

In the case of *MUDAN CHA*, the first two characters *MU DAN* refer to the tree peony, and *CHA* is camellia. The translation is *Peony Camellia.* On the other hand, in the case of *DATAOHONG*, the first character translates as large, the second as peach, and the last as red. So, *Large Peach Red* — but the Western synonym is *Crimson Robe*! The Chinese variety *HENTIANGAO* translates as *HEN* — hate or regret, *TIAN* — sky, *GAO* — high. Poetically, *Envious of Heaven's Height*, which is just another way of saying *The Dwarf*, its usual Western name.

The fruit of Camellia reticulata *are the size of a golf ball, and have a furry texture.*

CULTIVARS OF CAMELLIA RETICULATA
and hybrids with reticulata parentage

One of the showiest of modern reticulata hybrids, Aztec *was released in 1971.*

In this dictionary section, the Kunming reticulatas are included with the modern Western hybrids in a single, alphabetical listing. Kunming cultivars are described under their priority Pinyin Chinese names, but with cross references from their English synonyms and translations, and also from the earlier Wade-Giles system transliterations for readers more familiar with those old-style names from long usage. All Wade-Giles spellings are identified by the letters 'WG'. The date following each heading is the date of introduction in the West of the particular cultivar or hybrid.

At the top right hand of each entry is an indication of the plant's origin, *Yunnan reticulata* (imported); *Seedling* (Raised from a seedling of an imported reticulata, male parent unknown); *X reticulata hybrid* (Cross between a reticulata and another, different species); *Reticulata cross* (Cross between two named varieties of reticulata).

A number of the more recent reticulata imports listed in Mr Savige's introduction have not been included or described in the dictionary listing that follows, for several reasons. (1) They are not included in the official Chinese list of 105 known reticulata varieties. (2) Publication of incorrect or doubtful names with descriptions might later constitute a valid publication, leading to further confusion in nomenclature.

The Chinese government has announced that the Pinyin system shall be used in future, as standard, so that the Chinese transliterated names should finally be stabilised in this form.

BAOZHU CHA 宝珠茶

BUDDHA

Reticulatas

ARBUTUS GUM 1971
X reticulata hybrid

Not sufficiently unique either in colour or form to become an overnight sensation, the American reticulata hybrid *Arbutus Gum* has nevertheless charmed many growers since its introduction by Californian Frank Maitland. A hybrid of un-specified reticulata and japonica parents, it forms a medium-sized, upright-growing plant of aver-age growth, blooming in mid season. The large semi-double flowers vary from light to deep pink, and have upright petals.

ARCH OF TRIUMPH 1970
Seedling

The first of many listed reticulata varieties from the garden of Californian hybridist David L. Feathers, *Arch of Triumph* is a seedling of the wild reticulata form. It is a vigorous bushy plant, bearing very large, loose informal double blooms that shade from carmine-rose to wine-red. They feature the upright 'rabbit-eared' petals so be-loved of American camellia growers.

AZTEC 1971
X reticulata hybrid

1971 was a vintage year for camellia lovers, for it saw the introduction of the evocatively named *Aztec*. Its enormous blooms are a barbaric pink flushed with blood-red. They are semi-double, with irregular waved petals revealing a tantalising glimpse of rich gold stamens. California's Howard Asper was the hybridiser, using reticulata *DATAOHONG (Crimson Robe)* and japonica *Lotus*. Aztec blooms right through the season. (Photo p. 149)

BABY FACE (see TONGZIMIAN)

BAOZHU CHA (Vermilion Jewelry Camellia) 1980
Yunnan reticulata

(syn: *Jewelry, Noble Pearl, PAOCHUCHA* [WG], *Red Jewelry*) The true Yunnan variety known as *Red Jewelry* is at last revealed in our illus-tration, photographed on a visit to Yunnan by Tom Savige in early 1980. An unbelievably jewel-like red with overall iridescence, it is a large flower with deeply waved upright petals, and narrow foliage with pronounced edge ser-ration. It should be available to Western enthusi-asts within a few years.

BERNADETTE KARSTEN 1967
X reticulata hybrid

Introduced by Frank Maitland of Sylmar, California, the lovely *Bernadette Karsten* is the result of crossing unspecified reticulata and japonica varieties. The very large, carmine-pink flowers are semi-double, appearing mid season on a bush of strong upright growth.

BRIAN VARIEGATED 1958
X reticulata hybrid

Working from a favourite cross of *C. saluenensis* X *Captain Rawes*, New Zealander Brian Doak produced the charming semi-double hybrid

Brian, with medium-sized pale cyclamen-pink blooms on a plant of compact growth. From this subsequently sported *Brian Variegated*, in which the petals are occasionally flecked with pure white. It blooms mid to late season.

BRILLIANT BUTTERFLY 1969

X reticulata hybrid

After crossing the wild form of *C. reticulata* with its cultivar *HOUYE DIECHI (Butterfly Wings)*, Dr Jane Crisp of Tirau, New Zealand was rewarded with this delightful hybrid. An average grower of distinctively bushy habit, it bears large semi-double blooms of a vivid rose-red. The thick textured petals have deeply waved margins. (Photo p. 148)

BUDDHA 1948

X reticulata hybrid

One of the earliest reticulata hybrids to be introduced, and still among the most popular, *Buddha* bloomed for the first time in the West at California's famous Descanso Gardens. It is a hybrid between a Chinese reticulata variety and *C. pitardii Yunnanica*. The very large semi-double blooms are a brilliant rose-pink, fading to pale cyclamen. The petals are irregularly waved, and display a magnificent boss of gold stamens. Growth is vigorous and upright. (See also photo p. 146)

BUTTERFLY PEONY (see MAYE DIECHI)

BUTTERFLY WINGS (see HOUYE DIECHI)

CAMERON COOPER 1976

X reticulata hybrid

A recent introduction from Californian amateur Frank Pursel, *Cameron Cooper* is a cross between reticulata *DAMANAO (Cornelian)* and japonica *Mrs D. W. Davis*. A plant of dense upright growth, its enormous blooms vary from rose form double to peony form, their petals folded and swirled. *Cameron Cooper* is tinted a rich old rose with deep orchid tonings at petal tips.

CANADIAN CAPERS 1977

X reticulata hybrid

Developed by Vi Shuey of Temple City, California, the recent introduction *Canadian Capers* crosses an unnamed reticulata with the Chinese species *C. pitardii*. A plant of extremely vigorous open growth, it seems destined to achieve world popularity. The medium-sized semi-double flowers are tinted a light mauve-pink, their wide-tipped petals deeply notched. *Canadian Capers* is a fine, non-temperamental garden cultivar, flowering mid to late season.

CAPTAIN RAWES 1820

The very first reticulata to dazzle the eyes of Western gardeners, *Captain Rawes* was named for the East India Captain who brought it from Canton in 1820. As its blooms are sterile, that one plant became graft-parent to the enormous trees one still sees in many old gardens. Blooming late in the season, *Captain Rawes* bears large

CAMERON COOPER

CANADIAN CAPERS

CAPTAIN RAWES

semi-double blooms of carmine rose-pink. (See also photo p. 145)

CARL TOURJE 1960
X reticulata hybrid
Bred at the magnificent Huntington Camellia Gardens of San Marino, California, cultivar *Carl Tourje* is a cross between *C. pitardii Var. Yunnanica* and the reticulata *DAMANAO (Cornelian)*. A plant with strong, upright and open growth, it produces large, mid season semi-double blooms with deeply waved petals. These are soft pink with shadings of cyclamen.

CARMINE OSMANTHUS LEAF
(see MEIHONG GUIYE)

CHANGCHIACHA (WG) (see ZHANGJIA CHA)

CHANG'S FAMILY CAMELLIA
(see ZHANGJIA CHA)

CHANG'S TEMPLE (see ZHANGJIA CHA)

CHERRY GLOW 1970
Seedling
A splendid seedling from the Yunnan reticulata *DATAOHONG (Crimson Robe)*, *Cherry Glow* was introduced by Australian grower Edgar Sebire. Open and upright in growth, it blooms mid season like its female parent, producing very large loose peony form blooms of glowing cherry-red. A stunning garden variety.

CHINA LADY 1968
X reticulata hybrid
A most unusual cross between reticulata *Buddha* and the sensational *C. granthamiana* from Hong Kong (see chapter on camellia species), *China Lady* was introduced by California's Nuccio Nurseries. A strong grower with beautifully marked narrow foliage, it bears very large semi-double blooms of rich orchid-pink, shaded cyclamen. The petals are quite irregular.

CHINMEIHUNGKUEIYEH (WG)
(see MEIHONG GUIYE)

CHRYSANTHEMUM PETALS (see JUBAN)

CONFUCIUS 1948
X reticulata hybrid
A Chinese reticulata hybrid imported by Descanso Gardens of California, *Confucius* is claimed to be the result of a reticulata crossed with *C. pitardii Var. Yunnanica*. A medium-sized plant of compact growth and dark pointed foliage, it bears slender cyclamen-pink buds which open to large semi-double blooms of orchid-pink. These have fluted petals, and often mixed stamens and petaloids. It had no Chinese name.

CORNELIAN (see DAMANAO)

CORNELIAN CHRYSANTHEMUM PETAL
(see MANAO JUBAN)

CONFUCIUS

DALI CHA   大哩茶

CORNELIAN ROSE (see MANAO JUBAN)

CRIMSON BOWL CAMELLIA
(see HONGWAN CHA)

CRIMSON OSMANTHUS LEAF
(see MEIHONG GUIYE)

CRIMSON ROBE (see DATAOHONG)

DAGUIYE (Large Osmanthus Leaf) 1969
Yunnan reticulata
(syn: *TAKUEIYEH* [WG]) Another remarkable
Yunnan reticulata, though not one commonly
grown in the West, *DAGUIYE* (as the Chinese
call it) is a large, deep carmine bloom of semi-
double to peony form, flowering mid to late
season. The foliage is frequently variegated in
cream. (Photo p. 146)

DALI CHA (Tali Camellia) 1948
Yunnan reticulata
(syn: *Queen of Tali, Tali Queen, TALICHA*
[WG]) Each of the Yunnan reticulatas seems more
remarkable than the last, and *DALI CHA* is no
exception. An extraordinary, very large flower
with irregularly-shaped petals, it may vary from
turkey-red to deep pink. Classed as a semi-
double, it features textured outer petals and wavy
inner petals intermixed with golden stamens.
Growth is medium and upright, and the flowers
appear mid season.

DAMANAO (Large Cornelian) 1948
Yunnan reticulata
(syn: *Cornelian, Large Agate, TAMANAO*
[WG]) One of the most gorgeous Yunnan
reticulatas, *DAMANAO* was imported to
California in 1948, and subsequently propagated
world-wide. A plant of fast growth and large
drooping leaves, often heavily marked in yellow,
it was also incorrectly distributed under the
names *Chang's Temple* and *Lion Head* — synonyms belonging to two other cultivars. The very
large informal double blooms are glowing red to
deep pink, marbled white. The petals are fluted
and crinkled, standing high above the central
stamens to give an almost ball-shaped bloom.
Indeed a jewel of a flower.

DATAOHONG (Large Peach Red) 1948
Yunnan reticulata
(syn: *Crimson Robe, Great Peach Bloom,
TATAOHUNG* [WG]) Parent of many modern
hybrids, *DATAOHONG* was imported direct to
California from Yunnan in 1948 by Descanso
Gardens and Ralph Peer. A splendid plant of
preading open habit, it bears large reticulated
foliage, often strongly margined in cream and
yellow. The very large semi-double blooms are
coloured bright carmine-red, and the wavy crêpe-
textured petals surround a boss of golden
stamens.

DAYINHONG (Great Spinel Pink) 1948
Yunnan reticulata

DAMANAO   大玛瑙

Reticulatas

(syn: *Great Shot Silk, Shot Silk, TAYINHUNG* [WG]) Another of the 1948 wave of reticulata imports from China, *DAYINHONG* (or *Shot Silk*, as it is commonly known) seems one of the loveliest. A large semi-double bloom with petals loosely waved, it is tinted a brilliant spinel-pink with faded patches. Early blooming, *DAYINHONG* is a strong grower.

DICK GOODSON 1979
X reticulata hybrid
A brand new introduction from Oakland hybridist Frank Pursel, the reticulata hybrid *Dick Goodson* will be worth waiting for when it is distributed. It is a plant of excellent spreading growth, with enormous glossy foliage and flowers to match. They are semi-double, light red with occasional paler markings, and have a wonderfully heavy texture in the deeply fluted, high-standing petals.

DIECHI MUDAN (see MAYE DIECHI)

DR CLIFFORD PARKS 1971
X reticulata hybrid
Released by Dr Clifford Parks of the Los Angeles State and County Arboretum at Arcadia, and named for himself, this stunning reticulata hybrid is unusual both in form and colour. The very large semi-double blooms appear in different styles on the same plant. They may be loose peony form, full peony form or even anemone form, and they are coloured a brilliant flame-red with an almost orange iridescence. They bloom mid season on a plant bursting with hybrid vigour. A cross between reticulata *DATAOHONG (Crimson Robe)* and japonica *Kramer's Supreme*, it inherits the brilliant coloration from the latter.

DR LOUIS POLIZZI 1969
X reticulata hybrid
A release of the Tammia Nurseries in Louisiana, *Dr Louis Polizzi* is an interspecific hybrid of *C. saluenensis* and the older reticulata *Captain Rawes*. A variable, medium-sized flower of semi-double to full peony form, it is delicate orchid-pink, shaded in white. The plant is compact but vigorous, and blooms early to mid season.

DREAM GIRL 1965
X reticulata hybrid
Plant wizard Howard Asper's interspecific cross between sasanqua *NARUMIGATA* and reticulata *Buddha*, this delicate flower is one of the 'three girls' *(Dream Girl, Flower Girl, Show Girl)* which were a sensation when released in 1965. The pale satin-pink blooms (large to very large) have inherited the form of their sasanqua parent and the size of the reticulata, all on a plant of vigorous, upright growth. Sadly, like the sasanquas, they shatter badly.

DWARF ROSE (see HENTIANGAO)

EARLY CRIMSON (see ZAOTAOHONG)

EARLY PEACH RED (see ZAOTAOHONG)

EARLY PEONY (see ZAO MUDAN)

EDEN QUEEN 1973
Seedling
A chance seedling of reticulata *DAMANAO (Cornelian)* was propagated by J. J. Clark of Auckland, New Zealand to bring this unbelievably beautiful reticulata to enthusiasts worldwide. Very large and semi-double in form, it is a pure lustrous red, like an enormous artificial peony made of ruffled silk. All this on a plant of open upright growth is more than most camellia-fanciers can resist.

ELLIE RUBENSOHN 1963
Reticulata cross
Raised by Australian advertising tycoon Sim Rubensohn in 1963, this lovely flower was named for his wife. Resulting from a cross between reticulatas *DATAOHONG (Crimson Robe)* and *ZIPAO (Purple Gown)*, it is a medium-sized plant of spreading growth, with very large blooms of rosy-crimson. These have undulating petals and vary from semi-double to loose peony form.

ENVIOUS OF HEAVEN'S HEIGHT
(see HENTIANGAO)

FENHONG DIECHI (Pink Butterfly Wings) 1974
Yunnan reticulata
A Yunnan reticulata we are all waiting for and it should be available soon! *FENHONG DIECHI* is semi-double with wavy petals of 'rabbit's ear' form. It is pink and arrived in Japan in 1974.

FEN MUDAN (see YINFEN MUDAN)

FIRE CHIEF 1965
X reticulata hybrid
Here's a glorious hybrid for those who like their camellias deep glowing red! Again from hybridist Howard Asper, *Fire Chief* is the result of a cross between the japonica *Donckelarii* and reticulata *DAMANAO (Cornelian)*. Large in size, semi-double to peony form in style, *Fire Chief* blooms late season on a medium-sized plant of bushy growth. Introduced in 1965, it has a variegated form, moiréd in white.

FLAT PETAL TALI CAMELLIA
(see PINBAN DALI CHA)

FLORE PLENO (see ROBERT FORTUNE)

FLOWER GIRL 1965
X reticulata hybrid
Raised by Howard Asper, *Flower Girl* is the most stunning of blooms, with the best features of both its parents – sasanqua *NARUMIGATA* and reticulata *DAMANAO (Cornelian)*. From the first it inherits shining dark foliage of compact size and a free-flowering habit; from the latter, blooms of enormous size (13cm/5¼ in across is quite normal). These are loose, semi-double and a particularly rich pink, the colour of Thai silk. This is overlaid with a distinct cyclamen cast, glowing almost blue in shade. The flower is centred with brilliant gold stamens, and blooms over a long period. Growth is fast and tall.

FLUTED ORCHID 1960
X reticulata hybrid
A result of crossing the reticulata *DATAOHONG (Crimson Robe)* with *C. saluenensis, Fluted Orchid* is an early hybrid of delicate and unusual appearance. Medium in size, it is semi-double with deeply fluted pale pink petals, and a spectacular centre compounded of stamens and variable petaloids. It was raised by David L. Feathers in 1960. (Photo p. 148)

FORTYNINER 1969
X reticulata hybrid
California's Howard Asper was again the breeder of this outstanding informal double cultivar. A cross between reticulata *HOUYE DIECHI (Butterfly Wings)* and the darker japonica *Indian Summer*, it is a vigorous plant with bushy growth and foliage of japonica type. The large glowing red blooms are of peony form, and appear early to mid season. The foliage may sometimes be flecked with white or have a darker edge.

FRANCIE L. 1964
X reticulata hybrid
From the Nuccio Nursery at Altadena, *Francie L.* is the hybrid of reticulata *Buddha* and *C. saluenensis Var. Apple Blossom*. It is a tall, leggy grower with typical sparse reticulata foliage, flowering mid season. The very large blooms, semi-double and with delicately waved petals, are usually described as rose-pink, but I would think rose-madder was a better description as there seems to be almost a transparent red glow overlaid on the petals. *Francie L.* also has a variegated form.

GOLDEN HEART JEWELRY
(see JINXIN BAOZHU)

GOLDEN STAMEN HIBISCUS
(see JINRUI FURONG)

GRAND JURY 1962
X reticulata hybrid
A *pièce-de-resistance* from New Zealand hybridist Les Jury, his punningly named *Grand Jury* is a most unusual hybrid of *C. saluenensis* back-crossed with *X Salutation*, which is itself a cross

DATAOHONG 大桃红

DAYINHONG 大银红

DICK GOODSON

DR CLIFFORD PARKS

EDEN QUEEN

FIRE CHIEF

155

of *C. saluenensis* and reticulata *Captain Rawes*. The result is a large peony form to semi-double bloom of salmon-pink, opening mid season. The growth is open and spreading.

GREAT PEACH BLOOM (see DATAOHONG)

GREAT SHOT SILK (see DAYINHONG)

GREAT SPINEL PINK (see DAYINHONG)

HAROLD L. PAIGE 1972

X reticulata hybrid
The very large, deep rose-red blooms of *Harold L. Paige* (a cross between reticulata *DATAO-HONG* [*Crimson Robe*] and japonica *Adolphe Audusson*) have inherited the best features of both parents. They are double, with rose to peony form and ruffled petals, and peak late in the season. The size and colouring, allied to a spreading habit and vigorous growth, have made it a popular addition to the ranks of modern reticulata hybrids. It was introduced by J. Osegueda of Oakland, California, and named for the doyen of California camellians, now in his nineties.

HENTIANGAO (Envious of Heaven's Height) 1964

Yunnan reticulata
(syn: *Dwarf Rose*, *HENTIENKO* [WG], *The Dwarf*) One of the original Yunnan reticulatas imported to New Zealand in 1964, *HENTIAN-GAO* was subsequently lost. It blooms late season, with semi-double to rose form flowers in an interesting shade of light carmine, margined in white. The name is due to the dwarf size even of mature plants. The English name *The Dwarf* is a clever interpretation of the picturesque Chinese original, which means literally *Envious of Heaven's Height*. It has recently been re-imported to California and Australia, and should be available within a few years.

HENTIENKO (WG) (see HENTIANGAO)

HIGHLIGHT 1969

X reticulata hybrid
New Zealand grower Les Jury introduced this cultivar in 1969, having crossed reticulata *ZIPAO (Purple Gown)* with the species saluenensis. Vigorous, and with an open habit, it produces flowers mid to late season. They are semi-double, quite large, with brilliant rose-red wavy petals — but not sufficiently different to ensure its popularity.

HONGWAN CHA (Crimson Bowl Camellia) 1974

Yunnan reticulata
(syn: *Crimson Bowl*) A new variety from west Yunnan, *Crimson Bowl* has been propagated in Japan since 1974. It is a large, light crimson camellia of cupped form. The stamens are interspersed with a few petaloids.

FLOWER GIRL

FRANCIE L.

*HOUYE DIECHI (Thick Leaf Butterfly Wings)
1948*

Yunnan reticulata
(syn: *Butterfly Wings, HOYETIECHIH* [WG],
Thick Leaf Butterfly) Imported from China in
1948, the luscious Yunnan reticulata *HOUYE
DIECHI (Butterfly Wings)* displays a very large
semi-double bloom with deeply waved petals of
pure rose-pink. These are irregularly sized and
do perhaps resemble the wings of a horde of
brilliantly coloured butterflies. They appear mid
season on a bush of spreading, open growth.

HOWARD ASPER 1963

X reticulata hybrid
Possibly the fastest growing of all camellias (mine
shot up almost 2 m/6½ ft in a single year)
Howard Asper bursts with a vitality that gives it
also the largest known flower of any variety,
often 20 cm (8 in) and more across. The leaves
are large but rather narrow; the blooms open
from crimson buds to a beautiful deep salmon,
with upright waved petals. It is classed as an
informal double, and frequently reveals a mass
of golden stamens among the petals. *Howard
Asper* is a cross between reticulata *DAMANAO
(Cornelian)* and japonica *Coronation*, and was
named for its California breeder. It is remarkably
resistant to strong sun, and blooms mid to late
season.

HOYEHTIECHIH (WG) (see HOUYE DIECHI)

HSIAOKUEIYEH (WG) (see XIAOGUIYE)

INNOVATION 1965

X reticulata hybrid
Itself a charming innovation from Californian
hybridist David Feathers, *Innovation* has caught
many eyes with wine-red blooms of lavender
overtone. They are large and of peony form, with
a centre of twisted petals mixed with golden
stamens. The lavender toning comes from the *C.
saluenensis* X japonica hybrid *Williams' Lavender*, which was crossed with the reticulata
DATAOHONG (Crimson Robe). The plant on
which these unusual blooms appear is fast-
growing, with a slightly open habit.

INSPIRATION 1954

X reticulata hybrid
A brilliant phlox-pink cross between reticulata
and *C. saluenensis*, *Inspiration* is simply covered
in bloom mid season. Medium in size and semi-
double in form, it was a 1954 introduction by
English grower Francis Hanger.

JEAN PURSEL 1975

X reticulata hybrid
Named for the wife of northern California
hybridist Frank Pursel, this superb camellia has
won prizes everywhere since its 1975 introduction. *Jean Pursel* is a very large peony form
bloom with heavily textured petals in soft mauve-
pink. These frame a splendid centre of mauve-
pink and white petaloids swirling among golden

HOWARD ASPER

INSPIRATION

Reticulatas

JEAN PURSEL

JUBAN

stamens. Mid to late in bloom, *Jean Pursel* is a second generation hybrid of reticulatas *DATAOHONG (Crimson Robe)* and *DAMANAO (Cornelian)*, crossed with japonica *Mrs D. W. Davis.*

JEWELRY (see BAOZHU CHA)

JINGAN CHA (Tsingan Camellia) 1979
        Yunnan reticulata (syn: *TSINGANCHA* [WG] Imported by the University of California only in 1979, and to Australia in 1980, *JINGAN CHA* has not flowered in the West. It is a large red peony form bloom from the garden of the Tsingan Temple, and particularly beautiful.

JINRUI FURONG (Golden Stamen Hibiscus) 1979
        Yunnan reticulata Imported by the University of California in 1979, *JINRUI FURONG* has not yet been released to Western growers.

JINXIN BAOZHU (Golden Heart Jewelry) 1979
        Yunnan reticulata Not yet released in the West, *JINXIN BAOZHU* was imported from Yunnan in 1979 by the University of California.

JUBAN (Chrysanthemum Petals) 1948
        Yunnan reticulata (syn: *Rose Flower, TSUEBAN* [WG]) Imported jointly by the American grower Ralph Peer and California's Descanso Gardens, *JUBAN* is perhaps the smallest-flowered of the Yunnan reticulatas. The small to medium blooms are very pale carmine-pink, rose form to formal double, with notched petals. The early blooming plant on which they appear is of slender open growth.

K. O. HESTER 1972
        Seedling A seedling of the Yunnan reticulata *DALI CHA (Tali Queen) K. O. Hester* has abandoned the deep colouring of its parent in favour of a soft orchid pink. The large to very large blooms are semi-double, with tiers of lightly ruffled upstanding petals, and open mid season. This stunning camellia was named for its Californian originator and is borne freely on a plant of open upright growth.

KIRI TE KANAWA 1972
        X reticulata hybrid Appropriately named for the New Zealand soprano who rose to fame with her performance as the 'Lady of the Camellias' in Verdi's *La Traviata, Kiri Te Kanawa* is a most unusual hybrid between *C. pitardii* and reticulata *Buddha.* It is a medium-sized semi-double bloom of brilliant fuchsia-pink, introduced by Hollywood grower J. Sobeck. The flowers open early in the season on a bush of medium compact growth.

KOHINOOR 1968

Seedling

Like the previously described camellia, *KOHINOOR* is also an orchid-pink seedling, this time from reticulata variety *Buddha*. It is also a very large semi-double flower, with irregular upright petals of shimmering texture. The Indian name *Kohinoor* means 'Mountain of Light' and is quite appropriate for this introduction by Californian Ralph Peer.

KUNMING CHUN (Kunming Spring) 1970

Yunnan reticulata

A large red semi-double reticulata not yet (1981) released in the West, *KUNMING CHUN* is described as having wavy petals, and has been grown in Japan since 1970.

KUNMING SPRING (see KUNMING CHUN)

LARGE AGATE (see DAMANAO)

LARGE CORNELIAN (see DAMANAO)

LARGE OSMANTHUS LEAF (see DAGUIYE)

LARGE PEACH RED (see DATAOHONG)

LASCA BEAUTY 1973

X reticulata hybrid

Surprisingly, the apparently exotic name of this lovely hybrid turns out to be nothing to do with the colourful Asian race of the same name. It is a practical acronym for the Los Angeles State and County Arboretum, where it was introduced by Dr Clifford Parks. The result of crossing *DAMANAO (Cornelian)* with japonica *Mrs D. W. Davis*, it is a very large semi-double flower of soft pink with heavily textured petals. The blooms appear mid season on a strong-growing plant.

LEONARD MESSEL 1958

X reticulata hybrid

A most floriferous plant with bushy, spreading growth, *Leonard Messel* inherits a good measure of cold resistance from its parents, the wild form of *C. reticulata* and the *X Williamsii* hybrid *Mary Christian*. Large semi-double rose-pink flowers appear in profusion from early to late season, their petals prettily waved. This popular garden camellia was introduced by Mrs Leonard Messel of Sussex, England.

LILA NAFF 1967

Seedling

A seedling of reticulata *HOUYE DIECHI (Butterfly Wings)*, *Lila Naff* compensates for its unfortunate name (to Australian ears at least) with large blooms of incredible beauty. Averaging 12 cm (4¾ in) in diameter, these are semi-double and tinted a soft silvery-pink. The few petals are deeply waved and fluted around high central stamens. *Lila Naff*, a strong compact plant, was introduced by Louisiana's Tammia Nurseries.

K. O. HESTER

LEONARD MESSEL

Reticulatas

LION HEAD (see SHIZITOU)

LIUYEHYINHUNG (WG)
(see LIUYE YINHONG)

LIUYE YINHONG (Willowleaf Spinel Pink) 1948
Yunnan reticulata
(syn: *LIUYEHYINHUNG* [WG], *Narrow-leafed Shot Silk, Willow Wand*) *LIUYE YINHONG* or *Willow Wand* is a slender-leafed plant of strong growth. The large rose form double blooms are tinted delectable orchid-pink, and have petals of silken texture. Blooming mid season, it was imported by Californian growers in 1948.

LUANYE YINHONG (Ovate-leaf Spinel Pink) 1979
Yunnan reticulata
Imported only in 1979 by the University of California, *LUANYE YINHONG* has not yet bloomed outside its native China. It is described as being a large bowl-shaped single camellia, pink in colour.

MANAO JUBAN (Cornelian Chrysanthemum Petal) 1974
Yunnan reticulata
(syn: *MANAOTSUEBAN* [WG]) Another of the reticulata group imported to Japan in 1970, *MANAO JUBAN* has not yet been released to collectors. It is a medium-sized rose form double bloom of pink and white.

MANAOTSUEBAN [WG] (see MANAO JUBAN)

MANDALAY QUEEN 1966
Seedling
A seedling of *DALI CHA (Tali Queen)*, this interesting cultivar was raised by California's Shade and Shadow Nursery. It is a very large semi-double bloom with fluted petals, less elaborate than its parent. The colouring is a rich rose-pink, and the flowers open from mid to late season. The plant itself is of typical robust reticulata habit.

MARY STRINGFELLOW 1980
X reticulata hybrid
Another splendid introduction from the small garden of hybridist Frank Pursel, *Mary Stringfellow* shares the parentage of his other triumphs, *DAMANAO (Cornelian)* and japonica *Mrs D. W. Davis*. It is a very large semi-double hybrid, with brilliant stamens and heavily veined petals of rose-pink. The growth habit seems splendid in these early days.

MAYE DIECHI (Reticulate Leaf Butterfly) 1948
Yunnan reticulata
(syn: *Butterfly Camellia, DIECHI MUDAN, MAYEHTIECHIH* [WG], *Professor Tsai, TIEHTSEMOUTAN* [WG]) One of the most popular reticulata introductions, *MAYE*

DIECHI was named *Professor Tsai* in the West, for the Kunming botanist who produced it by crossing reticulatas *HOUYE DIECHI (Butterfly Wings)* and *MUDAN CHA*. It was imported to California in 1948 and has since spread worldwide. The original Professor Tsai will be long remembered from this medium-sized semi-double bloom with open tiers of waved petals. These are delicate rose-pink, often fading to silver-pink towards the flower's central stamens. The plant is of open bushy growth, and blooms mid season. (Photo p. 146)

MAYEHTIECHIH (WG) (see MAYE DIECHI)

MAYE TAOHONG (Reticulate Leaf Crimson) 1979
Yunnan reticulata
Imported by the University of California, *MAYE TAOHONG* is a large crimson semi-double camellia with waved petals. It is not yet in distribution.

MEIHONG GUIYE (Carmine Osmanthus Leaf) 1974
Yunnan reticulata
(syn: *QINGMEIHONG GUIYE, Crimson Plum Osmanthus Leaf*) A wavy-petalled, red semi-double reticulata imported to Japan in 1974. Not yet in general distribution.

MISS TULARE 1975
Seedling
Raised by M. W. Abramson of Tulare, California, the gorgeous *Miss Tulare* is a cross between *DATAOHONG (Crimson Robe)* and an unnamed japonica cultivar. It is a large, even very large flower, varying from rose form double to full peony form in style. The fluted notched petals shade from true red at the centre to deep rose margins. The plant is typically vigorous in growth. A variegated form was released in 1977.

MOUCHANG 1966
Reticulata cross
A most interesting reticulata released by Howard Asper in 1966, *MOUCHANG* is pure salmon-pink in colour, and almost completely single in form. This cross between Yunnan varieties *DAMANAO (Cornelian)* and *MUDAN CIIA* blooms mid season, and is a very large flower, appearing on a plant of robust upright growth.

MOUTANCHA (WG) (see MUDAN CHA)

MUDAN CHA (Tree Peony Camellia) 1948
Yunnan reticulata
(syn: *MOUTANCHA* [WG]) This brilliant reticulata was imported from Yunnan in 1948. Its Chinese name means 'peony flower', and that is just what it looks like — a very large bright pink peony, veined and occasionally striped with white, particularly on the inner petals. It is formal to rose form double, with wavy crêpe-textured petals and medium growth.

NARROW-LEAFED SHOT SILK (see LIUYE YINHONG)

NOBLE PEARL
It now appears that the Yunnan variety *Red Jewelry*, for a time known as *Noble Pearl*, was not imported to the West, and the plant sold as *Noble Pearl* for many years was actually *DALI CHA* or *Tali Queen*. Existing plants should therefore be known by that name. (See, however, *BAOZHU CHA* for the true cultivar, which has yet to be released in the West.)

NOTRE DAME 1977
Seedling
Northern California camellia patron and gridiron enthusiast Mrs Charles O'Malley developed this marvellous reticulata seedling and named it for her favourite team. A very large camellia of loose, dramatic peony form, it blooms mid to late season in a striking shade of deep pink, washed with silver. Certainly a top scorer for the 1977 season.

NUCCIO'S RUBY 1974
Seedling
A reticulata seedling of unspecified parentage, *Nuccio's Ruby* was propagated by the Nuccio Nursery of California. It is a large to very large bloom of true rich red. Semi-double, it has ruffled petals of irregular shape and size. There is a variegated form.

OSMANTHUS LEAF (see XIAOGUIYE)

OTTO HOPFER 1970
X reticulata hybrid
A truly dazzling camellia, *Otto Hopfer* is usually described as having light red blooms, but in my own garden these have a distinctly orange cast. Released in 1970 by D. Hopfer, it is a robust plant with large foliage, a cross between *DATAOHONG (Crimson Robe)* and the japonica *Lotus*. The flowers are large to very large, open semi-double in style, with irregular petals.

OVATE-LEAF SPINEL PINK (see LUANYE YINHONG)

OVERTURE 1971
Seedling
Introduced by F. S. Tuckfield of Berwick, Australia, the dazzling *Overture* is a chance seedling of reticulata *DATAOHONG (Crimson Robe)*, of most unusual form. The very large loose informal double flowers, which open mid season, have upstanding petals reflexed into tubular form. These are bright red with luminous overtones. The plant is a splendid robust choice for the collector.

PAGODA (see ROBERT FORTUNE)

PAOCHUCHA (WG) (see BAOZHU CHA)

PEONY (see MUDAN CHA)

LIUYE YINHONG　　　柳叶银红

MANDALAY QUEEN

MISS TULARE

MOUCHANG

MUDAN CHA　　　牡丹茶

OTTO HOPFER

OVERTURE

Reticulatas

PEONY CAMELLIA (see MUDAN CHA)

PHARAOH 1971

Seedling

A very large-flowered seedling of *DAMANAO (Cornelian)*, *Pharaoh* was introduced by Californian Howard Asper. The blooms are semi-double to rose form, with the petals deeply waved and tinted a rich old rose. They open mid season on a plant of medium upright growth.

PHYL DOAK 1958

X reticulata hybrid

An early reticulata cultivar, using the parentage of *C. saluenensis* and *Captain Rawes*, *Phyl Doak* was introduced by Dr B. Doak of Papetoetoe, New Zealand, and is widely grown in the southern hemisphere. The medium to large blooms are semi-double, and the colour is described as rose bengal — pale pink on my own observation. The plant is compact, and suitable for container use.

PINBAN DALI CHA (Flat Petal Tali Camellia) 1975

X reticulata hybrid

This is a light red, flat semi-double Yunnan reticulata which is not yet in wide distribution. It was imported to Japan by Dr Kinhachi Ikeda in 1975, and again to the University of California in 1979.

PINE CONE (see ROBERT FORTUNE)

PINE CONE SCALE (see ROBERT FORTUNE)

PINE CONE SHELL (see SONGZIKE)

PINE SHELL (see SONGZIKE)

PINK BUTTERFLY WINGS
(see FENHONG DIECHI)

PINK PEONY (see YINFEN MUDAN)

PROFESSOR TSAI (see MAYE DIECHI)

PURPLE GOWN (see ZIPAO)

QINGMEIHONG GUIYE
(see MEIHONG GUIYE)

QUEEN OF TALI (see DALI CHA)

RED JADE (see YUDAIHONG)

RED JEWELRY (see BAOZHU CHA)

RED WITH JADE BELT (see YUDAIHONG)

RETICULATE LEAF BUTTERFLY
(see MAYE DIECHI)

RETICULATE LEAF CRIMSON
(see MAYE TAOHONG)

RETICULATE LEAF SPINEL PINK
(see MAYE YINHONG)

ROB ROY 1970
X reticulata hybrid
Evocatively named for the Scottish folk hero Rob
Roy Macgregor, reticulata *Rob Roy* was a cross
between *DAYINHONG (Shot Silk)* and the hybrid *J. C. Williams*. The grower was T. E.
Croson of California. It is a medium to large
semi-double flower with irregular petals. These
are tinted a luscious pale pink, with deeper
tonings towards the notched petal tips. *Rob Roy*
is a plant of compact growth. (Photo p. 147)

ROBERT FORTUNE 1847
(syn: *Flore Pleno, Pagoda, Pine Cone, Pine Cone
Scale, SONGZILIN, SUNGTZELIN* [WG])
The second reticulata variety to reach the West,
Robert Fortune seems to have arrived in England
in 1847, in the effects of a noted plant collector
of the same name. Originally, the Chinese called
it *SONGZILIN* meaning 'pine cone', but the decision to name it for its discoverer seems appropriate. It is a magnificent large bloom of formal
double style, and deep pink in colour. There are
several very large trees of it in Europe.

ROSE FLOWER (see JUBAN)

ROSS CLARK 1967
X reticulata hybrid
A very large semi-double bloom with waved,
upstanding petals, *Ross Clark* was introduced by
New Zealander H. J. Clark in 1967. It is a cross
between *C. saluenensis* and the reticulata *Buddha*.
A strong upright grower, blooming mid season.

ROYALTY 1968
X reticulata hybrid
Very large, semi-double, and coloured a brilliant
red, the reticulata hybrid *Royalty* was introduced
by Californian T. E. Croson. This mid season
bloomer is a cross between the red japonica
Clarise Carleton and *Buddha*, from which it inherits strong medium growth, and open flower
shape. The outer petals are deeply notched, the
inner elegantly waved.

SAI MUDAN (Superior Peony) 1979
Yunnan reticulata
Imported by the University of California — not
yet flowered or released in the West. The
Chinese suggest the Western synonym *Super
Peony*.

SAI TAOHONG (Superior Crimson) 1979
Yunnan reticulata
Super Crimson is an English synonym suggested
by the Yunnan Chinese for this spectacular variety, which has not yet flowered in the West. It
was imported only in 1979 by the University of
California.

SALUTATION 1936
X reticulata hybrid

ROBERT FORTUNE

SAN MARINO

Reticulatas

A very early reticulata hybrid, *Salutation* was introduced in 1936 by Col R. S. Clarke of Sussex, England. It is a large delicate pale pink cross between the species *C. saluenensis* and reticulata *Captain Rawes*. The large blooms are single to semi-double, opening mid season on a plant of medium open growth. It is still popular in England, being somewhat cold-resistant.

SAN MARINO 1975
                                                    Seedling
This brilliantly coloured reticulata seedling was first shown in 1975 by Willard Goertz, a prominent camellian of San Marino, California. It shows a large semi-double bloom of vivid red. The deeply fluted and rolled petals are heavily textured and irregular in length. *San Marino* is a mid season bloomer, with strong spreading growth.

SATAN'S ROBE 1965
                                    X reticulata hybrid
A garish Oriental red hybrid by David Feathers, dramatic *Satan's Robe* is a cross between the hybrid *Satan's Satin* and *Crimson Robe (DATAOHONG)*. A large semi-double flower with silken sheen, it blooms mid season on a plant of bushy upright growth. A very eye-catching flower.

SHIHTZETOU (WG) (see SHIZITOU)

SHIZITOU (Lion Head) 1964
                                    Yunnan reticulata
(syn: *SHIHTZETOU* [WG]) The true Yunnan reticulata *SHIZITOU* or *Lion Head* has been the subject of much investigation. Experts have now decided it was *not* imported to the West in 1948, hence all plants of that name grown outside China must be classed as the variety *DAMANAO* or *Cornelian* (which see). The true *Lion Head* was finally imported to New Zealand in 1964, and has been available there for the last six years.

SHOT SILK (see DAYINHONG)

SHOWGIRL 1965
                                    X reticulata hybrid
Like a giant sasanqua in form, the Howard Asper hybrid *Showgirl* is in fact a cross between sasanqua *NARUMIGATA* and reticulata *DAMANAO (Cornelian)*. Dating from 1965, it is a large to very large semi-double bloom of loose peony form. The deeply waved pale pink petals have a cyclamen cast, and are quite irregular. Early blooming, *Showgirl* is a strong grower with a degree of sun-hardiness.

SMALL OSMANTHUS LEAF
(see XIAOGUIYE)

SONGZIKE (Pine Cone Shell) 1974
                                    Yunnan reticulata
(syn: *Pine Shell, SUNGTZEKE* [WG]) This precious Yunnan reticulata is not yet distributed to the world, but is described as a large rose form

double similar to *Robert Fortune*, but with smaller petals. The colour is deep scarlet-pink. It reached the United States only in 1979.

SONGZILIN (see ROBERT FORTUNE)

STAR OF INDIA 1971
                                    Seedling
A startling Oriental red reticulata from Australian hybridist Fred Tuckfield, *Star of India* does not seem to have achieved popularity outside its home state of Victoria. It is a large semi-double flower with fluted petals arranged 'hose-in-hose', and blooming mid season. It originated as a seedling of *DATAOHONG (Crimson Robe)*.

SUNGTZEKE (WG) (see SONGZIKE)

SUNGTZELIN (WG) (see ROBERT FORTUNE)

SUPER CRIMSON (see SAI TAOHONG)

SUPER PEONY (see SAI MUDAN)

SUPERIOR CRIMSON (see SAI TAOHONG)

SUPERIOR PEONY (see SAI MUDAN)

TAKUEIYEH (WG) (see DAGUIYE)

TALI CAMELLIA (see DALI CHA)

TALI QUEEN (see DALI CHA)

TALICHA (WG) (see DALI CHA)

TAMANAO (WG) (see DAMANAO)

TATAOHUNG (WG) (see DATAOHONG)

TAYINHUNG (WG) (see DAYINHONG)

THE DWARF (see HENTIANGAO)

THICK LEAF BUTTERFLY
(see HOUYE DIECHI)

THICK LEAF BUTTERFLY WINGS
(see HOUYE DIECHI)

TIEHTSEMOUTAN (WG) (see MAYE DIECHI)

TONGZIMIAN 1980
                                    Yunnan reticulata
(syn: *Baby Face, TUNGZIEMIEN*) Not as yet released in the West, the Yunnan reticulata *TONGZIMIAN* or *Baby Face* is known to have reached Australia in 1980, and is now in cultivation. It is described as a white flower, variegated with deep red, and sounds most spectacular. It is large, open and semi-double, blooming late in the season.

TREE PEONY CAMELLIA (see MUDAN CHA)

TSAOMOUTAN (WG) (see ZAO MOUDAN)

TSAOTAOHONG (WG) (see ZAO TAOHONG)

TSINGAN CAMELLIA (see JINGAN CHA)

TSINGANCHA (WG) (see JINGAN CHA)

TSUEBAN (WG) (see JUBAN)

TUNGZIEMIEN (WG) (see TONGZIMIAN)

TZEPAO (WG) (see ZIPAO)

VALENTINE DAY 1958
                                    X reticulata hybrid
To many people (including myself) the most perfect reticulata hybrid to date is *Valentine Day*, surely the high point of Howard Asper's career. In colour it is a medium pink with salmon tonings; in size, very large; in shape, formal double with the perfect centre of a half-open rosebud. The result of a cross between *C. saluenensis* and *Buddha*, it matches the beauty of its flowers with a fast-growing constitution.

VALLEY M. KNUDSEN 1958
                                    X reticulata hybrid
Popular wherever reticulata camellias are grown, the Howard Asper hybrid *Valley M. Knudsen* was named for a California garden-lover, and has the same parentage as *Valentine Day*. It is a smaller flower (though still large in size) with semi-double to peony form. The blooms of deep orchid-pink are borne profusely on a well-shaped fast-growing plant which may achieve considerable size.

VANNINE 1958
                                    X reticulata hybrid
Ninth and last of a series of nine seedlings crossing popular japonica *Lady Vansittart* with *Crimson Robe (DATAOHONG)*, *Vannine* was raised by that remarkable camellia-lover David Feathers of Lafayette, California, but as yet its circulation is limited to a few friends. A large single bloom with unusually thick petals of great substance, it has the vigour of a reticulata combined with the striking white, red and pink variegations of the japonica parent. It blooms mid to late season, and would seem to have a great future.

VERMILION JEWELRY CAMELLIA
(see BAOZHU CHA)

WELCOME SPRING (see YINGCHUN HONG)

WELCOME SPRING RED
(see YINGCHUN HONG)

WHITE RETIC 1977
                                    Seedling
Is this the long-awaited perfect white reticulata? Possibly, but as it was introduced only in 1977 (a chance seedling from the garden of H. Fish in Santa Cruz, California) it is perhaps too early

SHIZITOU 狮子头 *SONGZIKE* 松子壳

VALENTINE DAY *VALLEY M. KNUDSEN*

VANNINE *WHITE RETIC*

WILD SILK

WILLIAM HERTRICH

to tell. A plant of vigorous growth, *White Retic* has an open upright habit, and its large semi-double blooms are white with the softest pink shading on the reverse.

WILD SILK 1969

         X reticulata hybrid
A shimmering reticulata hybrid from the southern hemisphere, *Wild Silk* crosses the wild form with cultivar *Shot Silk (DAYINHONG)*. It was created by New Zealander Tom Durrant. *Wild Silk* is a large semi-double of vibrant Chinese rose. It has strong, upright petals and a husky growth. It blooms mid to late season.

WILLIAM HERTRICH 1971

         Seedling
Can there be no end to the brilliant contributions of hybridist Howard Asper? Here he gives us a marvel in deep cherry-red, named for the late great director of the magnificent Huntington Camellia Gardens. *William Hertrich* is a very large semi-double bloom with irregular petals, the outer somewhat reflexed; the inner upright and loosely interspersed with stamens. It is a seedling of Yunnan reticulata *DAMANAO (Cornelian)*, and if the flowers have a fault it is that they drop too soon and shatter as they do so. *William Hertrich* is a husky plant with strong growth.

WILLOW WAND (see LIUYE YINHONG)

WILLOWLEAF PINK (see LIUYE YINHONG)

WILLOWLEAF SPINEL PINK
(see LIUYE YINHONG)

XIAOGUIYE (Small Osmanthus Leaf) 1948

         Yunnan reticulata
(syn: *HSIAOKUEIYEH* [WG], *Osmanthus Leaf*) Another charmer imported both in 1948 and again by Colonel Durrant in 1964, *XIAOGUIYE* (or *Osmanthus Leaf* as you'll probably prefer to call it) is daintier and less opulent in all its habits. The growth is slender and open, and the leaves are like that of the sweet-smelling *Osmanthus fragrans*. The rose form double blooms are only medium in size, but coloured a vivid orchid-pink. They appear profusely mid to late season.

YINFEN MUDAN (Pink Peony) 1980

         Yunnan reticulata
Reportedly one of the best Yunnan reticulatas, *YINFEN MUDAN* or *Pink Peony* is not yet in Western distribution. It is a large pink peony form camellia — a first-class flower.

YINGCHUN HONG (Welcome Spring Red) 1974

         Yunnan reticulata
(syn: *Welcome Spring*) A reticulata from the Tunchun area, *Welcome Spring* has been pictured in several Japanese books, but is not yet grown in the West. It is a large, flattish, red camellia, semi-double.

YUDAIHONG (Red with Jade Belt) 1979
Yunnan reticulata
(syn: *Red Jade*) Not yet in Western distribution, reticulata *YUDAIHONG* arrived in California in 1979, and is currently being propagated. It is a red semi-double camellia, variegated with a white band.

ZAO MUDAN (Early Peony) 1964
Yunnan reticulata
(syn: *TSAOMOUTAN* [WG]) A Yunnan variety imported to New Zealand by Colonel Tom Durrant, *ZAO MUDAN* has not caught the public imagination like others of these magnificent flowers. It is a large semi-double bloom, with upright folded petals notched at their margins. They are tinted a brilliant China rose.

ZAOTAOHONG (Early Peach Red) 1964
Yunnan reticulata
(syn: *TSAOTAOHUNG* [WG], *Early Crimson*) Not commonly grown in the West, this decorative Yunnan cultivar is described as very large, semi-double and light crimson in colour. It blooms early on a shrub of strong growth.

ZHANGJIA CHA (Chang's Family Camellia) 1964
Yunnan reticulata
(syn: *CHANGCHIACHA* [WG], *Chang's Temple*) The true Yunnan reticulata variety *Chang's Temple* or *ZHANGJIA CHA* was imported directly from China to New Zealand in 1964 by Colonel Tom Durrant. It is a tall strong-growing plant, with particularly large leaves, and blooms mid to late season. The large open-centred semi-double blooms are coloured a brilliant China rose. Their petals are waved and deeply notched and the centre includes occasional petaloids. Plants grown outside China prior to 1964, and propagated from them, often have variegated colouring, and must now be regarded as specimens of the variety *DAMANAO* or *Cornelian* (which see).

ZIPAO (Purple Gown) 1948
Yunnan reticulata
(syn: *TZEPAO* [WG]) Yet another import from the Botanical Institute of Yunnan, *ZIPAO* or *Purple Gown* arrived in 1948, when Californian grower Ralph Peer imported it jointly with the Descanso Gardens. It is a large to very large flower, formal double to peony form. The lightly waved petals are coloured magenta (a deep red-purple) with radial flecks of white and occasionally wine-red. *ZIPAO* blooms profusely at mid season on a bush of rather compact habit. There is also a variegated form known as *ZIPAOYUTAI*.

ZHANGJIA CHA 张家茶

ZIPAO 紫袍

THE SASANQUAS

Including species C. sasanqua, C. hiemalis and C. vernalis

Free-flowering SHISHI GASHIRA *or* Lion's Head, *the most popular variety for espalier work, is not a true sasanqua, but the wild form of* Camellia hiemalis, *the 'Cold Camellia'.*

The delightful autumn and winter-blooming camellias known collectively to Western gardeners as sasanquas are not members of a single camellia species, but of three. They also include the hybrids between them and, less commonly, between the sasanqua and japonica species.

In Japan, they have a history in cultivation quite as old as that of *C. japonica*, but more often for practical rather than decorative reasons. Their leaves have been used for centuries to make a poorer grade of tea, and their generously produced nuts or fruit have been the basis of a thriving Japanese industry for a longer period than written records cover.

Before the advent of oil from whales and fossil fuels, oil from the camellia seed was used for lighting, lubrication, and above all, for cooking and cosmetic purposes. Camellia oil has a higher calorific content than any other edible oil available naturally in Japan, but its extraction is difficult and time-consuming. In the twentieth century, manufacturers have not been able to compete with sunflower, corn and other imported oils. Nor has the change to shorter Western hairstyles helped the industry. Time was when Japanese of both sexes wore their hair long, and dressed it regularly with perfumed camellia oil.

Today, the camellia seeds or nuts are used only in a variety of cottage industries — making dolls' eyes, beads, rings and many other novelties for the flourishing souvenir trade.

The true wild sasanqua *(Camellia sasanqua)* is a small tree growing in evergreen coastal forests of southern Shikoku, Kyūshū and many other minor islands as far south as Okinawa. It is found growing up to 900 metres (2,700 feet) above sea level, and is altogether a more delicate and slender plant than the commoner *C. japonica*. It is, in fact, not thought of by the Japanese as a true camellia at all. They call it *Sazankwa*, meaning the 'plum-flowered tea'. Its leaves are pointed and slender (less than a quarter of the size of those on a japonica) and their central rib bears fine hairs which are also found on young foliage and twigs. Sasanqua flowers are naturally white, single and from 4 to 8 centimetres (1½ to 3 inches) in diameter according to variety. They have five or six petals and loose golden stamens, and are often quite irregular in shape. They appear from late summer right into winter.

The second species, *Camellia hiemalis*, is called in Japan *KAN TSUBAKI*, meaning the 'cold camellia'. In its natural form, the variety known as *SHISHI GASHIRA* or *Lion Head*, it has a shrubby, spreading habit, and is often used in landscaping as a low, mushroom-shaped foliage plant or neatly trimmed to formal shape. The leaves are similar to those of the sasanqua, while the flowers are red-pink, informally double and about 6 centimetres (2½ inches) in diameter. The stamens are often developed as petaloids, and the variety is very fertile, being a parent of many other so-called sasanqua varieties. *C. hiemalis* flowers right through the winter months and makes an attractive container plant.

The third species included under the umbrella name sasanqua is *Camellia vernalis*, the spring sasanqua or *HARU SAZANKWA* to the

Japanese. This species is quite popularly grown in a number of decorative cultivars. They all withstand cold well, and bloom continuously from mid winter well into spring. Plant geneticists have discovered many intermediate characteristics among the varieties of *C. vernalis*, and these may yet turn out to be not a separate species but a group of natural hybrids between *C. japonica* and *C. sasanqua*.

All three species 'shatter' badly, dropping a petal at a time shortly after bud-opening until the ground beneath the plant is a sheet of colour. This habit is admired by the Japanese and by Australian gardeners as well; but not in the United States, where *Sclerotinia camelliae* (the fungus known as 'camellia blight'), has ravaged so many gardens. As this disease survives and develops on fallen, decaying flowers, 'shattering' can be a most unwelcome characteristic unless the hygiene of a daily clean-up of spent blooms is observed.

Decorative sasanqua cultivars are known to have been prized in Japanese gardens as far back as the Muromachi period of the fourteenth century, and there are ancient trees in the gardens of Kyōtō temples estimated to be 400 years old. They are mentioned in many seventeenth

century flower arrangement books, including the *Anthology of Beautiful Flowers* (1684), and a volume published in 1739, *Golden Flowers and Plants*, lists one hundred varieties. Later in the eighteenth century, the decorative sasanquas were out of favour, along with other camellias, and remained so during the turbulent decades leading up to the Meiji restoration of 1868. Shortly after this, a society was formed known as Menkōkai, with the aim of locating, preserving and propagating famous sasanqua varieties of bygone reigns and producing improved new varieties. It succeeded admirably, and to the devotion of its members we owe thanks for many of the exquisite cultivars we grow today.

As a climax to this renewed interest in sasanqua culture, a book named *Stories of the Mountain Plum* was published in 1899 which recorded many charming facets of sasanqua lore that underlined its importance to Japanese culture in olden times. These included two anecdotes of the former military dictator Kasai who, in contrast to the Western idea of a military man, was besotted with these beautiful blooms. One anecdote

One of the first-recorded sasanqua cultivars was MOMOIRO SAZANKA *(the* Peach-coloured Sasanqua*), here shown in this seventeenth century illustration from the* Chinka Zufu.

recounted that he boastfully named an especially gorgeous variety he had raised *Hooray for me!*; the other, that he paid 10 *ryō* (an enormous sum) for a plant of *YAMATO NISHIKI* 6 *shaku* tall. (Six *shaku* would be approximately 1.8 metres or 6 feet in modern terms.)

Though known to Western botanists from drawings and pressed specimens from the early eighteenth century, live sasanquas were not generally seen in the West until 1869, when some specimens were imported by Dutch traders. As they are native to warmer areas of southern Japan, they were not entirely successful in cold European winters, and have never achieved the popularity of the japonica camellias in that part of the world, except in Italy.

Sasanquas make charming pot subjects for winter bloom. Here is cultivar KANJIRO.

They have however become a great success in Australia, northern California and some southern states of the USA where the climate of certain coastal areas resembles that of the sasanqua's natural habitat. They grow far more rapidly than the japonicas, and because they are more resistant to full sun, have many practical uses in the open garden. Densely-foliaged varieties can be quickly trained as a loose, open screen, or clipped as a formal hedge. Sasanquas also perform splendidly as espaliers, where the additional warmth provided by a wall backing encourages remarkable feats of growth, particularly in cultivars with naturally pendulous growth such as *C. hiemalis Chansonette* and *SHISHI GASHIRA*, and *C. sasanqua Plantation Pink*. Wire frameworks for future training should be attached to the wall or fence first, and the soil enriched before planting with plenty of acid compost, manure and moistened peat moss. The sasanquas can be planted at any time of the year, but mid winter, before spring leaf-growth, is best.

Fruit of the sasanqua camellia is the source of much of Japan's famous camellia oil.

Specimens of naturally taller-growing sasanquas can be encouraged to assume a columnar shape, most useful for framing gateways or doors, or simply to punctuate an otherwise boring landscape. Varieties *MINE NO YUKI, Beatrice Emily,* and *Cotton Candy* are suitable for this.

The leading shoot should be tied at several points to a tall, strong stake, and the principal branches pruned annually in winter to encourage branching and denser growth. A light mulch of cow manure is beneficial.

Sasanquas are also much used for groundcover and in rockeries. Varieties with a naturally low, spreading habit should be selected, such as *Bonsai Baby*, *SHISHI GASHIRA* and *TANYA*.

Finally, because of their neat, dense, evergreen foliage, sasanquas are much favoured as container plants for terrace or courtyard display. They can be clipped and pruned to neat formal shapes or trained to a more romantic bonsai style. They look splendid at any time of the year, even when not in bloom. *Yuletide* is a popular container variety; others worth trying are *Eureka* and *Little Pearl*. Sasanquas do best in a container mix of seventy-five per cent acid compost-rich soil and twenty-five per cent sharp sand for improved drainage. Mulch with milled cow manure, and water more frequently than open-ground specimens. Moisture in containers tends to drain away from the roots, which as in all camellias, are close to the surface.

Except for shaping, no pruning of the many sasanqua varieties is needed; in fact, it would tend to limit flower production. The display varies from plant to plant, but in the best cultivars is almost unbelievably profuse. The colour range of the sasanquas is not as wide as in the japonicas, there being few of the really bright reds or striking variegations. But by way of compensation the delicate petals are often fluted and ruffled, and there are many 'sweet pea' types where the base colour fades gently into a contrasting border tone. Flower styles are mostly single or semi-double, with a small proportion of loose anemone types. Formals are rare indeed. The stamens however are particularly showy, often widely flared as in the Higo camellias, or with a display of petaloids.

The really charming difference is that many sasanqua varieties are distinctly fragrant. This is often quite noticeable when they are planted close to windows or by the terraces where so much of modern living takes place. Because fragrance is so common among sasanquas, the symbol used elsewhere in the book has not been included in individual entries.

I have not listed varieties and cultivars of the three species separately, but have run them together in alphabetical order, in the section that follows. Each entry indicates the species to which it belongs, and the varieties are cross-indexed by both Japanese and English names (when the latter exist).

The names of many Japanese sasanqua varieties are quite charming and evocative, and always to be preferred to the English translations which are often so lacking in poetic feeling, however accurate they may be. For this reason, I have taken the liberty of translating some of these names afresh, retaining more of the poetic feeling, sometimes at the expense of literal accuracy. I think few older sasanqua-lovers will object, and newer fanciers will perhaps realise more of the charm inherent in the original Japanese names, under which sasanquas should in any case be classified both at nurseries and shows.

Dates of introduction are not included in the sasanqua entries, as few of them are readily available. Size references are not as specific as with japonicas and reticulatas. Few of the sasanquas exceed medium size, and then only when grown in the most perfect conditions.

A modern Japanese woodblock print of sasanqua blooms by noted artist Shodo Kawarazaki.

Sasanquas

AZUMA NISHIKI 東錦

CHANSONETTE

CRIMSON TIDE

AKASHI BAY (see AKASHI GATA)

AKASHIGATA (Akashi Bay) *sp. sasanqua*
One of the original Japanese cultivars, this lovely
sasanqua bears very large flowers for the species.
These are semi-double, frosty white, shaded
toward the petal edges in a medium pink, and
occasionally striped in the same colour. The
petals are lavishly twisted and curled around a
widely flared boss of gold-tipped stamens. The
plant bears occasional double blooms.

AKEBONO (Dawn Pink) *sp. sasanqua*
One of the favourite older sasanqua types in
many parts of the world, *AKEBONO* (not to be
confused with the japonica variety of the same
name) is a plant of upright spreading growth,
quite suited to espalier or hedging work. The
clear pink flowers are single, and medium in size.
Leaves are small and dark.

APPLE BLOSSOM (see FUKUZUTSUMI)

ASAHI NO SORA (Sunrise Sky) *sp. sasanqua*
Curiously coloured for a sasanqua, and best described as lilac-pink, the large blooms of *ASAHI
NO SORA* are graduated from the almost transparent, fluted petal edges to a deep flush at the
centre, where the petals surround a prominent
mass of gold-tipped stamens. The flowers are invariably single.

ASTONISHMENT (see KENKYŌ)

AZUMA NISHIKI (Eastern Brocade)
 sp. sasanqua
Long twisted and fluted petals surround a prominent centre of gold stamens in this lovely
Japanese sasanqua cultivar. Generally single, occasionally semi-double, the flowers are large and
tinted rose-pink, shading deeper at the petal
edges.

BACKWARD GLANCE (see NODAMI USHIRO)

BEATRICE EMILY *sp. sasanqua*
Tall and open in growth, popular in espalier
work, the vigorous cultivar *Beatrice Emily* bears
medium-sized blooms in profusion. These are
almost magenta in bud, opening to loose informal
double flowers of creamy-white, with the outer
petals tinted a distinct lavender at their
margins.

BENI KAN TSUBAKI (see SHISHI GASHIRA)

BERT JONES *sp. sasanqua*
This strong-growing sasanqua is a great favourite
in Australian gardens, where its long, whip-like
lateral growth has made it a perfect choice for
espalier work. The leaves are dark, shining and
handsome, the flowers large. Each bloom is semi-
double, tinted a rich rose-pink with a delightful
silvery overcast. The flower centre is often a
mixed mass of pink petaloids and golden stamens.
Blooming period is particularly long, from beginning of autumn well into winter.

BETTIE PATRICIA *sp. sasanqua*
A popular sasanqua variety in the United States,
Bettie Patricia is noted for its rose form double
blooms of clear, light pink. These are borne lavishly on a plant of upright though spreading
growth.

BOASTFUL FLOWER (see HANA JIMAN)

BONANZA *sp. sasanqua*
Popular wherever sasanqua camellias are grown,
the dazzling *Bonanza* bears large, semi-double
peony form blooms of deep glowing red. Their
firm petals are both waved and fluted. The plant
is medium in height, upright in growth and particularly handsome pruned as a small specimen
tree. Blooming season begins early, and continues
for several months.

BONSAI BABY *sp. hiemalis*
A favourite for bonsai work, the dainty, deep red
cultivar of *C. hiemalis* has miniature blooms
which are so important when a plant is trained
to dwarf size. Each perfect flower is either formal
or rose form double. An American cultivar.

BUNDLE OF FORTUNE (see FUKUZUTSUMI)

CAMELLIA IN MIDWINTER
(see KAN TSUBAKI)

CHANSONETTE *sp. hiemalis*
One of the most popular hiemalis cultivars,
Chansonette has an extremely bushy growth, but
might be considered more suitable for espalier
work due to the rather rambling habit of its
branches. The long-lasting, medium-sized
blooms are formal double in style and tinted a
deep lavender-pink. As the flower opens, the
ruffled petals reveal small central stamens.

CHERIE *sp. sasanqua*
Spectacularly beautiful flowers of soft lavender-
pink make the sasanqua cultivar *Cherie* a conversation piece anywhere. They are semi-double to
rose-form double in style, the petals often slightly
fimbriated or fringed.

CHŌ ASOBI (Playful Butterfly) *sp. sasanqua*
What a splendid flower — and how I wish it were
available to gardeners in my part of the world!
The Japanese name means *Playful Butterfly* and
how like butterflies the delicate flowers seem,
fluttering over their dark foliage in the slightest
breeze. Single, and a delicate pink in colour, these
ravishing blooms are marked in white, sometimes
softly shaded, sometimes in dramatic moiré patterns. The petals are twisted, often with deeply
divided ends, and the stamens are a particularly
rich gold.

CHŌJI GURUMA (Wheel of Cloves)
 sp. sasanqua
The Japanese name of this unusual cultivar translates as *Wheel of Cloves*, but why it should be
called so must remain a secret to the Japanese.
The plant is vigorous and upright in growth, the

ENID REID

flowers are perfectly anemone form and rose-pink. The stamens are converted to a formal mass of rose-pink heart-shaped petaloids.

CHRISTMAS CANDLES   *sp. hiemalis*
Particularly favoured in the northern hemisphere, where it is often trained and pruned to formal shape as a winter cr Christmas decoration, *Christmas Candles* is a small-growing cultivar of *C. hiemalis* with very large blooms for the species. They are semi-double and coloured a brilliant red.

COLD CAMELLIA (see KAN TSUBAKI)

COTTON CANDY   *sp. sasanqua*
(syn: *Hyman's Semi-double Pink*) Popular in Australia and the United States, the modern cultivar *Cotton Candy* bears blooms of the same clear pink as that popular fairground confection. The plant's growth is upright and spreading, with a rather loose habit. The large flowers are semi-double to loose informal double in style, with ruffled and fluted petals. In some areas, the blooms develop a faint overtone of lavender.

CRIMSON KING   *sp. sasanqua*
Described in overseas volumes as a deep, mahogany-red, the single blooms of this handsome sasanqua tend more to a glowing crimson-red in Australian gardens. The flowers are medium in size, their petals interestingly twisted. The plant's low, spreading habit makes it a suitable choice as a low hedge, or for rockery work.

CRIMSON TIDE   *sp. sasanqua*
The wonderfully textured crimson-red blooms of this noble sasanqua cultivar are semi-double, each petal interestingly twisted and with a rippled surface reminiscent of crushed crêpe. The plant on which they appear has a dense spreading habit, and leaves of rich shining green.

CRIMSON VELVETTII (see VELVETY)

DAWN (see GINRYŪ; see also SHIN ONOME)

DAWN PINK (see AKEBONO)

DAZZLER   *sp. hiemalis*
Tall and vigorous in growth, rapidly spreading in habit, *Dazzler* is one of the most useful *C. hiemalis* cultivars for winter colour. The flowers, semi-double and with lightly waved petals, are medium in size and a brilliant cerise-rose.

DENSE HAILSTONE (see YAE ARARE)

EASTERN BROCADE (see AZUMA NISHIKI)

EDNA BUTLER   *sp. sasanqua*
A sasanqua of strong upright growth, *Edna Butler* has often been used as a dense, blooming hedge. The large, semi-double flowers are soft pink, their waved and crinkled petals often including a few petaloids.

ELEGANT FRIENDS (see SETSUGEKKA)

EMPIRE RED (see MIKUNI KŌ)

ENID   *sp. sasanqua*
Very popular as a specimen plant, the open-branching, upright-growing sasanqua cultivar *Enid* seems not to be listed in US catalogues. Its blooms are small, single, and tinted a delicate blush-pink.

ENID REID   *sp. sasanqua*
Enid Reid is another sasanqua cultivar that is popular in Australia, but seems not to be grown in America. Down under it is widely used for hedging because of a dense, upright growth. The medium-sized light pink flowers are semi-double, and borne in profusion at branch tips. Their petals are crimped and fluted, occasionally darkening in tone towards the edge.

EUREKA   *sp. sasanqua*
This most unusual sasanqua is a new introduction from Australia's Camellia Lodge Nursery, who seem to have found a plant headed for world favour. *Eureka* is dwarf and spreading in habit, clothed with dark leaves margined in golden-green. The small flowers, a vivid strawberry-pink in tone, are semi-double with occasional petaloids.

EXQUISITE   *sp. sasanqua*
A vigorous and handsome plant, the tall-growing cultivar *Exquisite* is useful for espalier work because it has spreading, heavily foliaged branches. The very large single blooms are palest silver-pink, their petals ruffled and with indented tips.

FANCY HAT (see TSUMAORI GASA)

FIVE CONTINENTS (see GODAISHŪ)

FLAMINGO (see FUKUZUTSUMI)

FLOWER IN WINE (see SHUCHŪ KA)

FLUTED WHITE (see SETSUGEKKA)

FLUTTERING SLEEVES (see MAI NO SODE)

FUJI NO MINE (Peak of Mt Fuji) *sp. sasanqua*
The Japanese cultivar *FUJI NO MINE* is a vigorous, attractive sasanqua with large, double flowers. These are pure white like the snows at the peak of Mt Fuji, and are quite informal in style. They have fluted, deeply notched outer petals surrounding a mass of white petaloids and gold-tipped stamens.

FUKUZUTSUMI (Bundle of Fortune)
          sp. sasanqua
(syn: *Apple Blossom, Flamingo, Zerbes*) A vigorous plant of upright spreading growth, this fine sasanqua is most commonly known in the West as *Apple Blossom* — the flower which it most closely resembles. Soft white, merely flushed pink and with a heart of golden stamens, it is invariably single.

EUREKA

EXQUISITE

Sasanquas

HANA JIMAN　　　　　　　　花自慢

HIRYŪ　　　　　　　　　　飛竜

IRIHI NO UMI　　　　　　　入日の海

GAUZY SLEEVES (see KASUMI NO SODE)

GIN RYO (see GINRYŪ)

GINRYŪ (Silver Dragon)　　　*sp. vernalis*
(syn: *Dawn*) A plant of compact bushy growth, the Japanese cultivar *GINRYŪ* or *GIN RYO* is what the Japanese call a *Haru sazankwa*, a spring-flowering species known to science as *Camellia vernalis*. The small to medium-sized blooms are white, suffused with blush-pink, and semi-double. Their fluted petals are arranged in a tiered formation. Unlike those of the true sasanquas, these exquisite flowers hold well and rarely shatter. In many English language catalogues it is listed as *Dawn*.

GLORY (see SHŌWA NO SAKAE)

GLORY OF SHOWA (see SHŌWA NO SAKAE)

GODAISHŪ (Five Continents)　　*sp. sasanqua*
One of the most striking cultivars from Japan, the sasanqua *GODAISHŪ* bears very large, semi-double blooms of vivid crimson-pink. These are slightly fluted, with an almost purplish overcast, and are set off to perfection by large, shining leaves. The plant is tall in growth, with an open habit.

GWEN PIKE　　　　　　　*sp. sasanqua*
A useful sasanqua with strong appeal to Australian gardeners, *Gwen Pike* has almost miniature foliage and makes a generally compact, bushy growth. It is suited either to container growing, or as a low border shrub. The shell-pink blooms are medium in size, and informal semi-double in style.

HANA DAIJIN (Noble Flower)　　*sp. sasanqua*
(syn: *HANA OTODO*) The Japanese sasanqua *HANA DAIJIN* is indeed, as its name translates, a noble flower. The dramatic semi-double blooms have deeply overlapping, almost circular petals of dark rose-pink. A centre of curved golden stamens and green pistils completes a picture of floral perfection.

HANA JIMAN (Boastful Flower)　*sp. sasanqua*
This Japanese sasanqua cultivar can be forgiven its boastful nature. The plant is quite compact, though with a vigorous habit of growth. The large semi-double flowers have deeply fluted irregular petals and are white, edged with a deep border of red-violet.

HEBE (see HUGH EVANS)

HIGH TIDE (see MOCHI NO SHIO)

HINODE NO UMI (Ocean Sunrise)
　　　　　　　　　　　　sp. sasanqua
A vigorous sasanqua with dense compact growth, *HINODE NO UMI* has possibly the deepest colour of any cultivar — a deep, glowing crimson. The flowers are large, single and of an interesting flat form.

HIRYO (see HIRYŪ)

HIRYO NISHIKI (see HIRYŪ NISHIKI)

HIRYŪ (Scarlet Dragon)　　　*sp. vernalis*
(syn: *HIRYO, Red Bird, Scarlet Bird*) Best known of the *Haru-sazankwa* or spring camellias, this *HIRYŪ* is not the same as the sasanqua commonly sold in Australia under that name (see *C. hiemalis* KANJIRO) but quite different both in species and appearance. It is a sun-loving plant of compact growth, bearing small rose form double flowers of deep crimson-red. These open from tight buds into flaring, open blooms with waved and twisted petals. The stamens are straight and borne in a tight, cylindrical mass.

HIRYŪ (Aust) (see KANJIRO)

HIRYŪ NISHIKI (Scarlet Bird's Brocade)
　　　　　　　　　　　　sp. vernalis
(syn: *HIRYO NISHIKI*) This is the variegated form of the previous variety, with the same growth habits and flower style — but crimson, splashed with white.

HUGH EVANS　　　　　　*sp. sasanqua*
(syn: *Hebe*) A tall-growing sasanqua cultivar with weeping branches, *Hugh Evans* is sometimes trained to 'climb' a post or column, particularly in a sunny position. There, in autumn, the weeping foliage is liberally scattered with the medium-sized, single pink flowers.

HYMAN'S SEMI-DOUBLE PINK
(see COTTON CANDY)

INAZUMA (Lightning Flash)　　*sp. sasanqua*
The large, semi-double blooms of this Japanese sasanqua cultivar are pure white, but reversed in pink which seems to bleed through the petals as an occasional irregular pink marking. The golden stamens are arranged flat in the style of Higo camellias. The logic of the name *INAZUMA* or *Lightning Flash* is not clear.

INU HARIKO (Papier Maché Dog)
　　　　　　　　　　　　sp. sasanqua
(syn: *Paper Tiger*) This charmingly named flower looks almost like a delicate fairy-tale illustration. Basically a pale pink shading to white, it is also flushed and striped with deeper pink. The large semi-double blooms are quite eye-catching.

IRIHI NO UMI (Sunset Sea)　　*sp. sasanqua*
A vigorous plant of vertical growth, with short, compact branches, gorgeous *IRIHI NO UMI* is often seen in Japan as a hedge in landscape work. The foliage is dark, and the medium to large flowers are semi-double and of a particularly vivid cerise shade.

JANE MORGAN　　　　　　*sp. sasanqua*
This sasanqua with dense, compact foliage bears

JANE MORGAN

semi-double flowers of most unusual shape. The white petals are almost circular, and quite irregular in size, gradually diminishing to occasional petaloids mixed with the mass of stamens. Outer petals are notched, and deeply bordered in rose-pink.

JEAN MAY
sp. sasanqua

A popular sasanqua cultivar all around the world, *Jean May* is used for espalier and tub planting, but should be placed in a partially shaded position, for the shell-pink blooms tend to fade in sun. The foliage is dark and glossy, the growth bushy, and the semi-double flowers frequently have an admixture of petaloids among the stamens.

JENNIFER SUSAN
sp. sasanqua

Widely valued because of its early-flowering habit, the modern cultivar *Jennifer Susan* is most often seen as a specimen or hedge plant, to which it is suited because of open, upright growth. The soft pink blooms are semi-double to peony form with a loose informal appearance. Outer petals are waved, and petaloids are loosely mixed among the stamens.

JULIE ANNE
sp. sasanqua

Large peony form flowers have won many hearts for this charming, modern sasanqua. Growth is tidy but vigorous, and the flowers are deep rosy-red with a silver streak centring each petal.

KAN TSUBAKI (Camellia in Midwinter)
sp. hiemalis

Possibly the longest-grown variety of *C. hiemalis*, KAN TSUBAKI takes its name from the original Japanese epithet for the species. The medium-sized flowers are semi-double, tinted a rich crimson-pink.

KANJIRO
sp. hiemalis

(syn: *HIRYŪ* [Aust]) Long known in Australia under the name *HIRYŪ*, this splendid camellia of the hiemalis species has proved to be the original Japanese cultivar *KANJIRO*. Growing vigorously to a tall, bushy shape, it makes an excellent garden subject, whether as a specimen tree or hedge. The foliage is dark and glossy, and the flowers are large for the species. Single to semi-double and coloured a deep cerise, they are shaded paler at the centre and base of the petals. (Photo also p. 170)

KASUMI NO SODE (Gauzy Sleeves)
sp. sasanqua

With their gift for picturesque nomenclature, the Japanese have suggested a delightfully feminine garment in the name of this most feminine of sasanqua cultivars. The large loose semi-double flowers are white, edged with softest pink, and their petal reverses are tinted a deeper shade.

KENKYŌ (Astonishment)
sp. sasanqua

One of the most striking blooms among the sasanqua group, *KENKYŌ* does indeed make one marvel as the small bush unfolds its enormous white flowers, flushed with pink. (The pink tends to disappear altogether as the bloom matures.) The petals are long, heart-shaped, deeply fluted and rippled at their margins. The long narrow leaves are widely spaced.

KINKA ZAN (Mount Kinka)
sp. sasanqua

Anemone form cultivars of the sasanqua species are sufficiently rare to render this charming flower worthy of collector's attention. Medium in size, its outer petals are tinted a rich rose-pink, deeply notched and sometimes marked in lime green. The spectacular centre is a mixture of gold stamens and loose ribbon-like paler pink petaloids, also deeply notched. The leaves are dark, narrow and not glossy.

KŌ GYOKU (Little Gem)
sp. sasanqua

(syn: *Ruby*) The dwarf bushy growth of cultivar *KŌ GYOKU* makes it a perfect choice for container work. Compact, curved leaves of rich dark green make a perfect foil for the brilliant pink buds, the colour of a Ceylon ruby. These open to medium-sized formal double blooms, with deeply notched petals which are white, shading to pink at the tips, particularly on the undersides.

LAVENDER QUEEN
sp. sasanqua

Tinted a unique shade of pale lavender, this large single cultivar sasanqua has great novelty value to the collector and may be the parent of more colour breaks to come. It is a plant of low horizontal habit, and vigorous spreading growth.

LIGHTNING FLASH (see INAZUMA)

LION HEAD (see SHISHI GASHIRA)

LITTLE GEM (see KŌ GYOKU)

LITTLE PEARL
sp. sasanqua

Highly recommended by California's Nuccio Nurseries, the charming introduction *Little Pearl* has a compact growth that should endear it to container growers. Flower buds are light pink, opening to medium-sized pure white flowers which are irregularly semi-double.

LUCINDA
sp. sasanqua

A favourite cultivar for hedge and espalier work, decorative *Lucinda* is tall-growing, and with a spreading habit. The medium-sized blooms are a bright lolly-pink in colour, and may be semi-double to informal peony form. There is often a loose group of petaloids waving gaily above the central stamens. The pink shade is quite unusual, seeming to be overlaid with a silvery-blue sheen.

MADO NO TSUKI (Moon at the Window)
sp. sasanqua

JULIE ANNE

KANJIRO　　　　　勘次郎

LUCINDA

Sasanquas

MADO NO TSUKI　　　　　窓の月

MIDGET

NAVAJO

Particularly effective when planted where the blooms can be viewed with light pouring through them, this appropriately named sasanqua is perfectly simple in flower style. Only small in size, the blooms are semi-double, with long petals of purest white, fluted, reflexed and sometimes tinted with blush-pink as they open. The stamens are sparse, long and moderately flared.

MAI NO SODE (Fluttering Sleeves)
　　　　　　　　　　　　　　　　sp. sasanqua
Very large for a sasanqua, the blooms of *MAI NO SODE* are bigger than many japonica varieties. The deeply curved, somewhat concave petals are irregularly fluted, with margins often twisted and overlapped like the tail of a fancy goldfish. Indeed they do resemble the voluminous, fluttering sleeves of a dancing girl, for which they were named. In colouring they are deep rose-pink, shading to white at the centre where they meet a widely flared boss of long gold stamens. A superb variety.

METHUSELAH'S ROBE (see OKINA GOROMO)

MIDGET　　　　　　　　　　　*sp. sasanqua*
A tiny bush with compact masses of long glossy leaves, the dwarf sasanqua *Midget* has to be the perfect choice for container work. The single star-shaped blooms have petals of irregular length with rippled and reflexed edges. These are graduated from white at the base to deep carmine at the tips. Stamens are graduated from white to pale yellow.

MIKUMIKO (see MIKUNI KŌ)

MIKUNI KŌ (Empire Red)　　　*sp. sasanqua*
(syn: *MIKUMIKO*) A Japanese cultivar that has achieved great popularity in Australia, the striking *MIKUNI KŌ* blooms early and long. Tall and bushy of growth, its flowers are medium-sized and single, with irregularly shaped petals of rich carmine, sometimes with a touch of mauve. These are deeply fluted and crimped.

MINAGAWA (see SHISHI GASHIRA)

MINE NO YUKI (Snow on the Mountain Peak)
　　　　　　　　　　　　　　　　sp. sasanqua
(syn: *White Doves*) Looking at my fine container specimen of *MINE NO YUKI*, I have often felt the American name of *White Doves* is more appropriate than the Japanese epithet. For one thing, the small to medium semi-double flowers are rather untidy, with notched feathery petals; they are not a snowy white at all, but rather a tarnished cream shade. It is a beautiful plant, with bushy pendulous growth and inclined to set too many buds. Flower size improves with disbudding.

MING BROCADE (see TAIMIN NISHIKI)

MIRANDY　　　　　　　　　　*sp. hiemalis*
Elegant and decorative, the large semi-double

blooms of *C. hiemalis Mirandy* shade from frosty white to a rich rose-pink. A good-sized bush will produce bloom throughout the winter months.

MISS ED　　　　　　　　　　　*sp. sasanqua*
A popular cultivar in all camellia-growing areas, the curiously named *Miss Ed* is a neat, bushy plant with noticeably small foliage. The medium-sized peony form flowers are tinted a light orchid-pink with occasional lavender and deeper pink overtones. The petals are wavy with notched edges, and open in many layers like a ballerina's tutu skirt.

MOCHI NO SHIO (High Tide)　　*sp. sasanqua*
A cup-shaped bloom of exceptional beauty, the Japanese cultivar *MOCHI NO SHIO* is medium to large in size, and semi-double. The somewhat rippled concave petals are frosty white, shaded pink on their reverses and sometimes on their tips. The flower most resembles a bowl of golden stamens which seem ready to overflow.

MOON AT THE WINDOW
(see MADO NO TSUKI)

MOUNT KINKA (see KINKA ZAN)

NARUMI BAY (see NARUMI GATA)

NARUMI GATA (Narumi Bay)　　*sp. sasanqua*
(syn: *Oleifera*) Named for a celebrated Japanese beauty spot, this sasanqua cultivar is vigorous in growth, and with an upright habit. The large white blooms are shaded delicate pink at the edges and do not open fully, remaining an attractive cupped form. The petals have a noticeably crinkled texture at all times. *NARUMI GATA* is prone to occasional foliage variegation, and is often sold under the synonym *Oleifera*.

NAVAJO　　　　　　　　　　　*sp. sasanqua*
A stunning large-flowered sasanqua cultivar, *Navajo* makes a compact, dense-foliaged shrub with plenty of strong upright growth. The flower colour is a strong rosy-red, fading to almost white at the centre of a rather flat flower. It is semi-double. Most highly recommended.

NOBLE FLOWER (see HANA DAIJIN)

NODAMI USHIRO (Backward Glance)
　　　　　　　　　　　　　　　　sp. sasanqua
Compact in size but vigorous in growth, this striking cultivar may be readily pruned to formal shape. The rose-pink flowers are perfectly single, and sufficiently large to elicit a backward glance from any camellia-lover.

OCEAN SUNRISE (see HINODE NO UMI)

OKINA GOROMO (Methuselah's Robe)
　　　　　　　　　　　　　　　　sp. sasanqua
This popular sasanqua cultivar forms an attractive small bush, often with variegated foliage. The flowers are single, medium-sized, and white shading to pink.

PLANTATION PINK

OLEIFERA (see NARUMI GATA)

PALE MOONLIGHT   *sp. sasanqua*
A useful dwarf-growing cultivar for places where sunlight is not too strong, *Pale Moonlight* combines a low spreading habit with small foliage. The medium-sized semi-double blooms are tinted a pale orchid-pink and have upward pointing inner petals.

PALE PINK (see SHŌWA NO SAKAE)

PAPAVER   *sp. sasanqua*
(syn: *Pink Poppy, Rosea Papaver*) Similar in flower colour to the variety *Rosea* (a soft rose-pink) the single blooms of this sasanqua remain semi-open in cup form. The habit is rounded and compact, the growth inclined to be slender.

PAPER TIGER (see INU HARIKO)

PAPIER MACHÉ DOG (see INU HARIKO)

PEAK OF MT FUJI (see FUJI NO MINE)

PINK POPPY (see PAPAVER)

PINK SHOWER   *sp. hiemalis*
The large fragile semi-double blossoms of *Pink Shower* do not hold well on the bush; nevertheless, they make a beautiful picture in areas free of the dreaded flower blight, as they scatter every which way, carpeting the ground for yards. The flowers are light pink, their petal edges delicately shirred, and the stamens widely flared.

PINK WINTER CAMELLIA
(see SHISHI GASHIRA)

PINSON'S LIGHT   *sp. sasanqua*
An attractive new sasanqua propagated by Sydney's Camellia Grove Nursery, *Pinson's Light* bears an eye-catching medium-sized white bloom of peony form. The reflexed outer petals are occasionally tinged with deep pink, and the inner growth consists of a mass of white petaloids, loose and notched. Flower buds are cherry-red.

PLANTATION PINK   *sp. sasanqua*
One of the most popular of the sasanqua group, and bred by the Camellia Grove Nursery of St Ives, New South Wales, *Plantation Pink* is notable for its rapid growth, tree-like habit and particularly large saucer-like single flowers in a showy, soft pink. *Plantation Pink* is often used for hedges.

PLAYFUL BUTTERFLY (see CHŌ ASOBI)

RAINBOW   *sp. sasanqua*
A vigorous plant with plenty of strong, upright growth, *Rainbow* may be trained to formal container shape or used as a vertical accent plant. The large white flowers are single, each petal bordered with a contrasting band of red.

RED BIRD (see HIRYŪ)

RED WILLOW   *sp. sasanqua*
As if the medium-sized flowers were not attractive enough (they are a particularly rich shade, more red than pink, and semi-double) this aptly named camellia brings the added bonus of dark, narrow foliage and a willow-like; weeping habit. Let it spill from a tall container, or over the edge of a terrace or bank.

RING AROUND THE MOON
(see TSUKI NO KASA)

ROSEA   *sp. sasanqua*
A favourite in colder areas, *Rosea* has a notable resistance to low temperatures, and maintains vigorous growth at all times. The large single flowers are deep rose-pink, with a noticeably sweet fragrance. The petal edges are reflexed, giving each a somewhat tubular appearance.

ROSEA MAGNIFICA (see ROSY MIST)

ROSEA PAPAVER (see PAPAVER)

ROSY MIST   *sp. sasanqua*
(syn: *Rosea Magnifica*) A soft misty pink, as their name implies, the blooms of this outstanding sasanqua cultivar are single and larger than average. The growth is strong, the habit spreading.

RUBY (see KŌ GYOKU)

RUSHAY   *sp. sasanqua*
Another innovation from Australia's Camellia Grove Nursery, the elegant sasanqua *Rushay* is semi-double, with petals that are long and deeply fluted, rather reminiscent of a reticulata. The colouring is pale pink, flushing deeper toward the flower centre. Dark foliage.

RYŌMEN KŌ (Two-faced Pink)   *sp. sasanqua*
A most attractive Japanese cultivar, *RYŌMEN KŌ* bears a medium-sized semi-double bloom of vivid crimson, occasionally seen with white shading. The flowers are generally cup-shaped, the foliage strong and broad, and the blooms are exactly the same shade, front and back.

SANDAN KA (Triple Tiara)   *sp. hiemalis*
A favourite Japanese cultivar for centuries, the unusual *SANDAN KA* bears flowers of deep pink with a striking 'hose-in-hose' effect. The Japanese name *SANDAN KA* means three-tiered flower, and it is a variety of the winter camellia, *C. hiemalis*.

SANDAN ZAKI (Triple Flower)   *sp. hiemalis*
Another favourite Japanese cultivar with a long history, the delicate *SANDAN ZAKI* bears rose-pink semi-double blooms, often three at a time from a single bud, hence its Japanese name meaning 'triple flower'. It is not common in Western collections.

RED WILLOW

RUSHAY

SETSUGEKKA   雪月花

SHISHI GASHIRA   獅子頭

SHŌWA NO SAKAE   昭和の栄

SHUCHŪ KA   酒中花

STAR ABOVE STAR

Sasanquas

SCARLET BIRD (see HIRYŪ)

SCARLET BIRD'S BROCADE
(see HIRYŪ NISHIKI)

SCARLET DRAGON (see HIRYŪ)

SETSUGEKKA   *sp. sasanqua*
(syn: *Elegant Friends, Fluted White, Wavy White*) A great favourite among the true sasanquas, as its many synonyms imply. The bloom is pure white, semi-double and larger than average, with the petals distinctively rippled and fluted. The plant is of vigorous growth and upright habit, but should be protected from morning sun which might burn the flowers.

SHIN ONOME (Dawn)   *sp. sasanqua*
Larger in diameter than many japonica cultivars, this elegant camellia should correct the beliefs of many growers that sasanquas bear only small flowers. The variety has strong upright growth, dense habit, and palest pink single blossoms. Each petal is deeply notched.

SHISHI GASHIRA   *sp. hiemalis*
(syn: *BENI KAN TSUBAKI, Lion Head, MINAGAWA, Pink Winter Camellia*) Not a true sasanqua, this cultivar is much valued as a winter's decoration in Japan, where it is called *BENI KAN TSUBAKI* (the red cold camellia). It is classed by botanists as a variety of *C. hiemalis*. The bloom is semi-double to almost double, of medium size and a glowing rosy-red. It is particularly decorative as a pot specimen, and may be trained as a hedge or espalier. The flowering period is long. (Photo also p. 168)

SHŌWA NO SAKAE   *sp. hiemalis*
(syn: *Glory, Glory of Showa, Pale Pink, USUBENI*) Again not a true sasanqua, though frequently sold as one, *SHŌWA NO SAKAE* is a cultivar of the winter-blooming *C. hiemalis*. The delicate flowers are a soft pink, occasionally with a faint, white marbling. Medium-sized, they may vary from semi-double to rose form double with many petaloids. *SHŌWA NO SAKAE* does not fade in full sun and flowers over a long period. A tendency to horizontal habit makes this cultivar useful as a ground cover, or in hanging baskets and other horizontal containers.

SHŌWA SUPREME   *sp. hiemalis*
One of the most valued of small winter-blooming camellias, *Shōwa Supreme* is an improved version of *SHŌWA NO SAKAE*, raised from a chance seedling. The colouring is the same soft pink, but in a larger peony form flower. It is often recommended as a container plant, or for ground cover, espalier and other horizontal usage.

SHUCHŪ KA (Flower in Wine)   *sp. sasanqua*
Not so commonly seen as many of the other Japanese cultivars, the delightful *SHUCHŪ KA* is worth seeking out for the beauty of its single to semi-double flowers. These are white,

of flat form, though the petals have a pronounced central rib and are edged with raspberry-pink.

SILVER DRAGON (see GINRYŪ)

SNOW (see MINE NO YUKI)

SNOW ON THE MOUNTAIN PEAK
(see MINE NO YUKI)

SPARKLING BURGUNDY   *sp. sasanqua*
Popular in many parts of the world, this American sasanqua cultivar is particularly eye-catching, provided its blossoms can be kept out of full sun. Growth is tall and spreading, though rather irregular. Blooming begins early and lasts for a long period. The small double blooms tend to peony form and are a rich ruby-rose when they first open. This fades to light red with a lavender sheen.

STAR ABOVE STAR   *sp. vernalis*
A remarkably late-blooming cultivar of the spring-flowering *C. vernalis*, *Star Above Star* features a tall bushy growth. The medium-sized semi-double blooms are lavender-white, flushed with pink at the tips of outer petals. These petals have crinkled edges, and are arranged in star-shaped layers, one above the other. A particularly charming novelty.

SUNRISE SKY (see ASAHI NO SORA)

SUNSET SEA (see IRIHI NO UMI)

TAIMIN NISHIKI (Ming Brocade)
    sp. sasanqua
The brocaded effect of this large single cultivar is one of texture, rather than pattern. The blooms are semi-double, the pale pink petals notched and fluted, with a finely embossed texture like that of expensive damask over all. Certainly a sasanqua for the collector of fine camellia quality — and check the width — over 10 cm (4 in) for each flower.

TAISHO BROCADE (see TAISHŌ NISHIKI)

TAISHŌ NISHIKI (Taisho Brocade)
    sp. sasanqua
This remarkable camellia cultivar does not appear to be grown in Western gardens, which is a pity. Its colour and patterning are unique. The bloom is large, single (generally with only five petals) and is basically a deep raspberry-pink, shading even darker at petal tips. Against this is set a moiré pattern of wave after wave of rippled white *across* the petals. These waves are closest together at the tips, gradually fading in frequency and contrast as they near the flower centre. *TAISHŌ NISHIKI* commemorates the reign of Emperor Taishō in whose time the sasanqua camellias were returned to favour.

TANYA   *sp. sasanqua*
Not *Tanya* as in Russia, but *Tanya* as in the title

VELVETY

of a Japanese drama, this popular sasanqua novelty is a semi-dwarf grower of slow, spreading habit and small sharp foliage. The small flowers are deep rose-pink and single. *Tanya* is much favoured for container planting and rockery work, and makes a decorative groundcover.

TRIPLE FLOWER (see SANDAN ZAKI)

TRIPLE TIARA (see SANDAN KA)

TSUKI NO KASA (Ring around the Moon)
                sp. sasanqua
Most imaginatively named, the delicate cultivar *TSUKI NO KASA* is surely one of the more charming Japanese varieties. The large blush-pink flowers are single, with the petal edges lightly frilled and twisted. Around the central mass of stamens there is a corona of deeper pink, surmounted with a halo of pink radiating veins. The foliage is long, dark and pointed.

TSUMAORI GASA (Fancy Hat) *sp. sasanqua*
How remarkable are the seemingly infinite variations in which nature can arrange a small group of petals. The flowers of this brilliant carmine cultivar are semi-double with about ten petals. The outer edges of these are rolled inward so the perimeter of the flower forms a perfect hexagon. White stamens, gold-tipped, complete the fashionable ensemble.

TWO-FACED PINK (see RYŌMEN KŌ)

USUBENI (see SHŌWA NO SAKAE)

VELVETY   *sp. sasanqua*
(syn: *Crimson Velvettii*) Richly coloured as a length of crimson silk velvet, the single to semi-double blooms of this splendid sasanqua truly glow. Occasional petaloids penetrate the corona of gold stamens, and the flowers appear on a bushy plant of generally upright habit.

WAVE CREST   *sp. sasanqua*
One of the most stunning sasanqua cultivars, and very like the original species, *Wave Crest* bears large semi-double blooms of purest white. The difference between it and other white cultivars is the petals, which are about twice as long as they are wide, twisted and raggedy-ended. The effect is very much that of the flying spume at the tip of breaking waves.

WAVY WHITE (see SETSUGEKKA)

WEEPING MAIDEN   *sp. sasanqua*
A dwarf-growing camellia of spreading habit and weeping growth, the cultivar *Weeping Maiden* makes an effective ground cover in neglected areas of the garden. The large single blooms are white, fading to blush-pink at the petal tips. They are noticeably fragrant.

WEROONA   *sp. sasanqua*
A brilliantly coloured sasanqua cultivar with strong bushy growth, *Weroona* bears large semi-double blooms with fluted and reflexed petals. These are white, shaded a deep raspberry-pink for about 1 cm (½in) in the petal tips. Under-petals are an even darker shade.

WHEEL OF CLOVES (see CHŌJI GURUMA)

WHITE DOVES (see MINE NO YUKI)

WHITE FRILLS   *sp. sasanqua*
A popular American cultivar, *White Frills* has the low spreading growth that particularly suits groundcover work. The blooms are large, pure white and peony form, with fluted petals.

WINSOME   *sp. hiemalis*
A delicate semi-double flower with a tendency to anemone form, *Winsome* is a cultivar of *C. hiemalis*, and bears medium-sized, pink-edged, white blooms. The bush is particularly charming with its mixture of dark buds and light flowers.

YAE ARARE (Dense Hailstone) *sp. sasanqua*
An extremely popular sasanqua wherever these beautiful flowers are grown, the stunning *YAE ARARE* is a vigorous plant with dense, upright growth. The white blooms are large and single, with rather long petals. These are tinted pink at their outer ends, and at the same point, they reflex. The stamens project in a large golden boss.

YULETIDE   *sp. sasanqua*
A splendid sasanqua for container or formal work, *Yuletide* is a great favourite in the northern hemisphere where its display coincides with the Christmas season. The small single flowers are perfectly regular in shape, with petals widest at their tips. They are coloured a glowing red with an occasional overtone of orange. They appear in great profusion over a long period, often blooming well into spring.

ZERBES (see FUKUZUTSUMI; also a Victorian synonym for KANJIRO)

WAVE CREST

YAE ARARE   八重霰

YULETIDE

THE HYBRID CAMELLIAS

Excluding reticulata hybrids

The good Abbé Berlèse's 1838 prediction that the future of the camellia lay in interspecific hybridisation was more accurate than he dreamed. But it was not to come true for more than a century after he wrote it.

The japonicas alone went on to achieve their glory for about another fifty years and then faded right out of fashion in Europe. There was a brief flutter of interest in the late Edwardian period, but this quickly came to an end with the outbreak of World War I, as a fickle gardening public's interest changed to the great wealth of *Rhododendron* species which flooded back to Europe from the Himalayan and Chinese expeditions of English plant hunters. Between 1918 and 1939, these numbered many hundreds. But among the loot of George Forrest's treks to outback China were the seed of many new camellia species as well. These included *C. saluenensis*, the wild form of *C. reticulata*, *C. tsaii* and *C. taliensis*. The first two were to prove of great importance in the raising of new and really different hybrids which would catch the imagination of the whole camellia world.

Plants of *C. saluenensis* were raised from Forrest's seed by J. C. Williams of Caerhays, Cornwall, who then proceeded to hybridise them with *C. japonica* varieties, to produce the first of the lovely *C. X Williamsii* hybrids.

These were vigorous plants, graceful and floriferous, and proved much more cold-hardy than either of their parent species. They bore a profusion of large pink flowers over many months, and found great favour among camellia-fanciers, even with the first varieties *J. C. Williams* (1940) and *Donation* (1941).

C. saluenensis was also crossed with the reticulata *Captain Rawes* to produce, in 1936, the large-flowered hybrid *Salutation*, followed shortly by a recross of the *X Williamsii* hybrid *Mary Christian* with the wild form of *C. reticulata* to produce the first of the true reticulata hybrids, *Leonard Messel*, still a favourite in many gardens.

In quick succession, stimulated by the success of these early crosses, hybridists set to work crossing established species and varieties with *C. cuspidata*, *C. fraterna*, *C. granthamiana*, *C. heterophylla*, *C. irrawadiensis*, *C. lutchuensis*, *C. oleifera*, *C. pitardii*, *C. rosaeflora*, *C. tsaii* and many other new species hot from the hands of the plant hunters.

Together with the post-World War II hybrids of *C. reticulata* from Yunnan, these new camellias have fascinated a whole generation of camellia-lovers, for whom this book may serve as a new iconography of these wonderful blooms.

The dictionary of interspecific hybrid camellias that follows includes all crosses except those involving reticulata parentage. These are in the separate chapter on reticulatas and their hybrids on page 142.

Indicative of future possibilities are these two unnamed hybrids of the Black Camellia, KURO TSUBAKI. *The first has dark red foliage, the second gold-variegated foliage.*

Opposite: A beautiful seedling from the early X Williamsii *hybrid* Donation, *raised by California hybridist David Feathers.*

X ANGEL WINGS

Hybrids

X ACK-SCENT 1978   FRAGRANT
Most successful of the fragrant hybrids to date,
W. L. Ackerman's *Ack-scent* was developed from
crossing two earlier fragrant camellias, *Kramer's
Supreme* and *X Fragrant Pink*. The medium-
large peony form blooms are tinted delicate pink,
exude a delicious spicy fragrance and flower mid
to late season. An all-round success with great
promise for the future. (Photo p. 194)

X ALICE K. CUTTER 1972   FRAGRANT
One of the more successful attempts to breed
maximum fragrance into a camellia, *Alice K.
Cutter* was a 1972 breakthrough by Dr R. Cutter
of California. It is a medium pink of large
anemone form, crossing *C. japonica Mrs Bertha
A. Harms* with hybrid *Parks 69 (2) (Reg Ragland
X C. lutchuensis)*. Blooming period is mid
season.

X ANGEL WINGS 1970
A delicate feminine hybrid, *Angel Wings* crosses
japonica *Dr Tinsley X C. saluenensis* to produce
a medium-sized semi-double bloom of orchid-
pink, shading white. Flowering mid season, it
shows unusual upright and deeply fluted petals.
From Kramer Bros, California.

X ANNE HAZLEWOOD 1967
Originating as a seedling of hybrid *Donation*,
Anne Hazlewood produces large, double blooms
of warm red, mid to late season. Introduced by
Walter Hazlewood of New South Wales.

X ANTICIPATION 1962
A deserving success for New Zealander Les Jury,
Anticipation is a large peony form bloom of deep
rose-pink, achieved by crossing *C. saluenensis X
C. japonica Leviathan*. *Anticipation* blooms mid
season.

X ARMSTRONG'S SUPREME 1970
A 1970 release from Armstrong's Nurseries of
California, *Armstrong's Supreme* is a medium to
large camellia hybrid of bright currant-red. A
cross of *C. japonica Ville de Nantes X hybrid J. C.
Williams*, it is a showy semi-double bloom with
upright petals and wavy margins. Mid season is
blooming time.

X AUTUMN GLORY 1967
Popular with Australian gardeners, *Autumn
Glory* was bred by Erica McMinn of Noble Park,
Victoria, crossing *C. japonica Spencer's Pink X
C. granthamiana*. It is a large single bloom,
flushed pink at petal edges, shading to white
toward a widely flared boss of superb gold
stamens.

X AVALON 1962
Propagated by Pasadena's McCaskill Gardens,
the 1962 release *Avalon* is a large rose-pink
camellia with cerise overtones. Semi-double, it
has irregular notched petals, and blooms mid
season.

X ANTICIPATION

X BIG MO

X BONNIE MARIE

X BABY BEAR 1976
A dainty miniature, *Baby Bear* resulted from a cross of *C. rosaeflora X C. tsaii*, made in 1976 by N. Hayden of New Zealand. The tiny blooms vary from pink to white and open on a dwarf plant, mid season.

X BALLET QUEEN 1976
New Zealander Les Jury raised the splendid *Ballet Queen* from crossing *C. saluenensis X C. japonica Leviathan*. The large peony form blooms are salmon-pink, and open mid to late season.

X BELINDA CARLYON 1972
A single red camellia of medium size from the surprising cross *C. japonica X C. heterophylla Barbara Hillier*, the hybrid *Belinda Carlyon* was released in England in 1972.

X BIG MO 1960
A medium-sized semi-double camellia, *Big Mo* is usually mistaken for a super-sized sasanqua. It is in fact a cross between *C. oleifera X C. hiemalis SHŌWA NO SAKAE*, raised by R. Carr of California. Colouring is soft rose-pink.

X BLACK KNIGHT 1965
A cross between hybrid *X Philippa Forwood (C. saluenensis X C. japonica) X C. japonica KURO TSUBAKI, Black Knight* was unveiled in 1965 by American hybridiser McCaskill. It is a large rose form double of black-red, and blooms mid to late season.

X BLUE DANUBE 1960
Again from McCaskill of Pasadena, *Blue Danube* is a hybrid crossing an earlier *C. X Williamsii X C. japonica*. Launched in 1960, it is a medium-sized camellia of peony form, coloured an unusual rose-lavender. Blooms mid season.

X BONNIE MARIE 1959
Crossing the earlier *C. cuspidata X C. saluenensis Robbie* with *C. japonica Charlotte Bradford*, the James Rare Plant Nursery of California produced *Bonnie Marie*. A large bloom of delicate phlox-pink with fluted petals, it varies from semi-double to anemone form, blooming throughout the season.

X BOWEN BRYANT 1960
A large semi-double hybrid bloom, *Bowen Bryant* was originated in 1960 by Australian Professor E. G. Waterhouse, who crossed *C. saluenensis* with a *C. japonica*. It is a sturdy open plant with deep pink blooms. Mid season.

X BOWEN BRYANT VARIEGATED 1964
A pink and white variegated form of the previous entry, *Bowen Bryant Variegated* was released in 1964 by Australia's Hazlewood Nursery.

X BRIGADOON 1960
Crossing *C. saluenensis X C. japonica Princess*

X CORAL DELIGHT

X CORNISH SNOW

X DEBBIE

X DONATION

Hybrids

Baciocchi produced this lovely rose-pink semi-double hybrid of medium size. Armstrong Nurseries of California released it in 1960.

X BURMA BABY 1965
Crossing *C. japonica X C. irrawaddiensis* resulted in a small white flower flushed and veined pink. Appropriately, Dr P. L. Hilsman of Georgia named it *Burma Baby*. An early bloomer.

X BUZZ ALDRIN 1971
One of several camellias named for American astronauts, *Buzz Aldrin* is a 1971 cross of *japonica Reg Ragland X C. granthamiana*. A light pink anemone form bloom of large size.

X CAERHAYS 1948
One of the original *X Williamsii* hybrids developed by J. C. Williams of Cornwall, *Caerhays* is named for the garden where he carried out his life's work. It is a rose-coloured semi-double camellia resulting from the cross *C. saluenensis X C. japonica Lady Clare*.

X CELEBRATION 1962
An uncommon semi-double hybrid of light orchid-pink, *Celebration* is a *C. saluenensis X C. japonica* cross by R. Veitch of England. The blooms are medium size.

X CHARLEAN 1963
A large semi-double hybrid of medium pink, *Charlean* shows pink stamens tipped with yellow when it opens mid to late season. Developed by W. Stewart of Georgia, it is a cross between *C. japonica Donckelarii X C. X Williamsii Donation*, from which it inherits a faint orchid shading.

X CHARLES COLBERT 1959
The *C. saluenensis X C. japonica* cross produced no finer camellia for Australian Professor E. G. Waterhouse than the radiant *Charles Colbert*. It is a medium-sized semi-double bloom of amaranth-rose. The petals are notched. A late bloomer.

X CITATION 1950
An early *C. X Williamsii* cross *(C. saluenensis X C. japonica)*, *Citation* was produced by Lord Aberconway of Bodnant, North Wales. It is a large semi-double camellia with irregular petals of silver blush-pink. Flowers mid season.

X CORAL DELIGHT 1975
A colourful break in the line of *C. saluenensis X C. japonica* crosses, *Coral Delight* is a warm coral-red bloom introduced by Kramer Bros of California. A medium-sized semi-double bloom, it opens mid season.

X CORNISH SNOW 1950
A popular hybrid from English grower J. C. Williams, *Cornish Snow* is small in size, profuse in flowering habit. The open single blooms have an occasional pink flush, and appear mid season from the leaf axils. *Cornish Snow* is a *C. saluenen-*

X E. G. WATERHOUSE VARIEGATED

sis X C. cuspidata cross.

X CREATION 1958
McCaskill Gardens introduced this worthwhile hybrid between *C. japonica Elegans* and *C. saluenensis Apple Blossom.* It flowers mid season, a large semi-double to anemone form bloom of luminous soft pink.

X DEBBIE 1965
Les Jury of New Zealand again. His 1965 creation *Debbie* is a true *X Williamsii* hybrid crossing *C. saluenensis X C. japonica Debutante.* It is a large spinel-pink bloom of semi-double to full peony form, with petaloids.

X DONATION 1941
One of the earliest and best loved *X Williamsii* hybrids, *Donation* resulted from a cross between *C. saluenensis X C. japonica Donckelarii* made by Colonel R. S. Clarke of Sussex. It is a large semi-double bloom of orchid-pink, blooming mid season. There is a variegated sport.

X DREAMBOAT 1976
Bright pink with a fascinating lavender cast, *Dreamboat* was launched in New Zealand by grower Jury. It is a large formal double with incurved petals, opening mid season. It crosses *C. saluenensis X C. japonica K. Sawada.*

X E. G. WATERHOUSE 1954
A great camellia from a great camellian, *E. G. Waterhouse* is a 1954 production of its late Australian namesake. A medium-sized formal double of light pink, it is a true *X Williamsii* cross, blooming mid to late season. (Photo p. 50)

X E. G. WATERHOUSE VARIEGATED 1960
Very popular in the United States, the light pink and white variegated sport of *E. G. Waterhouse* was released in 1960.

X EL DORADO 1967
C. pitardii crossed with *C. japonica Tiffany* produced this large, light pink camellia of full peony form. Blooming mid season, its 'godfather' was Howard Asper of California.

X ELEGANT BEAUTY 1962
Les Jury of New Zealand produced this striking deep rose camellia and named it *Elegant Beauty* as a tribute to its parents *C. japonica Elegans* which he crossed with *C. saluenensis.* It is a large anemone form hybrid, and blooms mid season.

X ELSIE JURY 1964
Jury of New Zealand backed a winner with his 1964 introduction, *Elsie Jury,* a cross of *C. saluenensis X C. japonica Pukekura.* A large ruffled bloom of deep pink and full peony form, it flowers mid to late season.

X FALLEN ANGEL 1974
A surprising colour break is noticeable in this hybrid between *C. japonica X C. granthamiana.*

X ELEGANT BEAUTY

X FREEDOM BELL

X HONG KONG

X INFATUATION

X JAMIE

X JURY 216

Hybrids

Fallen Angel is medium-sized, varying from semi-double to full peony form. Its colouring is distinctly lavender, with a greenish-yellow tone toward the centre. Dr W. Homeyer of Georgia registered it. Blooms mid season.

X FLIRTATION 1961
Armstrong Nurseries of Ontario, California are strongly behind their 1961 cross between popular *C. japonica Lady Vansittart X C. saluenensis.* They call it *Flirtation,* and it is a medium-sized single camellia of pale silvery-pink, with cupped form. It blooms early to mid season.

X FRAGRANT PINK 1968   FRAGRANT
Hybridist W. L. Ackerman of Maryland produced this charming scented bloom by crossing *C. rusticana X C. lutchuensis.* A miniature deep pink bloom of peony form, it flowers throughout the season, and will be the basis of many fragrant cultivars to come.

X FRAGRANT PINK IMPROVED 1975
                       FRAGRANT
Chemically produced in 1975 by the original hybridiser of *Fragrant Pink,* this improved version is in every way a better bloom, larger and more shapely than the original. (Photo p. 192)

X FREEDOM BELL 1965
Small to medium in size, delightful in shape and texture, *Freedom Bell* was produced by Nuccio Nurseries of California. It is a semi-double of 'hose-in-hose' form, tinted a bright coral-red. Exact parentage is not disclosed, but it flowers early to mid season.

X GALAXIE 1963
A medium-sized semi-double bloom of deeper striped medium pink, *Galaxie* presents an unusual colour effect because its darker petal reverses roll slightly inward. An American cross between *C. saluenensis X C. japonica Finlandia Variegated,* it blooms mid to late season.

X GARDEN GLORY 1974
A *X Williamsii* cross from the Nuccio Nursery, *Garden Glory* was registered in 1974. It is a medium rose form double bloom of rich orchid-pink with notched petal tips, and blooms throughout the season.

X GLAD RAGS 1969
An Australian contribution to the hybrid range, *Glad Rags* was first shown by H. K. Dettman of New South Wales. It is a large semi-double bloom with irregular petals and occasional petaloids, all in rich soft pink. Blooming early, it crosses *C. japonica Party Girl X C. saluenensis.*

X GLENN'S ORBIT 1967
Another astronaut is remembered in the remarkable *Glenn's Orbit* — a chance seedling from the *X Williamsii* hybrid *Donation.* It is a larger camellia of glowing orchid-pink, varying from

X PINK BOUQUET

X SAYONARA

semi-double to loose peony form. Blooming at mid season, it was originated in 1967, in Cornwall, England.

X HONG KONG 1960
Developed by North California hybridist Dave Feathers, *Hong Kong* is a stunning, small, bell-shaped bloom with outwardly flaring petal tips. It crosses *C. hongkongensis X C. saluenensis*, and its early blooms are irregularly variegated in white, pale pink and cerise.

X HUNTSMAN 1975
A more vivid colour than most of the *X Williamsii* hybrids, *Huntsman's* brilliant red tonings are the result of crossing *C. saluenensis X C. japonica*

ARAJISHI. It is a large peony form bloom, developed by New Zealander Les Jury. It blooms right through the season.

X INFATUATION 1980
A delightful new cultivar from California's David L. Feathers, *Infatuation* has already won prizes and is sure to attract many growers in years to come. Medium-sized, single and with long two-toned petals that are both ruffled and reflexed, it is a cross between *C. saluenensis* and *C. japonica Debutante*. The colour is basically a pale musk-pink, with deeper veining and occasional flushes of raspberry. Gold-tipped stamens project in a tight cylindrical mass.

X JAMIE 1968
A second generation *X Williamsii* hybrid from Professor Waterhouse of Sydney, *Jamie* is a gorgeous semi-double bloom of medium size and 'hose-in-hose' form. Colouring is vivid dark red, and the flowers peak mid season.

X J. C. WILLIAMS 1940
The original *X Williamsii* cross, hybrid *J. C. Williams* commemorates the man who began a new era in camellia hybridisation. A plant of pendulous growth, it is crowded all season with medium-sized single blooms of pale phlox-pink, often tipped with red.

X JOYFUL BELLS 1962
Cross *C. saluenensis* with the miniature *C. japonica FUYAJŌ* and you get *Joyful Bells*, a small six-petalled bloom of glowing wine-red. New Zealander Les Jury did it in 1962, and the hybrid has great popularity. Blooms mid season.

X JURY 216 1969
Hybridist Les Jury of New Zealand seems to have run out of names with this splendid *X Williamsii* hybrid, but as Shakespeare said, 'a rose by any other name . . .'. *Jury 216* is a large flower of most variable form, but invariably beautiful. A loose semi-double bloom of elegant mauve-pink, it has notched petals, and is often a darker tone in semi-shade.

X LADY CUTLER 1971
Named for the wife of the New South Wales

governor during the 1970s, *Lady Cutler* is a hybrid between *C. saluenensis* and *C. japonica Ville de Nantes*. It is very suitable for espalier because of its spreading habit. The mid season blooms are bright rose-pink, semi-double and large in size. New Zealander Les Jury introduced it.

X LADY GOWRIE 1954
Another *X Williamsii* hybrid from Professor Waterhouse, *Lady Gowrie* has a bushy habit with rather pendulous branches, and is much used as a tub specimen. The large semi-double blooms are clear cyclamen-pink, from medium to large in size. Mid season. (Photo p. 51)

X LAMERTSII 1952
Named for its hybridiser, Dr W. E. Lammerts of California, *Lamertsii* was introduced in 1952. It is a small single flower of blush-pink, with matching stamens tipped with a distinctly reddish tone. The plant is very sturdy and densely foliaged.

X LITTLE LAVENDER 1965
Introducing a charming lavender-pink colouring into the hybrid range, *Little Lavender* is a miniature anemone form bloom, peaking mid season. It is a cross between the earlier hybrid *X Philippa Ifould X C. japonica*, and was introduced by California's McCaskill Gardens.

X MARGARET WATERHOUSE 1954
One of the most widely grown *X Williamsii* hybrids, *Margaret Waterhouse* was named by its propagator E. G. Waterhouse in 1954. It is an early blooming semi-double flower of light pink.

X MILKY WAY 1965
A dainty miniature plant from Dr P. L. Hilsman of Georgia, *Milky Way* was registered in 1965 — a cross between *C. cuspidata* and *C. fraterna*. The flowers are small, white and single.

X MIRAGE 1975
Crossing *C. saluenensis X* the flame-coloured *C. japonica MOSHIO* resulted in colourful *Mirage*, a 1975 bloom of bright rose-red by New Zealander Les Jury. The flowers are large and semi-double, and bloom throughout the season.

X MONA JURY 1976
A 1976 introduction from Jury of New Zealand, *Mona Jury* took an earlier cross between *C. saluenensis X C. japonica* and recrossed it with the japonica *Betty Sheffield Supreme*. The resultant hybrid is a large peony form bloom of apricot-pink, flowering all season long.

X MONTICELLO 1957
A rich pink peony form bloom with loose petals, *Monticello* was introduced in 1957 by David Feathers. Parentage is not announced for this wonderful large hybrid, which blooms mid to late season, and is named for the Virginia home of American President Thomas Jefferson.

X SPRING FESTIVAL

X SYLVIA MAY WELLS

X TINY PRINCESS

Hybrids

X TIP TOE

X UTSUKUSHI ASAHI

X WALTZ DREAM

X OLÉ 1978

A newcomer to the garden scene, the *C. saluenensis* hybrid *Olé* was introduced only in 1978. It flowers very late indeed and provides a welcome extension to the camellia season. The flower is small, rose form, and tinted a delicious icecream-pink. It was raised by Hamilton Fish of Santa Cruz, California, and flowers profusely.

X PINK BOUQUET 1975

The exceptionally profuse blooming habit of this spectacular hybrid is suggested by its name. *Pink Bouquet* (introduced by the Monrovia Nursery of Azusa, California) is a cross of *C. japonica Pink Parfait X C. saluenensis*. It bears masses of medium to large blooms of light rose-pink with a fluorescent sheen. The flowers vary from rose form to fully double and bloom mid season.

X PINK CASCADE 1965

C. saluenensis X C. japonica Spencer's Pink produced *Pink Cascade*, a fine hybrid with an interesting weeping habit. Dr J. Rayner of New Zealand was the 'godfather', and the miniature pale pink flowers (single, with six petals) seem to form all over the plant in mid season.

X POLARIS 1964

A marvellous second generation hybrid, *Polaris* resulted from the crossing of *C. japonica HISHI KARAITO* with the earlier hybrid *J. C. Williams*. The flower form is delightful: large, semi-double to peony form blooms with long, narrow petals, scalloped at the tips. The colour is radiant pink, and mid season is the time to see them. J. L. Sparkman of Florida bred it.

X RED QUEEN 1960

A deep cherry-red single bloom of medium size, *Red Queen* was a *C. saluenensis X C. japonica Apollo* cross. R. Veitch of Exeter, UK was the hybridist.

X ROBBIE 1958

Very large semi-double blooms of deep orchid-pink open mid season when you plant *Robbie*, a seedling of the earlier hybrid camellia *Sylvia May*. It was released in 1958 by the James Rare Plant Nursery of California.

X ROBYN McMINN 1970

Robyn McMinn is a medium-sized formal double seedling from *Donation*, and tinted a soft clear pink. It blooms throughout the season, and was named by Mrs Erica McMinn of Noble Park, Australia.

X ROSE PARADE 1969

Less active in the general hybrid field than with japonicas and reticulatas, the Nuccio Nursery of Altadena, California have produced no more beautiful flower than the deep rose-pink stunner they've named *Rose Parade*. It is a vigorous compact cross between *C. X Williamsii Donation* and *C. japonica*. The medium-sized formal double blooms open all season long.

X SAYONARA 1965

A *X Williamsii* hybrid by E. G. Waterhouse, *SAYONARA* was first shown in 1965. It is a medium semi-double bloom of clear pink, flowering mid season. Growth is dense and bushy.

X SHOCKING PINK 1955

A popular *X Williamsii* hybrid (*C. saluenensis X C. japonica*) Professor Waterhouse's *Shocking Pink* was shown in 1955. It is a medium-sized semi-double flower with ruffled, notched petals and petaloids intermixed with gold stamens. The blooms are deep Tyrian rose in colour, and bloom mid to late season.

X SOUTH SEAS 1967

A cross between *C. saluenensis* and *C. japonica C. M. Wilson*, the medium-sized hybrid *South Seas* was registered in 1967 by New Zealander F. Jury. It is a semi-double to loose peony form flower of silver-pink, blushing to deeper rose at notched petal margins. Blooming mid season.

X SPRING FESTIVAL 1975

A seedling of *C. cuspidata* propagated by Toichi Domoto of California, *Spring Festival* is a dainty miniature camellia of rose form double style. Colouring is medium pink with a paler centre; growth is narrow and upright. *Spring Festival* blooms mid to late season.

X SWEET BIRD OF YOUTH 1960

A large lavender-pink hybrid with a centre of swirling golden stamens and petaloids, *Sweet Bird of Youth* is a variant seedling of the *X Williamsii* hybrid *J. C. Williams*. It blooms early to mid season and was registered in 1960 by R. Carr of Tulare, California.

X SYLVIA MAY 1950

An interspecific hybrid between *C. cuspidata* and *C. saluenensis*, *Sylvia May* was released by Dr W. M. Wells of California. The plant is slow and upright in growth, the mid season blooms single, of medium size with long narrow petals. Colouring is pale pink, and *Sylvia May* has itself become the parent of many newer, second generation hybrids.

X SYLVIA MAY WELLS 1966 FRAGRANT

An utterly ravishing hybrid produced by Harold R. Paige of Lafayette, California, *Sylvia May Wells* is a large loose peony form bloom of palest blush, shading to light lavender-pink. It flowers mid season on.

X TINY PRINCESS 1961

One of the best known miniature camellias, *Tiny Princess* is the result of a 1961 cross by American hybridist K. Sawada. The blooms are semi-double to peony form, often with loose petaloids. The whole flower is shaded a most delicate pink. Growth is rapid on this cross between *C. japonica AKEBONO X C. fraterna*. *Tiny Princess* blooms early to mid season.

X WATERLILY

X WILBER FOSS

X TIP TOE 1965

Tip Toe is a sweet second generation cross between *C. japonica* and the *X Williamsii* hybrid *Farfalla*. The profuse blooms are medium in size and semi-double. Colour is a light silver-pink, deepening almost to raspberry at petal edges. It is a product of Camellia Grove Nursery, New South Wales.

X TURKISH DELIGHT 1968

Named for the popular confection whose colouring it shares, *Turkish Delight* is a 1968 seedling of hybrid *Cornish Snow*, propagated by F. S. Tuckfield of Australia. It is a medium-sized semi-double flower, with narrow fluted petals of light lavender-pink. Peaks mid season.

X UTSUKUSHI ASAHI 1970s

Not a Japanese variety, *UTSUKUSHI ASAHI* was propagated by Kramer Bros Nursery of California, and is the result of crossing *C. saluenensis X C. japonica Dr Tinsley*. Salmon-pink semi-double, with medium-sized blooms borne profusely on a strong, bushy plant, its Japanese name means 'beautiful morning'.

X VILIA 1961

Named for a forest spirit of old European legend, *Vilia* is the product of California's McCaskill Gardens, a daring cross between the hybrid *X Williams' Lavender* and *C. japonica KURO-TSUBAKI*. The experiment produced a large semi-double bloom, with warm velvet-textured petals of soft lavender-pink. These shade to a variable darker tone at petal edges.

X VIRGINIA W. CUTTER 1972

FRAGRANT

A large red camellia of anemone form, *Virginia W. Cutter* is one of the fragrance experiments of Dr R. Cutter of Berkeley, California. It blooms mid season, and is a cross between *C. japonica Mrs Bertha A. Harms* and *C. lutchuensis Ackerman's E3-32*. A vigorous plant, it is destined to be the parent of many hybrids. (Photo p. 190)

X WALTZ DREAM 1961

A product of the same cross as *Vilia* (which see) *Waltz Dream* was produced by McCaskill Gardens in the same year. It is a very large camellia indeed, semi-double and tinted orchid-pink. Blooming time is mid season.

X WATERLILY 1967

This exquisite hybrid needs no explanation for its name *Waterlily*. Jury of New Zealand crossed *C. saluenensis X C. japonica K. Sawada*, and the result is a formal double bloom of medium size with bright pink petals shadowed faint lavender. *Waterlily* has tightly rolled petal edges and blooms early to mid season.

X WILBER FOSS 1971

A full peony form hybrid of brilliant pinkish-red, *Wilber Foss* is in fact the end product of a *X Williamsii* cross between *C. saluenensis* and *C.*

japonica Beau Harp. Large in size, it blooms early to late and was registered by New Zealand grower Les Jury.

X WILLIAMS' LAVENDER 1950

More popular with hybridists than it is among the general public, *Williams' Lavender* was a 1950 introduction by Georgia's Fruitland Nurseries. The medium-sized single blooms are a distinct lavender-pink and bloom mid season.

X WILLIAMSII ALBA 1960

When hybrid *J. C. Williams* produced this brilliant white seedling in 1960, its American propagator R. Carr immediately named it *Williamsii Alba*. A compact bushy specimen, its medium-sized blooms are single to semi-double with fluted petals, and open early to mid season.

X WIRLINGA BELLE 1973

An original cross between *C. rosaeflora* and *C. X Williamsii*, *Wirlinga Belle* is named for the Australian home of hybridist Tom Savige, who produced the bloom in 1973. It is a medium-sized single of soft pink, blooming early.

X WYNNE RAYNER 1967

The lavender-pink hybrid *Wynne Rayner* was produced in 1967 by New Zealand grower B. J. Rayner. It is a medium to large bloom of semi-double to anemone form. Mid season is its best blooming time.

X WYNNE RAYNER

FRAGRANT CAMELLIAS

On the scent of the future

by Kenneth C. Hallstone

The source of floral fragrance in plants, including the camellia, comes from a mixture of the various essential oils found in the flower. These oils appear as esters, alcohols, aldehydes, ketones, benzines and terpines. The predominant oil present in this complex mixture generally determines that particular flower scent. For example, one of the terpines is the basis for the fragrance in orange blossoms.

It is surprising to me that more of the camellias do not emit floral fragrance, because the seeds have been cultivated for centuries so that their delicate oil could be used in the blending of perfume. The oils are produced by the epidermal cells of the petals near the ovary. When the right combination of oils is formed, it may appear as an aromatic, mobile liquid. This material is called nectar, and is highly sought after by insects such as bees and ants. Whether the nectar is fragrant to humans depends on the combination of the volatile oils, the temperature, and the humidity. The scent of the flower generally develops after the flower opens, and seems to be strongest when the temperature is warm (above 15°C/60°F) and moist. For example, I have noticed when fragrant camellia blooms have been packed the night before in boxes with moist, shredded paper, the trapped, volatile oils give a very pungent fragrance that is quite easy to detect the next day, when the cover is removed at a show.

Before discussing floral fragrance in camellias though, some terminology should be established so that the writer and the reader understand one another. Hereafter, when a smell is discussed that is pleasing, it is referred to as a scent, if very delicate and light; and as a fragrance if more pronounced. When the smell is negative — not generally liked — it is described as an odour. For example, the musty smell found in most *C. sasanqua* varieties is said to be an odour, while the smell of *C. lutchuensis* is expressed as a fragrance.

Hybridisers, like the makers of fine perfume, are blending various camellia smells in hopes of developing one that is universally pleasing and in sufficient strength to be easily detected. This is important, because floral fragrance is a very subjective matter. The sense of smell varies with each individual, ranging from those who lack it entirely, to those who are supersensitive. In addition, the same smell may be described as pleasing to one person, only so-so to another, and unpleasant to still others. Along this line, two other facts are worth noting: (1) women generally have a keener appreciation of smell than men; (2) heavy smokers usually have a very poor sense of smell. Obviously, a heavy smoker would not be a good choice as a judge of fragrance at a camellia show!

Camellia japonica, the most popular and widely grown species, is not known for its floral fragrance. When a scent is present it is generally pleasing, yet rather thin. Growers and developers have been aware of this floral scent when it occurs in unusual strength, and have given their flowers names that point this out; names such as *Aroma, Fragrant Star, Fragrant Jonquil, Fragrant Pink, Scented Treasure* and *Sweet Delight*, to name a few.

Mr Hallstone, a Director of the International Camellia Society, lives at Lafayette, California, where his extensive camellia collection includes most camellia cultivars and species in which fragrance has been reported. Taking over the work of the late Dr Robert Cutter, he is devoting his hybridising efforts to the maximisation of fragrance in future camellia cultivars.

Opposite: Four fragrant camellias which are helping to put us on the scent of the future. They are (clockwise from top left) Blood of China, *a 1928 japonica cultivar;* Scentsation, *a 1967 japonica from the Nuccio Nurseries;* Scented Treasure, *originated by hybridist Harvey Short in 1950; and David Feathers'* Temple Incense *of 1955.*

All species and cultivars pictured in this book that have been reported as possessing scent have been clearly designated by the use of the word FRAGRANT, at the top, right-hand corner of their appropriate entry in the book's dictionary sections.

In addition to *C. japonica*, there are at least eight other species reported to be fragrant, namely *C. fraterna, C. kissi, C. lutchuensis, C. miyagii, C. oleifera, C. sasanqua, C. tsaii* and the recently discovered *C. yuhsienensis*.

Now that the bamboo curtain is lifted and China is trading again with the rest of the free world, there is very little doubt that we will discover many additional species there possessing a degree of floral fragrance that the hybridiser will be able to incorporate into his breeding programme.

Most of the early hybridisation for fragrance was done in the United States, but now, with the free exchange of breeding material, it has spread to the entire camellia world. The hybridist's goal has been to develop a show quality flower with a fragrance that is not only pleasing, but easily detected, and growing on an excellent garden plant. So far, twenty years of serious work have been dedicated toward this goal, yet success may still be five years or more away.

Above: Fragrant Pink Improved *is a colchicine-induced sport of the original* X Fragrant Pink *which W. L. Ackerman of Maryland produced in 1968 by crossing* C. rusticana *with fragrant* C. lutchuensis.

Right: Virginia W. Cutter, *a hybrid produced by Dr Robert Cutter in 1972. Photo by Kenneth Hallstone.*

Early hybridising for floral fragrance, particularly in the United States, began during the 1960s. The first efforts were made by combining the best of the *C. japonica* cultivars known to have fragrance. For example, *Scented Treasure* was crossed with *Fragrant Jonquil*. These crosses proved to be disappointing, but with the advent of the new species *C. lutchuensis* from Okinawa during the early 1960s, breeders for fragrance turned to interspecific crosses, using the pollen of this tiny, white flower. The *lutchuensis* species was evaluated to have the strongest and most pleasant fragrance, and thus became the standard for comparing the many hybrids that followed. The first F_1 crosses using *C. lutchuensis* as the pollen parent were found to be seed sterile (would not set seeds) and possessed a low percentage of viable pollen. Fortunately, in most cases the fragrance came through equal to that of lutchuensis itself. These plants became the basis for many of the fragrant crosses to follow.

So that you may understand the hybridiser's problem in up-grading a fragrant flower, and appreciate his diligent work, let us look pictorially at a cross that took five years to bloom.

Shown on the left is the seed parent *C. japonica Reg Ragland Variegated*, a semi-double 12.5 centimetre (5 inch) flower. On the right is the tiny pollen parent *C. lutchuensis*, a white miniature single bloom. The resulting offspring is the interspecific hybrid in the middle. It is a rose-pink single bloom 7.5 centimetres (3 inches) in diameter. Fortunately the fragrance came through equal to that of *C. lutchuensis*. This new hybrid was given a number *69(2)* and became the pollen parent for the hybrid *Alice Cutter* which was named and introduced in 1972. The pedigree of *Alice Cutter* is shown pictorially in figure 2.

Japonica Reg Ragland Variegated *(left) was crossed with* C. lutchuensis *(right) to produce the fragrant hybrid* 69(2) *at the centre. Photo Kenneth Hallstone.*

The seed parent, *C. japonica Mrs Bertha A. Harms*, a large semi-double white flower with wavy petals and a slight scent, is shown on the left. It was crossed with our hybrid *69(2)*, described above and shown on the right, resulting in the semi-double rose-pink flower named *Alice Cutter*, shown in the centre. In cooler climates and moist areas, this flower is larger, and takes an anemone form with excellent lutchuensis fragrance. The two crosses illustrated in the two colour plates represented ten years of work! Let me say at this point, that it is obvious camellia hybridisers are direct descendants of Job!

The previously shown hybrid 69(2) *was used as the pollen parent in a cross with japonica* Mrs Bertha A. Harms *(left) to produce the second generation fragrant hybrid* Alice K. Cutter *(centre) in 1972. Photo Kenneth Hallstone.*

Top: The fragrant Japanese Higo camellia NIOI FUBUKI (Scented Storm) *has been used in many fragrance-hybridising projects.* 匂吹雪

Above: X Ack-Scent *is the latest (1978) and most successful of the fragrant hybrids produced by W. L. Ackerman of Maryland, USA. Photo R. B. Hoedel.*

Besides the fragrance of the species *C. lutchuensis*, an equally popular one used by the breeder has been the scent expressed by the hybrid *Appleblossom* (a *C. japonica X C. saluenensis* cross). In 1960, *Appleblossom* was successfully backcrossed with the species *C. saluenensis*. This medium-sized pink single flower was given the name of *Salab (Saluenensis X Appleblossom)* and has proved to be an excellent breeding plant, with ample pleasing fragrance. Many crosses have been made combining the *C. lutchuensis* hybrids with the best of the *Salab* hybrids, and we are anxiously waiting for these seedlings to bloom.

In striving for his goal of developing a fragrant show flower, the hybridiser naturally turned to the very large blooms of species *C. reticulata*. In 1969, the first successful cross (using the cultivar *Crimson Robe* [*DATAOHONG*] as the seed parent) was made with *C. lutchuensis* as the pollen parent. The resulting F_1 generation of plants had few characteristics of *C. lutchuensis* and only a trace of its fragrance.

Subsequent crosses using these plants with other fragrant hybrids should show improvement both in size and scent. Crosses with *C. reticulata* and the fragrant *Salab* hybrid have been most encouraging. One such cross was a recent winner in the fragrance division of one of the camellia shows in northern California.

Japan's contribution to fragrance in camellias stems from their many delightfully scented Higo and Higo-type camellias. Such varieties as *AKATSUKI NO KAORI (Fragrance at Dawn), KINGYO TSUBAKI (Goldfish Camellia), KŌSHI (Fragrant Purple), KŌUN (Fragrant Cloud), NIOI FUBUKI (Scented Storm), ŌDAIRA KAORI (Odaira's Fragrance)* and *TAMA IKARI (Precious Anchor)* have all been used by the hybridist to blend delicacy and subtleness to the fragrance.

In the hands of hybridisers are several new and exciting crosses which will appear soon for testing at the show tables, with the hope they will be worthy of naming. *Ackscent* is the latest named fragrant flower to appear on the American scene. It is described as a large flower (11 centimetres or 4½ inches), deep shell-pink, in a loose peony form having 18 petals and 16 petaloids, some with 'rabbit ears'. It possesses a deep spicy fragrance derived from the blending of earlier fragrant camellias. Its parentage is *C. japonica Kramer's Supreme* crossed with the polyploid hybrid *Fragrant Pink Improved (C. rusticana X C. lutchuensis)*.

An eager camellia 'sniffer' can be identified by a dusting of yellow pollen on his nose as he asks 'what fragrance is that?' or 'doesn't this one have a lovely perfume?'.

Soon you will hear people talking and asking these questions as they lean over to smell an exotic camellia flower on the show table, or in gardens throughout the world.

CAMELLIA RELATIVES

In addition to the true camellias, the botanical family *THEACEAE* includes another 25 genera of plants, some of them containing a large number of species of great botanical interest. Mostly they are from tropical and subtropical Asia, with a few outlying species to be found on the east coast of North America, and in tropical South and Central America. Many of them enjoy the same climatic and growth conditions as the more popular camellias.

Though all of these camellia relatives taken together have not generated the same interest or the same passion as the true camellias, at least eight of the genera are well represented in ornamental horticulture. These are *Cleyera, Eurya, Franklinia, Gordonia, Schima, Stewartia, Ternstroemia* and *Tutcheria,* of which *Gordonia* and *Tutcheria* have proved compatible and have actually been used in some camellia hybridisation programmes (though so far to no great effect).

The whole family, however, cannot be ignored when considering the future of the camellia, and I take pleasure in introducing some of the more attractive representatives of the non-camellia genera to those who may not have run across them. The *Gordonia* in particular, does very well in Australia, and seems worthy of a great deal more attention both from horticulturists and home gardeners.

CLEYERA

Easy to grow from cuttings, the genus *Cleyera* is represented in cultivation by only one species, *Cleyera japonica,* which is grown in two varieties, largely for foliage interest. Known in Japan as *Sakakia,* it is an evergreen shrub with shiny, alternate camellia-like leaves which are also used in Japan in Shintō rituals. The tiny flowers are fragrant, but almost invisible with their creamy-yellow petals and brown stamens. These are followed by small black fruits. The cultivar *Tricolor* has bright green leaves variegated yellow and pale pink.

EURYA

A genus of some 70 small evergreen trees and shrubs found in tropical Asia, and out into the Pacific Islands, *Eurya* is represented by two or three garden species which enjoy the same conditions as their camellia relatives. *E. japonica* has shining, elliptical, lightly toothed leaves, small greenish flowers with an unpleasant odour, and minute berries.

FRANKLINIA

The monotypic genus *Franklinia* consists of one species, *Franklinia alatamaha,* a deciduous North American camellia relative with glossy 15 cm (6 in) leaves that turn scarlet in autumn. It bears showy white 7.5 cm (3 in) single flowers in the leaf axils. These are followed by woody five-celled seed capsules with up to eight seeds per capsule. The lovely *Franklinia* is now found only in cultivation, having completely disappeared in the wild in the last century.

Cleyera japonica *(Japan)*

Gordonia axillaris *(Taiwan and Vietnam)*

GORDONIA

The showy *Gordonias* are found both in Asia and North America, can easily be mistaken for camellias, and have in fact been hybridised with them. The Asian *G. axillaris* is a large shrub or small tree with shiny, oblanceolate leaves and crêpe-textured white flowers borne at the leaf axils in late summer. These are almost stalkless and drop in a single piece like camellias. It is found naturally from Taiwan to Vietnam and makes a fine garden specimen, especially in deep, rich soils. The related *G. lasianthus* is native to south-eastern USA, bears long, serrated leaves and long-stemmed white 6 cm (2½in) flowers. Both *Gordonia* species are colourful in winter when many of their evergreen leaves turn scarlet and gold.

Above: Schima superba *(India to South-East Asia)*

Right: A fifty-year-old tree of Gordonia axillaris *in the Sydney garden of Sir Alex and Lady Beattie.*

Stewartia pseudocamellia *(Japan)*

SCHIMA

The largest-growing genus in the camellia family, *Schima superba* is a stunning flowering tree found variously from India to Vietnam. It may grow to 40 m (130 ft) and has broadly elliptic 17.5 cm (7 in) leaves which are often reddish when young. The flowers open a dull scarlet, and fade to purplish-cream. They are 6 cm (2½ in) across and fragrant, and are followed by colourful fruits. Suitable for the tropics only.

STEWARTIA

Like the *Gordonia* (which see) the genus *Stewartia* is represented in east Asia and in North America. The American *S. ovata* or Mountain Camellia is a 5 m (16 ft) camellia-like shrub with deciduous 12.5 cm (5 in) leaves and white flowers. The Japanese species *S. pseudocamellia* may grow larger (it is a small tree), and has 7.5 cm (3 in) pointed deciduous leaves that turn purple in autumn. The 6 cm (2½ in) white flowers are exactly like single camellias with orange anthers, but the petals are furry on their reverses. A very lovely plant.

TERNSTROEMIA

Named for Christopher Ternstroem, an eighteenth century Swedish naturalist who spent much time in China, *Ternstroemia* is a genus of some 85 evergreen camellia relatives scattered about the warmer parts of Asia,

Africa and tropical America. Only two species are much cultivated: *T. sylvatica* from Mexico, and *T. gymnanthera* (syn: *T. japonica*) from Japan. Both are similar large shrubs (or small trees) with alternate, oblong, spirally arranged leaves, leathery and shining. The small flowers appear at leaf axils on drooping stems. They are five-petalled and yellowish-white, followed by berries.

Tutcheria spectabilis *(South-East Asia)*: *Left*

Ternstroemia sylvatica *(Mexico)*

TUTCHERIA

A small genus with eight species, the *Tutcherias* are found in many parts of South-East Asia, and were at one time classed as camellias. *T. spectabilis* is a small, evergreen tree with shining, short-stemmed alternate leaves. These have a distinctly V-shaped section, and hang loosely from the branches. The flowers, which appear at terminal leaf-axils, are cream-coloured, and marked radially in rich butterscotch-yellow. They are 7.5 cm (3 in) wide, and open from a pair of woolly sepals in mid summer (right at Christmas in the southern hemisphere). The seed capsules are quite large, and may also be 7.5 cm (3 in) in diameter. The related *T. virgata* has been used in camellia hybridisation.

Tutcheria spectabilis *(South-East Asia)*: *Below*

GLOSSARY

ACID: deficient in lime (of soil), pH value less than 7.0.

ACUTE: sharp, tapering with straight sides to a point (of a leaf).

ADULT: mature (of a plant).

AFICIONADO: an enthusiast (Spanish).

AIR LAYERING: a method of propagation which stimulates root growth from a plant above the ground.

ALCOHOL: a colourless, flammable liquid formed from certain sugars by fermentation (in fragrance).

ALDEHYDE: one of a group of organic compounds with the general formula R-CHO, which yield acids when oxidised, and alcohols when reduced (in fragrance).

ALKALINE: rich in lime (of soil), pH value more than 7.0.

ALTERNATE: arranged singly on different sides of a stem, and at different levels (of leaves).

ANTHER: the pollen-bearing part of a stamen.

APEX: the tip or point of a twig or branch.

APICES: plural of the above.

AROMATIC: a plant or drug yielding a fragrant smell.

ASYMMETRICAL: not evenly balanced or divided (of a flower or leaf).

ATROPHY: waste away. Reduce in size and power through lack of use (of plant parts).

AUXIN: a class of substances which in minute amounts regulate or modify the growth of plants, especially bud growth, leaf or fruit drop, etc.

AXIL: the upper angle that a leaf stem makes with the stem from which it appears.

AXILLARY: in or from an axil.

BASAL: at the bottom.

BENZINE: a colourless, volatile, flammable, liquid aromatic hydrocarbon.

BIGENERIC: a hybrid between two genera of plants as opposed to more common hybrids between species or varieties, e.g. Camellia X Gordonia.

BLOOM: (1) a flower. (2) a fine powdery coating.

BLUNTED: having an obtuse, rounded, thick or dull edge or tip (of a leaf).

BOSS: a knoblike projection or protuberance of ornamental character (of a cluster of stamens).

BOTANICAL: pertaining to plants.

BOTANIST: one who is skilled in botany.

BOTANY: the branch of science that deals with plant life.

BUD: a small axillary or terminal protuberance, containing rudimentary foliage (leaf bud), or rudimentary inflorescence (flower bud) or both.

BUD SPORT: a mutation. A singular or unusual deviation from the normal type, occurring from one bud or part of a plant.

BUSH: a low, thick shrub with indistinct trunks.

CALLUS: new tissue that grows over injured surface of a plant.

CALYX: the outer row of a flower, composed of separate or united sepals.

CAMBIUM LAYER: in trees, the thin layer of live growth cells between bark and heartwood.

CAMELLIA BLIGHT (Sclerotinia camelliae): a fungus disease that affects camellia blooms, particularly in the United States, discolouring the flower and reducing it to a sticky mess. Perfect hygiene and disposal of all damaged blooms is the only relief. To date, there is no cure.

CAMELLIAN: a camellia hobbyist or enthusiast.

CAPSULE: a dry, divisible fruit composed of one or more sections.

CARDINAL: a deep rich red (of a colour).

CHIMAERA or CHIMERA: an organism composed of two or more genetically distinct tissues or having tis-

sues of several species. A sport sometimes produced from the grafting point of two dissimilar camellia varieties, but differing from each.

CHLOROPHYLL: a green pigment, produced by plants from inorganic material.

CHROMOSOME: any of several bodies in a plant cell nucleus which will readily absorb a stain, and may thus be counted and compared with similar bodies in a different cell nucleus. Containing the genes.

CLEFT GRAFT: a graft in which a wedge-shaped scion is inserted in a stock so that the cambium layers touch and blend.

CLONE: a group of plants originating as parts of the same individual, from buds or cuttings.

CLUSTER: a number of things of the same kind growing together — as in a bunch of grapes (of flower buds).

COLCHICINE: a yellow, crystalline alkaloid, used to obtain new horticultural varieties because it causes abnormal division of some living cells.

COLD HARDY: resistant to low temperatures, not destroyed by frost.

COMPATIBILITY: the suitability of two plant species for hybridisation.

CONCAVE: curved like the interior of a hollow sphere.

CONSERVATORY: a glass-covered house or room into which plants or blooms are carried for display from a greenhouse.

CONVEX: curved like the outside of a sphere or globe.

COROLLA: the petals of a flower, collectively.

CREPE: a fabric with a finely crinkled or ridged surface to which petals are sometimes compared.

CULTIVAR: a variety of a plant that has been produced only under cultivation, as opposed to a natural variety. Cultivars can generally be propagated only by vegetative means.

CULTIVATE: to promote or improve the growth of a plant by labour or attention.

CULTIVATED: produced or improved by cultivation (of a plant).

CUPPED: hollowed out like a cup (of a flower).

CUSHION: a soft, compact, raised mass (e.g. of petaloids).

CUTTING: a cut section of a plant which will develop new roots and become self-sufficient.

DECIDUOUS: a tree or shrub which sheds all leaves at the same time.

DEHISCENT: splitting naturally on an existing seam (of seed capsules).

DIPLOID: an organism or cell of a plant containing double the basic number of chromosomes.

DISBUD: to increase flower size and quality by selective thinning of multiple bud clusters.

DIVISION: (1) the act of dividing into two or more parts. (2) one of the parts into which a thing is divided. (3) one of the major groupings of plant classification.

DOUBLE: having a number of petals greatly increased from the natural species. Often sterile, with stamens converted into petal form (of a flower).

ELLIPTIC: oblong, but narrowing to rounded ends (of a leaf).

ELLIPTICAL: having the form of an ellipse.

ENDEMIC: native to a particular, restricted area.

ENTIRE: with a continuous, unbroken margin (of a leaf).

ENVIRONMENT: the sum of surrounding conditions and influences which affect plant growth.

EPIDERMAL: of the outer and living layer of a plant or animal; of the skin.

ESPALIER: (1) to train a tree or shrub in two dimensions, e.g. along the wall of a house. (2) a tree or shrub so trained.

ESTER: a chemical compound formed by the reaction between an acid and an alcohol.

EVOLUTION: the continuous genetic adaptation of a species to its environment through the agencies of selection, hybridisation, inbreeding and mutation.

FAMILY: the major subdivision of a botanical order, comprising any number of genera, e.g. THEACEAE is the family to which the genus Camellia belongs.

FEATHERED: fringed, something like a bird's feather.

FERTILE: (1) stamens bearing functional pollen or

fruits containing viable seed. (2) capable of growth or development (as a seed).

FERTILITY: (1) the power of reproduction. (2) the quality of supplying nutriments in proper amounts for plant growth.

FILAMENT: a threadlike organ; loosely, the stamen of a flower.

FIMBRIATED: fringed (of a leaf or flower).

FISHTAILED: said of a leaf whose tip is divided into several parts, each with a separate vein. Resembling the tail of a goldfish.

FLACCID: weak or limp.

FLARED: spread gradually outward like the end of a trumpet.

FLORIFEROUS: flower-bearing, but by common usage, abnormally so.

FLOWER: an arrangement of a plant's sexual organs, consisting of pistils and stamens, usually surrounded by decorative, highly coloured petals and calyx.

FLOWER BUD: the rudimentary inflorescence from which a flower will develop and finally open.

FLUTED: having grooves or waves (of a petal).

FOLIAGE: the leaves of a plant, collectively.

FORM: external shape or appearance considered apart from the colour. Orderly arrangement of the parts.

FRAGRANCE: a pronounced, pleasant smell.

FRAGRANT: possessing a pleasant smell.

FRUIT: the ripened ovary of a plant, usually seed-bearing.

FUNGICIDE: any substance that kills fungi.

GENE: the unit of inheritance, transmitted by the chromosome and which develops into a hereditary character as it reacts with the environment and with other genes.

GENERIC: (1) pertaining to a genus. (2) referring to all the members of a genus.

GENETIC: pertaining to genes.

GENETIC INSTABILITY: a hereditary tendency toward mutation.

GENETICIST: one versed in genetics.

GENETICS: the science of heredity, dealing with resemblances and differences of related organisms developing from the interaction of their genes and the environment.

GENUS: the major subdivision of a botanical family, consisting of more than one species. The genus designation is the first part of a species' botanical name, e.g. Camellia in Camellia japonica.

GIBBERELLIC ACID: a metabolic product of the fungus Gibberella fujikuroa, used to stimulate plant growth. In camellias especially, it is used to bring forward the flowering period and to increase the size of the bloom to an unnatural degree.

GLABROUS: smooth, without hairs of any kind.

GLASSHOUSE: a glass-enclosed structure for the cultivation of plants, particularly in a climate generally outside their normal outdoor range.

GLAUCOUS: covered with a bloom which is easily rubbed off.

GRAFT: when a bud or shoot of one plant is joined to a rooted section of another for purposes of propagation.

GROWTH: the process or manner of growing.

GROWTH HORMONE: a substance found in a plant which specifically governs its increase in size.

GROWTH POINT: an embryo bud, usually in a leaf axil, from which further growth can be expected or even stimulated.

GUARD PETALS: the inner row of petals which protect the flower's sexual parts before the bloom is fully developed.

HABIT: general manner of growth of a plant.

HABITAT: the native environment where a plant naturally lives and grows.

HABITUAL: fixed by or resulting from a habit.

HAPLOID: pertaining to a single set of chromosomes.

HARDY: able to survive winter cold in the open air, but in Australia for instance, also used to describe plants able to survive a dry, hard summer. Sturdy (of plants).

HEEL: (1) a portion of harder, previous year's wood attached to a cutting of new growth. (2) to plant temporarily to prevent drying out of roots.

HEREDITY: (1) the transmission of genetic characteristics from parents to progeny. (2) the characteristics that are so transmitted.

HIGO: (1) an old name for Japan's Kumamoto province on the island of Kyūshū. (2) specifically, a flat style of camellia raised in that province.

HORMONE: any of various substances formed in a plant which activate specific organs when transported to them by the sap.

HORTICULTURE: the art and science of cultivating garden plants.

HORTICULTURIST: an adept in such cultivation.

HUMUS: a rich, organic debris, resulting from the rotting down of vegetable and other matter.

HYBRID: (1) a plant resulting from the crossing of parents that are genetically dissimilar. (2) a plant bred from two distinct varieties, species or genera.

HYBRIDISE: to cause the production of hybrids by crossing different species, etc.

HYBRIDISER: one who causes the production of hybrids.

HYBRIDITY: hybrid character.

IMBRICATION: an overlapping as of tiles or shingles (of petals). Usually understood to mean overlapping in a formal pattern.

INARCHED GRAFT: a graft which unites a growing point of the scion to another stock without separation from its own roots.

INCOMPLETE DOUBLE: a flower that has only partly developed the characteristics of a double bloom.

INCURVED: curving inward; concave (of petals).

INFLORESCENCE: (1) the arrangement of flowers on the stem of a plant. (2) the flowering part of a plant. (3) a flower cluster. (4) a plant's flowers collectively. (5) a single bloom.

INSTABILITY: the state of being unstable (with particular reference to a specific camellia variety's tendency to throw variant sports).

INTERCROSSING: cross fertilisation.

INTERMEDIATE: between two recognised or established states or forms (of a flower).

INTERSPECIFIC: between two species (of a hybrid).

INTRASPECIFIC: within a single species.

IRIDESCENCE: a play of lustrous, changing colours.

JUVENILE: the form of a young plant or its leaves when these vary from the adult form.

KETONE: any of a class of organic compounds having the general formula R-COR.

LANCEOLATE: several times longer than broad (of a leaf).

LATERAL: (1) on or at the side. (2) a shoot developing from a main stem or trunk generally at right angles.

LAYERING: propagation of a new plant by bending a low branch toward the ground or a pot, splitting the bark and pinning down until root growth has taken place.

LEAF: one of the expanded, usually green organs borne by the stem of a plant for the purpose of converting sunlight to energy.

LEAF AXIL: the upper angle that is formed between a leaf-stem and a twig from which it appears. Usually the site of new growth or an inflorescence.

LEAF BUD: the rudimentary leaf growth. On a camellia, often difficult to distinguish from the flower bud in its embryonic form.

LILY SHAPE: shaped like a lily. In camellias, tubular, with flaring petal tips.

LINEAR: long and narrow.

LOAM: a friable soil containing topsoil, sand, clay and silt particles, usually with decayed vegetation.

LOBE: a major segment of a petal or organ.

MATURE: ripe or of adult form.

MICROCLIMATE: a localised subdivision of a climatic area, often caused by proximity to the sea, or protection from a prevailing wind.

MINIATURE: an artificial classification for camellia flowers less than 6 cm (2½ in) in diameter.

MOBILE: flowing freely (of a liquid).

MOIRÉ: having a wavelike pattern, as in watered silk.

MONSOON: the seasonal wind of South-East Asia, blowing from the south-west in summer, and from the north-east in winter. Commonly accompanied by heavy rain.

MUTANT: a sport; a plant or flower differing genetically and often visibly from its parent, and arising spontaneously.

MUTATION: a sudden departure from the parent type, caused by a change in a gene or a chromosome.

NATURAL CROSS: a hybrid which has occurred spontaneously.

NATURAL HYBRID: as above.

NECTAR: a saccharine secretion of a plant which attracts the insects or birds that pollinate the flower. Named for the drink of the gods in classical mythology.

NOMENCLATURE: a set or system of names or terms, as those used in a particular science. Particularly, the rules of priority names agreed to by international camellia bodies.

NOTCHED: with a regular indentation on the edge or tip (of a petal or leaf).

OBLANCEOLATE: several times longer than broad, but wider at the tip than at the base (of a leaf).

OBLONG: longer than wide, with the sides almost parallel (of a leaf).

OBSCURE: inconspicuous or almost unnoticeable (of leaf serration).

OBTUSE: rounded, blunt.

ODORIFEROUS: giving out an odour.

ODOUR: a smell, generally one not pleasant.

OPPOSITE: two at each node on opposite sides of the stem (of leaves).

ORGANIC: composed of live or formerly living tissue.

ORGANISM: any form of animal or plant life.

OUTCROSSING: hybridisation of unrelated plants within a botanical family.

OVARY: the basal, seed-developing part of a pistil (of a flower).

OVATE: with a shape like that of a hen's egg, rounded both ends but broadest below the middle.

PARENT: any organism or plant that produces or generates another.

PEDICEL: the stalk of an individual flower.

PENDENT: hanging or suspended (of a flower or leaf).

PENDULOUS: hanging or swinging freely (of a flower).

PEONY FORM: shaped like a peony flower (of a flower).

PERFECTION: a formal, double camellia, especially in nineteenth century.

PERIPHERY: the external boundary of any surface or area.

PERSISTENT: not falling off (of a leaf, flower or organ).

PETAL: one decorative unit of the corolla (in a flower).

PETALODY: a condition in flowers where the stamens assume the form or appearance of petals; hence petaloded.

PETALOID: an organ that has the appearance of a true petal, whether it be a stamen or a sepal.

PETIOLE: the stalk of a leaf.

PHOSPHORESCENCE: (1) the property of being luminous at temperatures below incandescence. (2) a luminous appearance (of flowers).

PICOTEE: a flower whose petals have an outer margin of another colour, usually red.

PISTIL: the prominent female organ of a flower, generally projecting beyond the stamens. Consisting of stigma, style and ovary.

PLANT: (1) any member of the vegetable group of living organisms. (2) a seedling or growing slip. (3) to put or set in the ground for growth.

PLANT GENETICIST: one who makes a study of plant heredity.

PLANT HUNTER: a professional gatherer of rare plants or seeds, acting in a commercial interest.

PLANTATION: (1) a group of deliberately planted trees or other plants. (2) the planting of seeds, etc.

POLLEN: the spores or grains borne by a flower's male anthers (equivalent to mammalian sperm).

POLLEN DONOR: male parent of any plant.

POLYPLOID: a plant with more than twice the haploid number of chromosomes.

POT SPECIMEN: a plant grown permanently in a container.

PRIORITY NAME: the earliest recorded synonym of any camellia variety consistent with the rules of nomenclature as to date, description and publication.

PROPAGATE: to reproduce a plant, generally by means of cuttings or division, so that it comes true to type.

PROPAGATION: (1) the act of propagating. (2) multiplication by natural reproduction.

PROSTRATE: lying flat on the ground.

PUBESCENT: softly downy.

PUNGENT: sharply affecting the organs of taste or smell, as if by a penetrating power (of a fragrance or smell).

QUILTED: resembling a padded quilt in texture.

'RABBIT'S EARS': upstanding petals with a crowded, fluted effect (of camellia petals).

RADIAL: radiating from a central point, like the arms of a starfish.

RAINFOREST: a dense forest found in tropical or temperate areas with high humidity and heavy rainfall occurring throughout the year.

RANDOM: occurring without definite aim, purpose or reason (of hybrids).

RECURVED: curved downward or backward (of petals).

REFLEX: (1) bent or turned back. (2) to bend, turn or fold back (of a petal or leaf) hence, reflexed.

REPRODUCTION: (1) the act or process of reproducing. (2) the natural process among plants by which new individuals are generated.

RETICULATED: having the veins or nerves disposed like the mesh of a net (of leaves).

RIB: the primary vein or any prominent vein (of a leaf).

ROLLED: formed into a roll, or curved up from itself (of a petal or leaf).

ROOT: a part of any plant which, typically, grows downwards into the soil, fixing the plant and absorbing nutrients and moisture.

ROOTSTOCK: a root used as a stock in plant propagation; also a subterranean stem or rhizome.

ROSE FORM: shaped like a rose flower.

RUFFLED: drawn up, as if by gathering along one edge (of a petal).

RUGOSE: rough and wrinkled.

SCALE: one of a number of plant pests, clustered on stems or reverses of leaf. Unsightly rather than dangerous.

SCENT: a delicate, light smell.

SCION: a cutting. A shoot or twig cut especially for grafting.

SEED: a structure containing an embryo plant and food reserves, formed from an ovule after it has been fertilised.

SEED CAPSULE: the ripened walls of the ovary or pericarp.

SEED STERILE: incapable of developing seeds.

SEEDLING: a young plant developed from the embryo after germination of a seed.

SEGMENT: one of the parts of a petal that is deeply divided.

SELF COLOURED: coloured in a single tone without variegation or marking, e.g. solid red.

SEMI-DOUBLE: a flower made of more than nine petals, yet not fully double in form (of camellias).

SEPAL: one of the separate units of a calyx, often green and leaflike.

SERRATED: having saw-toothed edges (of a leaf).

SERRATION: one of the notches or teeth of such an edging.

SERRULATE: finely or minutely serrated (as a leaf).

SHADE: a degree or darkening of the colour (in a flower).

SHATTER: a flower's habit of disintegration and fall, petal by petal, rather than the whole faded bloom falling in one piece.

SHEATH: any more or less tubular structure surrounding an organ or part of a plant.

SHEEN: lustre, brightness, radiance.

SHRUB: a woody plant, generally lower growing than a tree, and with multiple trunks (a very generalised term).

SIMPLE: neither compound nor divided (of a leaf or petal).

SINUATE: with wavy or indented margins.

SINGLE: a flower consisting of nine or fewer petals (in camellias)

SOMATIC: pertaining to the walls, hence the shape of a flower.

SPATULATE: spatula shaped, oblong with the point rounded (of a leaf or petal).

SPECIES: the basic or minor unit in plant nomenclature.

SPECIFIC: of a species.

SPECIMEN: a plant grown separately as a show piece, or focus of garden design.

SPINEL: an ornamental stone in jewellery, coloured a vivid bluish pink. Hence the colour description, spinel pink.

SPONTANEOUS MUTATION: a change produced by natural process, independent of external agencies.

SPORT: a natural mutation, generally in a flower. Capable of propagation)see chapter on sporting in camellias).

SPORT PARENT: the plant on which a sport appears.

STALK: a non-technical term for the elongated support of any plant organ (as in leaf or flower).

STAMEN: the male or pollen-bearing organ of a flower, consisting of filament and anther.

STAMINATE: having stamens, but no pistils.

STAND: a grouping of any plant species in a natural habitat, developed by natural increase.

STELLATE: star shaped (of a flower).

STEM: the main leaf or flower-bearing axis of a plant.

STERILE: (1) a plant incapable of reproduction by a seed, generally a hybrid. (2) not functional, not producing flowers.

STIGMA: the top of the female pistil which receives the pollen.

STOCK: the plant or rooted part of a plant onto which another plant is grafted.

STRAIN: (1) an artificial variety of a species or plant. (2) a group of plants distinguished from other plants of the variety to which it belongs by some intrinsic quality, such as a tendency to flower freely, or to sport.

STRIATED: with fine, longitudinal lines (as a petal).

STUNT: to check the growth or development of; to dwarf.

STYLE: (1) the elongated part of the pistil between ovary and stigma. (2) a particular kind, sort or form with reference to appearance or character.

SUBSPECIES: a major division of a large species.

SUBTROPICAL: a plant native to areas outside the true tropics, but not able to survive cold winters.

SUCCULENT: juicy, fleshy, rather thick (of a plant or any part of a plant).

'SWEET PEA': in camellia nomenclature, a colouring which shades gradually from the base of the petal to a deeper tone at the petal margins.

SYMMETRICAL: capable of division into identical halves.

SYNONYM: a word of expression accepted as an alternate name of a camellia variety.

TAXON: an individual member of a classification.

TAXONOMIST: one who classifies plants, or identifies them from examination of their tissues.

TAXONOMY: the science of nomenclature.

TEMPERATE: mild or coastal (of a climate).

TERMINAL: (1) at the end or tip. (2) a shoot appearing at the end or tip of a branch or twig.

TERMINAL SPORT: the ultimate or 'end of the line' possibility in a standard 'sporting' sequence of camellia flowers. Normally, in white camellias with a single red marking, the terminal sport would be a flower of pure red, with all the variegated, margined and pink sports as intermediate types.

TERMINALLY: (1) the end. (2) at the end of a twig or branch.

TERPINE (or TERPENE): any of certain monocyclic hydrocarbons with the formula $C_{10}H_{16}$, occurring in essential or volatile oils.

TIER: one of a series of separate rows or ranks rising one behind or above another (as in petals).

TINT: (1) a hue or variety of a colour. (2) a colouring diluted with white or of less than maximum purity. (3) a delicate or pale colour.

TOMENTOSE: woolly (of a leaf or stem).

TOOTH: a clearly defined projection on the edge of a leaf.

TREE: (commonly) a large, woody plant that produces one main trunk and a distinct, elevated crown.

TRIPLOID: possessing triple the basic number of chromosomes (of a plant).

TROPICAL: a plant native to the warm zone between the Tropics of Capricorn and Cancer, needing a wet summer and a warm, dry winter.

TUBERCLE: a small, warty excrescence on a leaf or other organ of a plant.

TULIP SHAPED: a tubular shape with the petal tips turning slightly inward (of camellias).

TWIG: the shoot of a woody plant or tree representing the growth of a single season.

TYPE SPECIMEN: the individual, original species from which the botanical description was prepared (of a plant).

UNDER GLASS: in a glasshouse or other sheltered position.

UNDULATE: having a wavy surface or edge, or both at once.

UNSTABLE: not finally fixed, liable to change.

UPSTANDING: standing erect, well grown and vigorous.

VALID NAME: the earliest recorded name to be accompanied by a clear description and date in publication.

VARIANT: that which varies from the norm.

VARIEGATION: a condition of a petal or leaf where the natural colour is broken by another colour. The part is said to be variegated.

VARIETAL: of a variety.

VARIETY: (1) the subdivision of a species. (2) a recognisably different member of a plant species, capable of propagation.

VEGETATION: plants collectively; the plant life of a particular area considered as a whole.

VEGETATIVE: (in reproduction) asexual multiplication from cuttings, layers or other parts of an existing plant.

VIABILITY: the physical ability to grow or increase.

VIABLE: fresh, capable of germination (of a seed).

VIRUS: an infectious agent requiring living cells for multiplication.

VOLATILE: evaporating rapidly.

VOLATILE OIL: an essential oil produced from plant tissue, distinguished by its failure to remain liquid or to solidify.

WABISUKE: a generalised Japanese epithet for certain very small, simple camellia varieties used in the tea ceremony. Believed not to be members of a single species.

WALL SPECIMEN: a tree or shrub trained in espalier fashion against a wall.

WILLOW-LIKE: slender and weeping in habit.

BIBLIOGRAPHY

Amoenitarum Exoticarum E. Kaempfer, London, 1712

Camellia Cultivars of Japan Takasi Tuyama and Yoshio Futakuchi, Heibon-Sha Ltd, Tokyo, 1966

Camellia Journal, The American Camellia Society (Quarterly)

Camellia News Journal of the Australian Camellia Research Society (Twice yearly)

Camellia Nomenclature Ed. William E. Woodroof, Southern California Camellia Society (Triennial)

Camellia Quest E. G. Waterhouse, Ure Smith, Sydney, 1950

Camellia Review, The Southern California Camellia Society (Bi-monthly)

Camellia, The. Its History, Culture, Genetics And a Look Into Its Future Development Feathers, David L., and Brown, Milton H., Editors, American Camellia Society, 1978

Camellia Trail E. G. Waterhouse, Ure Smith, Sydney, 1952

Camellias Beryl Leslie Urquhart and Paul Jones, The Leslie Urquhart Press, Sussex, 1964

Camellias in America H. Harold Hume, Harrisburg, Pennsylvania, 1946

Camellias in Huntington Gardens 3 Vols, William Hertrich, Huntington Botanic Gardens, San Marino, California, 1954

Chinka Zufu, Japanese Camellias — The Imperial Collection Ed. Takeshi Watanabe, Kodansha, Tokyo, 1969

Chubu Camellias Seibundo Shinkosha

Encyclopedia of Camellias in Color Tadao Tominari, Japan Camellia Society, Vol 1, 1972; Vol 2, 1978

Higo Camellias Taizo Hiratsuka, Seibundo Shinkosha, Tokyo

History and Description of the Species of Camellia and Thea; and of the varieties of Camellia japonica *that have been imported from China* William Beattie Booth, read August 18, 1829 before the Royal Horticultural Society, London

How to Grow and Use Camellias Lane Books, California

International Camellia Journal ICS, Sydney (Annual)

Ishii's Selected Japanese Camellias Including Sasanquas Takasi Tuyama and Toshio Yamada, Tokyo

Japanese Camellias Seibundo Shinkosha, Tokyo

Magic of Camellias, The Norman Sparnon and E. G. Waterhouse, Ure Smith, Sydney, 1968

Monograph of the Genus Camellia Samuel Curtis, London, 1819

Notes on Georgia Camellias James Stokes, American Camellia Yearbook, 1949

Nouvelle Iconographie des Camellias A. Verschaffelt, Van Geert, Paris, 1848

'Observations on the Camellia and its Varieties, with some Account of its introduction into Great Britain and this Country' Wilder, M. P. Esq, *The American Garden Magazine*, January, 1835

Revision of the Genus Camellia, A Robert J. Sealy, Royal Horticultural Society, London, 1955

Some Chinese Ghosts Lafcadio Hearn, Little Brown & Co., New York, 1896

Tsubaki Ningen Yoshiaki Andoh, Color Books, Japan, 1974

World of Plants, The Asahi Hyakka, Tokyo, 1976

Together with the catalogues of the following nurseries:
Camellia Grove, St Ives, NSW
Camellia Lodge Nursery, Noble Park, Victoria
Nuccio's Nurseries, Altadena, California

GENERAL INDEX

CULTIVAR INDEX

Every camellia species and every cultivated variety of camellia mentioned or described anywhere in this book is listed alphabetically below, together with cross-references to the pages on which they will be found. Page numbers in normal type refer to a written entry or description; page numbers in bold type refer to illustrations. The index also includes a number of synonymous names, each of which is cross-referenced to that camellia variety's currently accepted priority name, under which any entry appears. Japanese and Chinese names and synonyms are shown in italic capitals as elsewhere in the book. Nearly 1,800 names are included.

207

ACKNOWLEDGEMENTS

Planning a dictionary of camellias is one thing; tracking down many of the varieties to photograph is another, as I soon found when I began work for this book. I am indebted to many camellia friends, both old and new, who helped locate my planned subjects, leaving me with an embarrassment of riches. While many readers may regret the omission of some personal favourite, I have hoped to blunt their disappointment by including at least a few exquisite blooms that will be unfamiliar to enthusiasts in every individual country where these beautiful flowers are grown. The final selection is my own, and I can only hope that I have chosen well.

My unpaid helpers then, included:

In Australia Alex and Joy Beattie, Pat Clifton, Eric Craig, Mary Davis, Brian Donges, Eddy Graham, Peter Landers, Jack and Isobel Lee, John and Annette Riddle, Rick Roberts, Tom Savige, Barry Stern, Paul Vlasic.

In Japan Yoshiaki Andoh, Hirofumi Chonan, Kazuo Iida, Eishin Kamioka, Professor Futoshi Murayama, Tsugio Ohta and family, Peter Okumoto.

In the USA Dave Feathers, Dave and Barbara Goux, Willard Goertz, Ken and Kay Hallstone, Dr Fred Heitman, Ray Hornyak, Betty Klein, James F. Lichtman, Edith Mazzei, Professor Milton Meyer, Julius and Tom Nuccio, Charles and Marge O'Malley, Harold and Mary Paige, Frank and Jean Pursel, Terry Scalese, Irene Teachout, John Winston, David Wittry.

The camellias were mostly photographed at:
Australian Camellia Research Society shows at Myer Ltd, Sydney; Camellia Grove Nursery, St Ives, NSW; Descanso Gardens, La Canada, California; E. G. Waterhouse Memorial Camellia Garden, Yowie Bay, NSW; 'Eryldene', Gordon, NSW; Huntington Gardens, San Marino, California; Kadoorie Farm and Botanic Gardens, Hong Kong; 'Kewita', Somersby, NSW; Kinkakuji Temple, Kyōtō, Japan; Kyōtō Botanic Garden, Kyōtō, Japan; Los Angeles State and County Arboretum, Arcadia, California; Milton Park, Bowral, NSW; Monrovia Nursery, Azusa, California; Nagoya Botanic Garden, Nagoya, Japan; Nuccio's Nursery, Altadena, California; Ohta's Nursery, Kumamoto, Japan; Royal Botanic Garden, Kew, England; Royal Botanic Gardens, Sydney, NSW; Shinjuku Go-en, Tokyo, Japan; Strybing Arboretum, San Francisco, California; The Imperial Palace, Tokyo, Japan.
Pictures were also taken at shows of the Northern California Camellia Society at Concord and Oakland, the Australian Camellia Research Society at Gordon and Miranda Fair, NSW, and in my own garden.

I am particularly indebted to the managements of Camellia Grove Nursery, St Ives, NSW; Camellia Lodge, Noble Park, Victoria; and Nuccio's Nursery, Altadena, California for permission to draw from their vast experience of camellia cultivation by quoting liberally from their catalogues and cultivation booklets. These extracts are found principally in the introduction to the Japonica camellias.

Milton Brown, Executive Editor of the American Camellia Society, was generous in supplying rare early illustrations of the camellia from the society's library; Yoshiaki Andoh contributed some wonderful pictorial material from Japan, including the *Fifteen Mysteries of Maria* which is reproduced with the permission of the University of Kyōtō. Colonel Tom Durrant supplied the marvellous pictures of reticulata camellias in his New Zealand garden; the staff of the Kunming Botanical Institute in China indirectly supplied the Chinese character names and Pinyin transliterations of Chinese reticulata varieties, and the photograph of *Camellia chrysantha*, which nicely proves the accuracy of Paul Jones' beautiful painting of the same flower. Anita Byrnes translated research material from the Japanese.

My warmest thanks to them all.